Cybercrime and Cybersecurity Research

nova
science publishers
New York

Cybercrime and Cybersecurity Research

Cybersecurity in the Current Framework of the EU and Italian Criminal Justice Systems. A Focus on Digital Identity Theft
Clara Anna Pettoello-Mantovani
2022. ISBN: 978-1-68507-583-5

Cybersecurity Risk Management: An Enterprise Risk Management Approach
Kok-Boon Oh (Editor)
Bruce Ho (Editor)
2022. ISBN: 978-1-68507-428-9 (Hardcover)
2022. ISBN: 978-1-68507-505-7 (eBook)

Weapons Systems: Annual Assessment and Cybersecurity
Dale R. Copley (Editor)
2019. ISBN: 978-1-53615-595-2 (Hardcover)
2019. ISBN: 978-1-53615-596-9 (eBook)

Cyber-Security and Information Warfare
Nicholas J. Daras (Editor)
2018. ISBN: 978-1-53614-385-0 (Hardcover)
2018. ISBN: 978-1-53614-386-7 (eBook)

Security and Authentication: Perspectives, Management and Challenges
Ong Thian Song (Editor)
Tee Connie (Editor)
Mohd Shohel Sayeed (Editor)
2018. ISBN: 978-1-53612-942-7 (Hardcover)
2018. ISBN: 978-1-53612-943-4 (eBook)

More information about this series can be found at
https://novapublishers.com/product-category/series/microbiology-research-advances/

Clara Pettoello-Mantovani

Cybersecurity in the Current Framework of the EU and Italian Criminal Justice Systems

A Focus on Digital Identity Theft

nova
science publishers
New York

DOI: https://doi.org/10.52305/IURB6396

NOTICE TO THE READER

Library of Congress Cataloging-in-Publication Data

ISBN: 978-1-68507-583-5

Published by Nova Science Publishers, Inc. † New York

Contents

Foreword

This book, written by Clara Pettoello Mantovani, a scholar at the LUISS School of Law, focuses on the important topic of cybercrime, within the big picture of cybersecurity. Over the past two decades, the increasingly digitized world around us has pushed notions of cybersecurity to emerge as structural factors within private and public social domains. Repeated attacks by powerful viruses on computers and computer systems in general have revealed cyber threats to be a main global risk, as shown by recent cases involving public administration institutions worldwide.

The exponential multiplication of computer crimes has highlighted the need to punish such illicit actions. The need to contrast computer crimes has emerged strongly since the late 1980s, when the migration of most of our work and social activities to computer networks began. However, the regulatory framework of most nations has proven to be insufficient and often culturally unprepared to effectively contrast illicit activities revealing the need for ad hoc protection. For example, within the European context and more precisely in Italy, the first legislation against cybercrime was established in 1993 with Law 547. However, similar to other countries, even though the new law introduced important changes and additions to the criminal code provisions related to cybercrimes, the legislative effort seems to remain insufficient for effective protection from crimes perpetrated against individuals.

In her book, Clara Pettoello-Mantovani addresses these important concepts, starting from the observation that the complex reality of cyberspace, which is constantly evolving and expanding, requires a continuous adaptation of criminal law. The author also correctly points out that this process of adaptation must maintain its typical normative and protective function. In this book, Pettoello Mantovani also points out that the activities that take place within cyberspace seem to redefine the relationship between technology and law. The operating conditions and functions of this new space, in which licit and illicit actions take place, risk competing with the primary normative rules of law. In this regard, Pettoello-Mantovani emphasizes the risk pointed out by

Lessig, that the development of a new "technical code" endowed with its own intrinsic universality, may be progressively accredited and presented as a "new legal code" for the globalized world.

This book can provide a useful insight for those interested in understanding the current issues and controversies related to cybercrimes and clarifies the notion that cybersecurity is in its essence the activity of prevention, detection and, ultimately, intervention in attacks that revolve within cyberspace. Ensuring not only the protection of information but also that of individuals. The important and agreeable conclusion by Pettoello-Mantovani is that the role of legislators remains essential due to the need to constantly update and/or develop legal statutes aimed at regulating the activities that take place within cyberspace. Activities that must be subtracted to the regulatory influence of private enterprises.

Maurizio Bellacosa
Professor of Criminal Law and European Criminal Law
LUISS "Guido Carli" School of Law, Rome, Italy

Preface

This book deals with the complex and often challenging topics of cybersecurity and cybercrimes.

The continuous increase in the use of the internet and thus of Cyberspace as a whole, has led to an exponential growth in threats, vulnerabilities and risks to which one may be subjected to. Cyberspace has therefore become a sort of battlefield where, in addition to different interconnected computer systems, hardware and software devices are able to incapacitate or destroy physical or virtual infrastructures.

The complex and constantly evolving reality of Cyberspace, requires a continuous adaptation of criminal law. The author emphasizes that the role of lawmakers remains essential due to the need to update and/or develop legal standards designed to regulate activities that take place in Cyberspace.

This book provides a useful insight for those interested in understanding the current issues related to cybercrimes and clarifies the notion that cybersecurity is in its essence the activity of prevention, detection and finally intervention in the attacks that take place in cyberspace, ensuring not only the protection of information but also of the person.

List of Abbreviations

AgID	Agency for Digital Italy
AI	Artificial Intelligence
ANR	National Regulatory Authority
ARPANET	Advanced Research Projects Agency Network
BSPA	Baseline Security Product Assessment
CEF	Coordinated Enforcement Framework
CERN	European Organization for Nuclear Research
CERT	Computer Emergency Response Team
CFR	Code of Federal Regulations
CIA	Confidentiality Integrity and Availability
CIT	Cyber Intelligence Team
CoC	Convention on Cybercrime
CNP	Card Not Present
COVID-19	Coronavirus disease 2019
CSA	Cybersecurity Act
CSDP	Common Security Defense Policy
CSIRT	Computer Security Incident Response Teams
CSPN	First Level Security Certification of Information Technology Products *(France)*
DOS	Denial of Service
DDOS	Distributed Denial of Service
DNS	Domain Name System
DPCM	Prime Minister Decree *(Italy)*
DPR	Presidential Decree *(Italy)*
DSM	Digital Single Market
EC3	European Cybercrime Centre
ECI	European Critical Infrastructures
eIDAS	electronic IDentification Authentication and Signature
EMPACT	European Multidisciplinary Platform

	Against Criminal Threats
EPRS	European Parliamentary Research Service
ENISA	European Network and Information Security Agency
EUROPOL	European Police Office
GAN	Generative Adversarial Networks
GDPR	General Data Protection Regulation
ICCPR	International Covenant on Civil and Political Rights
ICT	Information and Communications Technology
IIoC	Indecent Images of Children
IoT	Internet of Things
ISCOM	National Institute for Communication and Technology Information (*Italy*)
ISP	Internet Service Provider
ICT	Information Communication Technology
IT	Information Technology
MISE	Ministry of Economic Development (*Italy*)
MitM	Man-in-the-middle
NCP	Non Consensual Pornography
NIS	Network and Information Security
OECD	Organization for Economic Co-operation and Development
PC	Personal Computer
TCP/IP	Transfer Control Protocol/Internetwork Protocol
T-CY	Cybercrime Convention Committee
UDHR	Universal Declaration of Human Rights
UNODC	United Nations Office on Drugs and Crime
VAWG	Violence against Women and Girls
VoIP	Voice over Internet Protocol
WIPO	World Intellectual Property Organization
WWW	World Wide Web

Introduction

An Introduction to Cybersecurity and Cybercrimes: The Birth of Cyberspace

The birth of the internet dates back to the 1960s. It was developed as a way for government officials and researchers to facilitate information sharing and was initially used primarily among academic circles to exchange scientific data. However, it had limited mainstream utility. In the 1960s, computers were large, immobile devices with limited memory potential, and until the 1970s punch cards were used by computer programmers to store data. To use the information stored in any computer, users had to physically travel to the computer site or mail magnetic tapes using the conventional postal system.

A major stimulus to the development of the Internet was the acceleration of the Cold War. The Soviet Union's launch of the Sputnik satellite prompted the U.S. Department of Defense to consider alternative ways to disseminate information even after a nuclear attack. That possibility prompted the formation of the U.S. Advanced Research Projects Agency Network (ARPANET), which eventually evolved into what is now known as the Internet. ARPANET proved to be a great success because of its use for the rapid exchange of documents and information. However, membership was required to access its use, which was still limited to certain academic and research organizations that had contracts with the U.S. Department of Defense. In response to these limitations in access to and use of the ARPANET, other networks were developed to provide broad and accessible information sharing.

January 1, 1983 is globally considered the official birth date of the Internet. The computer networks that existed at the time did not have a standard way to intercommunicate before this date, so a new communication protocol called Transfer Control Protocol/Internetwork Protocol (TCP/IP) was established. This arrangement allowed different types of computers connected to different networks to "talk" to each other. ARPANET and the Defense Data Network also aligned themselves and officially switched to the TCP/IP standard. As of January 1, 1983, all networks could then be connected by a universal language.

During the early 1990s, the European Organization for Nuclear Research (CERN) announced that the World Wide Web (WWW), as we know it, would become of public domain, therefore accessible to anyone and everyone. Making the "web" a public domain system meant that it was open to anyone with a computer, resulting in a massive impact on how people lived and communicated in their normal lives. This process gave rise to a so-called technological revolution, which is commonly referred to as the Cyber-revolution. What was once a small national interactive network was transformed by the Cyber-revolution into a global communication system, characterized by constant communication and exchange of information. This network is now widely known as *Cyberspace,*[1] a term developed during the first decade of the Internet's spread to describe a widespread, interconnected digital technology. From its inception, the concept of cyberspace referred to the web as a separate world, unrelated to reality, that allows people to hide behind false identities.

To better understand this revolution and the impact that cybernetics[2] has had in our daily lives, we must first analyze its etymology. Mathematician Norbert Wiener first coined the term "cybernetic," deriving it from the Greek word "kyber" meaning helmsman or pilot. According to Wiener, cybernetics studies the way humans and animals in general communicate with the outside world. It is a multidisciplinary science with many strong interactions with other disciplines and technological areas such as philosophy, psychology, mathematics, biology, physics, and so on.[3] The terminology of "Cyberspace" was first coined by Canadian writer William Gibson, in his short story "Burning Chrome," defining it as a "consensual hallucination" in computer networks. Gibson described cyberspace as an illusion, consensually experienced every day by billions of legal practitioners in every nation. He viewed cyberspace as a graphical representation of data obtained from the desks of every computer in the human system.[4] With the advent of the internet

[1] See A.CADOPPI-S.CANESTRARI-A.MANNA-M.PAPA, *Cybercrime,* Milano 2019.

[2] The word cybernetics comes from the Greek word "*kybernetes,*" meaning *rudder, pilot,* a device used to steer a boat or to support human governance; Dan C. Marinescu, in Complex Systems and Clouds, 2017. N. Wiener defined cybernetics as "the study of control and communication in the animal and the machine (1947). Cybernetics is "the art of creating equilibrium in a world of constraints and possibilities," according to the philosopher Ernst von Glasersfeld. The famous mathematician Andrey Nikolaevich Kolmogorov defines cybernetics as the "*science concerned with the study of systems of any nature which are capable of receiving, storing, and processing information so as to use it for control.*" In www.sciencedirect.com.

[3] WIENER, *Humans and the use of Human Beings,* 1950.

[4] W.GIBSON, *Burning Chrome*, in *Omni magazine*, 1982; GIBSON W., *Neuromancer*, 1984.

age, this term was then used to refer to the virtual place where communication occurs through computer networks. A more recent definition of cyberspace was provided by a panel of experts from the U.S. Pentagon, who defined cyberspace as the "global domain within the information environment consisting of the interdependent network of information infrastructures, including the Internet, telecommunications networks, computer systems, and embedded processors and controllers." According to this definition, cyberspace is considered to be the realm of computer networks in which information is stored, stored, shared, and disseminated.

The expansion of Internet use has exposed cyberspace to exponential growth in threats, vulnerabilities, and risks. Cyberspace has thus become a kind of battlefield where, in addition to several interconnected computer systems, there are hardware and software devices capable of rendering inefficient or destroying physical or virtual infrastructures.

Today cyberspace is increasingly structured as a huge database whose contents are indexed and processed by powerful search engines and AI systems that correlate keywords and syntax. Given the high level of technological automation reached by this process, it is not only able to retrieve and process information, but also allows users to create so-called "digital alter-egos," which gradually replace individuals, especially in terms of their knowledge and decision-making. The personality of each individual, which includes the ability to express, communicate, inform and develop, is thus enhanced but also exposed to continuous and systematic collection of its data, information, traces and attacks. As a result, the personality of individuals can be influenced, subjugated and even dispossessed because of the relationships that occur in cyberspace and of which it becomes an integral part, often unable to escape its constraints. The user thus becomes a potential victim and target, as well as a possible perpetrator of abuse and crime, which increasingly take place in cyberspace.[5]

[5] L. PICOTTI, *I diritti fondamentali nell'uso e abuso sui Social Network. Aspetti Penali*, in Giur. di Merito, 2012, n. 12, 2522 s.

Chapter 1

Cybersecurity in the European and National Context

1. Cybercrimes – A New Generation of Crimes

Crime is, as it has always been, a structural element of our society. The efforts to uncover, prevent and punish criminal activities, in whatever form they may present themselves, are often overwhelming, and the struggle for justice is demanding, as keeping up with it requires a complete visual, wide flexibility and constant rational changing.

Technology and its advancements have always provided individuals with the opportunity to find new ways to exploit and commit various crimes. The immediate reflection that this cyber revolution and therefore the opening of the internet to the public has had in the field of criminal law is mainly represented by the fact that now criminals, commonly known as hackers, have the ability to commit "cyber-attacks," giving rise to a new form of crime commonly known as cybercrime1. Cybercrimes are thus a particular type of "new generation crime" committed primarily by using a computer particularly to illegally access, transmit or manipulate data.

Cybercrime is commonly regarded as a specific type of crime or a group of crimes, where an electronic device, able to store and/or process data (typically a computer), is the object of the crime or is used as a tool to commit an offense. However, as with traditional crimes, cybercrime has many different features and takes place in a wide variety of scenarios and environments. In this regard, we may use cybercrime as an umbrella term to describe two main closely linked, yet distinct, ranges of criminal activity: cyber-dependent crimes and cyber-enabled crimes.

Cyber-dependent crimes include crimes that can be committed only through the use of information and communications technology (ICT) devices, where the devices are both the tool for committing the crime and the target of the crime (e.g., developing and propagating malware for financial gain;

hacking to steal, damage, distort or destroy data and/or network or activity). Typically, they broadly fall into two main categories: illicit intrusions into computer networks (e.g., hacking) and the disruption or downgrading of a computer's functionality and network space (e.g., malware and denial of service [DoS] or distributed denial of service [DDoS] attacks).

Cyber-enabled crimes instead incorporate traditional crimes that can be increased in scale or reach by the use of computers, computer networks or other forms of ICT systems (such as cyber-enabled fraud and data theft). Therefore, these crimes do not rely on computers or networks but have been transformed in scale by the constant use of the internet and communications technology. Hence, cyber-enabled crimes have de facto expanded the magnitude of cybercrimes from the original and traditional perimeter of economic related crimes,[6] to include offenses committed against individuals or which indirectly involve them.

---

[6] Economic Related Cybercrimes include unauthorized access, sabotage or use of computer systems with the intention to cause financial gain to the perpetrator or financial loss to the victim. It may involve computer fraud or forgery, hacking to steal personal or valuable data for commercial gain or the distribution of viruses.

Cyber criminals may seek to obtain personal and financial data for fraudulent purposes. Valuable forms of data may include: personal information (names, bank details, and National Insurance numbers); company accounts, client database, and intellectual property (for example, new company products or innovations).

Victims may not report these crimes if, for example, they feel that the issue is trivial or do not actually recognize that what has happened to them is in fact a crime. Additionally, where individuals have had their bank account details accessed or hacked, either the bank or the individual or both may not report the crime if the individual is reimbursed by their bank. Similarly, some businesses may not report for the same reasons, or for fear of reputational damage, or may choose to deal with such issues internally. List of these crimes include:

Fraud: Cyber-enabled fraud is possibly the most common of all cybercrime offences. The internet allows offenders to hide their identities behind websites and email addresses, providing a forum in which they never have to meet a victim in person to commit the crime. Some offenders may also be part of a wider criminal gang who may also never meet each other, with members based anywhere in the world. Online fraud can be committed in a number of ways. For example:

Electronic financial frauds, for example, online banking frauds and internet enabled card-not-present (CNP) fraud. Internet-enabled CNP fraud involves transactions conducted remotely, over the internet, where neither cardholder nor card is present Related to this are e-commerce frauds, which refer more generally to fraudulent financial transactions related to retail sales carried out online. Both businesses and customers may be victims.

Fraudulent sales through online auction or retail sites or through fake websites, which may offer goods or services that are not proved. Alternatively buyers may be led to purchase a counterfeit product (when led to believe it was an original). This may also include other retail misrepresentations, such as online ticketing fraud.

Mass-marketing frauds and consumer scams, including but not limited to: Phishing scams; Pharming, and Online romance (or social networking/dating website) frauds. In this

There is no universally accepted definition of cybercrime; in fact, there are many different definitions, which vary in relation to their degree of specificity and breadth.[7] A traditional approach one can take in defining what constitutes a cybercrime is to consider it as the digitalization of already well-known traditional offences. Therefore, cybercrimes may be considered offences committed by anyone who has the possibility of connecting to the web, and therefore connecting into "cyberspace," via computer.[8]

Computer crimes are represented by peculiar characteristics that differentiate them from so-called offline crimes. These specific characteristics are the de-localization of resources and the de-temporalization of activities as well as de-territorialization. In other terms, these peculiar traits symbolize the fact that cybercrimes can easily be committed from any part of the world, without a necessary physical connection between the user and the system.

These new-generation crimes can be divided into the following two categories: cybercrime in a narrow sense (computer crimes) and cybercrimes in a broad sense (computer-related crimes). The term computer crime identifies any illegal behavior directed by means of electronic operations that targets a computer system's security and the data it possesses. Computer-related crimes instead describe any illegal conduct committed by means of, or in relation to, a computer system or network, whereas computer crimes consists of those offenses that have at least one essential element that explicitly refers to ICT in the description of the mode of conduct—that is, the means, the objects, the event itself or a different condition of the offense that must be considered as an element that necessarily must be integrated for the purpose of perpetrating the offense itself. Cybercrimes intended in a broader sense can instead be qualified as those crimes that may be committed with the use of internet technology (IT) tools or computer objects—that is, with a mode of conduct involving ICT systems, including the web. Its distinctive elements therefore appears in the formulation of the legal case only as a possible mode, object, instrument or result of the conduct. These are alternative to other elements that are considered legally "equivalent" and do not take into account ICT. Therefore, only in the light of the concrete methods of the commission of the offense will it be possible to consider whether the offense should be

context, individuals may be contacted via social networking or dating sites and persuaded to part with personal information or money following a lengthy online relationship.

[7] EMILIO C. VIANO, *Cybercrime: Definition, Typology, and Criminalization*, 2016, 3.

[8] See also: L. PICOTTI, *I diritti fondamentali nell'uso ed abuso dei Social Network. Aspetti penali*, in Giurisprudenza di merito, n. 12-2012, p. 2522-2547, L. PICOTTI, Internet e responsabilità penali, in G.PASCUZZI.*Diritto ed informatica*, Milano, 2002, p. 117-146, L.PICOTTI, *Studi di diritto penale dell'informatica*, Verona, 1992, p. 111-148.

classified and examined as an IT offense in its broad sense or in its narrow sense.

From this distinction, we can detect, therefore, how technology plays a major role in the definition of cybercrimes. In some cases, electronic devices and the data they contain are the intended target of the crime. However, in other situations, electronic or digital devices are the actual tools that the offender (hacker) uses to perpetrate the crimes, which are intended to directly affect individuals, organizations or governmental entities.

Therefore, not only data but also individuals, whether directly or indirectly, may become the subjects of electronically perpetrated crimes.

Within this category of crimes directed at or involving individuals may fall a wide range of conditions, which include a) intellectual property crime (piracy, counterfeiting and forgery); b) online marketplaces for illegal items provided by dark web areas; c) malicious and offensive communications (inappropriate use of social media, cyberbullying/trolling, virtual mobbing, false accounts); d) offences that specifically target individuals (including cyber-enabled violence against women and girls [VAWG], disclosing private sexual images without consent, cyberstalking and online harassment, coercion and control); e) child sexual offences and indecent images of children (IIoC; child sexual abuse, online grooming, circulation of IIoC); and f) extreme pornography and obscene publications.

Intellectual property is defined as the right to copyright, design, patent or trademark. Intellectual property crimes can cover a wide range of activities, such as the unauthorized use of another's intellectual property through the manufacture, use and/or sale/import of the property without prior permission. Most intellectual property crimes fall under the umbrella of counterfeiting goods,[9] where trademarks are willfully infringed and there are breaches of copyrights, usually defined as "piracy."[10]

---

[9] Counterfeiting is when money or currency is forged but may also relate to goods if they are not manufactured or produced by the designated manufacturer or producer given on the label or flagged by the trademark symbol The internet may be used as a way of counterfeiting goods, and physical copies of pirated media through:

- offering items, either billed as genuine, or clearly fake, for sale through online shops and auction sites, or on social networking sites;
- Setting up and running sophisticated websites, for example which purport to be genuine retail outlets; and
- Using easily available technology to set up websites offering fake goods, either billed as genuine, or clearly fake

[10] Piracy is the unauthorized copying of an original recording for profit. Pirated products will often have different packaging to the genuine product and may often take the form of newly

Criminals use online marketplaces not only as a place to trade cyber skills, tools and techniques but to trade and sell other illegal items, such as stolen credit card details, drugs and firearms. These marketplaces are often "hidden" online and facilitated by individuals coordinating the trading of these goods. Where more than one individual is collectively running such a website, a charge of conspiracy against those doing so may be considered. However, when considering a case involving the online trading of illegal goods, it is advisable to consider charges against individuals "selling" or facilitating the online selling of objects as distinct from those who are "buying." Each case must be considered on its merits; however, in many instances, there may not be sufficient evidence to demonstrate a large conspiracy between multiple users of one marketplace where a number of seemingly distinct transactions have been made. Marketplaces for online trading are usually hosted in areas of the web called dark web zones, which are mainly comprised of internet sites and contents that are generally illegal, intentionally hidden and inaccessible through standard web browsers. The dark web is used to facilitate criminal activity across a wide range of threats and can be used by criminals to create so-called "safe spaces" for conspiring to commit offences, such as child sexual exploitation or the sale and purchase of illegal items (such as drugs or firearms).

Malicious and offensive communications include millions of communications sent everyday via the internet and online platforms such as social media apps. Some individuals use these online forums to send abusive, threatening, indecent, offensive and/or false messages that could be capable of committing a criminal offence. Offences committed through the use of social media include a variety of conditions targeting individuals, such as threats (violence to the person or damage to property), harassment or stalking, controlling or coercive behavior, disclosing private sexual images without

created compilations. The internet may be used to distribute, share or make available pirated music, films, games or other items in the following ways:

- Use of legitimate file sharing technologies to share copies of music and films e without permission of the intellectual property right holder;
- Posting protected content on a webpage without permission, for example, uploading a copy of a new cinema release;
- Streaming live sports matches, or concerts, out to audiences directly over the internet without permission; and
- Putting protected content, like a video game, into a cyber- locker, or online storage system, and providing the details on how to access the content on the internet, or a specific group of people.

consent, blackmail or other offences and information that are grossly offensive, indecent, obscene or false.

A typical example may be cyberbullying, a phenomenon, already present in our physical lives, that takes place using communication technology, such as social media and other forms of communication. Depending on the nature of the act, it may also constitute a criminal activity, and prosecutors should apply the principles outlined in the legal guide on communications via social media when considering allegations of this nature. For example, cyberbullying might involve harassment, threatening behavior, sending false information about someone, impersonation, cyberstalking or grossly offensive messages.[11]

Offences that specifically target individuals are facilitated by technological developments and create a new landscape for controlling, sexually motivated or other forms of interpersonal relationship offences. Disclosing private sexual images without consent, cyberstalking, harassment and coercive and controlling behavior crimes are predominately, but not exclusively, perpetrated against women and underage girls, whom are typically humiliated, controlled and threatened. In this regard VAWG includes the potential use of social media to exert power and control. For instance, in cases of "honor-based violence" and forced marriage, threats to post personal information on social media can be used to bring shame on victims in order to silence and coerce them.

Offences such as unauthorized access to computer material with the intent to commit further offences are also often part of a wider pattern of coercive and controlling behavior, such as offending, stalking and harassment. For example, stalking victims may have their bank or social media accounts compromised or private intimate photographs copied from their computer hard drive, leading to a range of harm from said theft and defamation to a physical attack.

Such crimes are often part of a wider pattern of behavioral activities. Therefore, these incidents should be viewed within a wider context, which can encapsulate both online and offline activities, including physical abuse.

Disclosing private sexual images or videos without the consent of the individual who appears in them and with intent to cause distress is a typical example of a crime perpetrated against individuals. This type of offence is colloquially known as "revenge pornography"—a broad term that usually refers to the actions of an ex-partner who uploads a sexually intimate photograph or a video in which the victim is engaged in a sexual activity on

---

[11] For more on the notion and discipline of Cyberbullying see Chapter III of this book.

to the internet, or shares it by text or email, with the intent of causing the victim humiliation or embarrassment as revenge for the breakup of their relationship.[12]

Cyberstalking and other forms of online harassment are generally described as a threatening behavior or unwanted advances directed at another using forms of online communications. They are often combined with other forms of traditional stalking acts such as being followed or receiving unsolicited phone calls or letters as well as traditional forms of harassment. Examples of cyberstalking may include threatening or obscene emails or text messages, spamming (where the offender sends the victim multiple junk emails), live chat harassment or flaming (a form of online verbal abuse), leaving improper messages on online forums or message boards, trolling or cyberbullying, sending electronic viruses, sending unsolicited email and cyber identity theft.[13]

The circumstance of "coercion and control" closes a gap in the law around patterns of coercive and controlling behavior in an ongoing relationship between intimate partners or family members. The use of the internet, social media, spyware and software to track and monitor the whereabouts of a victim and control their contact with others is a common finding in these cases.

Child sexual offences and the sharing of IIoC are rapidly growing in parallel with the growth of cyberspace, the latter of which has given perpetrators of child sexual abuse and those who create and disseminate indecent images a range of new tools to facilitate their offending. These crimes can be perpetrated through various social media, such as chat rooms, social networking sites and gaming devices that connect to the internet as well as through direct email addresses or mobile numbers belonging to victims. Child sexual abuse through cyberspace has the potential to allow offenders to target hundreds of children at a time, and once initial contact with a child is made, these children may be subject to threats and intimidation. The online abuse can be an end in itself without any physical-contact offences taking place. However, such physical-contact offences may occur by arranging to meet up with the child or persuading them to engage in sexual activity whilst they are being filmed or photographed. Further offences may also occur through the subsequent dissemination of these films or photographs. Offenders, for example, may use various control elements as a tool to stop a victim from reporting the sexual abuse, and the control might take the form of threatening

---

[12] For more on this topic see Chapter III §1.3.4.
[13] For more on this topic see Chapter III §1.3.3.

to publish the photographs or recordings of them, including images of the victim being naked or being abused. Undercover cyber zones may also function as available pedophile manuals or any item that contains advice or guidance on sexually and materially abusing children, giving advice on how to entrap or groom a child, commit other child abuse offences and escape capture.

In online grooming cases, predatory individuals may access internet sites that children and young people visit in order to search for potential victims by location or interest. Children and young people may often reveal personal information online, such as where they live or go to school or their family name, which is consequently used to manipulate behaviors and build relationships with their victims. Information may be published through a number of different online platforms that are accessible to others, including social networking sites, multi-player gaming portals and other web-based forums.

The spread of IIoC is facilitated by the use of cyberspace, and the variety of digital tools available has further facilitated the taking, making, showing and distribution of IIoC. Advances in digital programs, technological solutions and enhanced computer graphics have also made it easier to create "pseudo-photographs" of children.[14]

The dissemination of extreme pornography and obscene publications is also an important part of cybercrimes that may involve individuals as passive subjects of a criminal offence. Such dissemination can be committed via various avenues such as chat rooms, social networking sites and gaming devices that connect to the internet as well as through a direct email address or mobile number.

However, cybercrime is constantly expanding and is taking over new and more dangerous paths that not only affect individuals, as described above, but also organizations, governments and entire nations. The spread of this particular form of crime has forced institutions, in their various articulations, to develop a series of containment and intervention plans, which ensure an effective legal protection not only at the national level but also and especially at supranational level.[15]

---

[14] See, L.PICOTTI, *Online child pornography offences. A brief overview*, in Festschrift fur FRIEDER DUNKEL zum 70. Kriminologie und Kriminalpolitik im Dienste der Menschenwürde, Forum Verlag Godesberg, Monchengladback, 2020, pp. 207-208.

[15] SOAFER A.D., GOODMAN S.E., *The Transnational Dimension of Cyber Crime and Terrorism,* Hoover Press, 2005; GRABROSKY P.N.; *Global Dimension of Cybercrime, Global Crime*, 2004.

The need for an internet bill of rights was therefore authoritatively promoted and shared, providing for a clear set of rules, which offers, recognizes and guarantees, on a global scale, a system of fundamental rights regarding this new social dimension. In view of the need to ensure, at the global level, the protection of these fundamental rights and interests, there is a need to make operational "harmonized systems" aimed at sharing efficient, civil and criminal application practices, consequently strengthening the necessary international cooperation. The basic criterion that we must keep in mind is that what is lawful offline cannot be lawful online.

According to some authoritative scholars, including Lessig, the difficulty of network regulation marks the transition from the "rule of law" to the "rule of code." Everything that is allowed online is technically possible. According to Lessig, cyberspace is made up of a particular software or hardware that forms a set of rules and constraints on how one may behave in cyberspace. The substance of these constraints may vary; nevertheless, they are all considered to be the circumstances according to which one may access cyberspace since they limit some behaviors by making others possible or impossible.[16] Lessig's teaching suggests that the peculiar characteristics of the virtual space advise the criminal law scholar not to rely solely on traditional dogmatic categories.

The spread of the concept of cybersecurity reflects a cultural phenomenon and a need of the modern information society, in which cyberattacks have become the most pervasive and perceived risk.

In such context, cybersecurity is not only a technical subject but rather the social response to the growing computerization of communication and economics processes as well as the increased risk of cybercrime.

The latest statistics show that cybercrime is destined to grow exponentially if we do not adopt adequate preventive measures. Therefore, we can detect that the core of cybersecurity is that of risk prevention in its broadest sense. Economic operators will have to take action to make the network a safer place so as to discourage cybercriminals[17] from committing online crimes.[18]

---

[16] L. LESSIG, *The Law of the Horse. What Cyberlaw Might Teach*, in Harvard Law Review, 1999.

[17] "*Cybercriminals are individuals or group of people whom use technology to commit a cybercrime with the intention of stealing sensitive company information or personal data and generating profits*," in www.javapoint.com.

[18] P. SEVERINO, "Cybersecurity: Regulation and Policy," Luiss Law School seminar, 2019-2020.

1.1. The Criminological Profile of Cybercriminals

From a strictly criminological point of view, some authors have argued that traditional crimes have not substantially changed over time. They have adapted in response to broader social and technological changes and to the opportunities that modern computer applications have introduced in managing daily activities.[19] Some of the peculiarities of computer crimes have favored their proliferation even in subjects who otherwise would not have carried out the conduct in the most traditional form.

According to a careful analysis, cybercrimes differ from traditional crimes in that a) they are a net of basic computer skills and are technically easier to commit, b) they do not require a large initial criminal investment especially in comparison with the profit that can be derived from them, c) they can be committed in any part of the world without the necessary physical presence at the time the act occurs and d) there is not always clarity and regulatory uniformity at the European and international levels.[20]

In addition, the apparent separation between the physical and the virtual world in which criminal activities take place has extremely significant psychological implications, which manifest themselves, for example, in the lack of emotion and the lack of perception of the criminal negligence of one's conduct. In fact, the author often works alone with his PC and does not understand how his activity can be criminally likened to that of the street snatcher or the robber with a balaclava. The new criminal opportunities have also given rise to real phenomena of transnational crimes, as in the case of credit card fraud carried out in the e-commerce sector.

Returning to the subjective profile of cybercriminals, it has had an indicative and peculiar evolution following the spread of new technologies. Indeed, the internet seems to have initiated a sort of "democratization" of both the crime and the reasons for which it is committed. That is to say that there are some forms of abuse of the internet and new technologies that massively involve the so-called "unsuspected" as opposed to "professional" criminals.

Recent studies[21] have found that the cybercriminal has a medium-high education level, does not exhibit violent or antisocial behavior, has a reduced

---

[19] See F.BOSCO-C.COCCIADIFERRO, *L'evoluzione del crimine informatico: dall'hacking all'underground economy*, Unicri, Emerging Crimes Unit, 2011.

[20] See M.CHAWKI, *A Critical Look at the Regulation of Cybercrime: A Comparative Analysis with suggestions for Legal Policy*, 2004.

[21] Cassazione Penale, Sezione V. Sentenza 26 ottobre 2012, n. 42021. Also see N.MALIZIA, 25.10.12 Lesson "*La criminalità informatica: forme di manifestazione, prevenzione e repression.*" In: I° Corso di Approfondimento in Criminologia e profili penalistici –

perception of crime and has a good capacity for premeditation, organization and pre-ordination. He/she generally works in solitude and increases his self-esteem (even in a group) through the practice of what he/she considers to be an "exciting game."

Just to complete these brief general considerations of the criminological nature, it should be added that the repression of cybercrime required a specialization of the skills of the judicial police and criminologists, who had to adapt the old traditional theories and build new criminological schemes. The scene criminis can also be informatics or human relationships. Moreover, the habits of individuals have changed, the lack of real context attenuates the perception of crime and, therefore, the internet has brought subjects who were distant from illegality into this new category of criminals.

1.2. The Transition from the Original Computer Crimes into the New Dimension of Cybercrimes

During the last 30 years, there has been an important social phenomenon represented by the progressive public availability of the internet. This constantly expanding phenomenon has had an important impact on the field of criminal law. In fact, there has been a transition from the conceptual category of computer crimes—that is, computer crimes sensu stricto—to the broader one of cybercrimes.[22] TThis transition cannot be considered only from a criminological standpoint but also from a judiciary perspective.

The Council of Europe referred to the initial typology of crimes (computer crimes) with the initial Recommendation of 1989 on "computer or computer crime," in which a limited number of crimes were listed for which the Council of Europe suggested to the Member States their introduction in the various national legislations.[23] However, the rapid development that characterized the internet in the 1990s suggested the importance of the fundamental Cybercrime Convention of 2001, which included a much more articulated and systematic corpus of provisions and that, although just being a recommendation, was binding on the European Union (EU) Member States. The Convention

processualpenalistici," organized in 2012 dal "Dipartimento IURA - Diritti e tutele nelle esperienze giuridiche interne e sovranazionali" directed by Prof. Vincenzo Militello.

[22] L.PICOTTI, Presentation, in ID., *Il diritto penale dell'informatica nell'epoca di Internet*, Padova, 2004, p. VII.

[23] See CONSEIL DE L'EUROPE, Recommandation n. R(89) 9 sur la criminalité en relation avec l'ordinateur, Starsburg, 1990, containing a minimum list of eight indictments and an optional list of further four offenses.

contains innovative and fundamental indications concerning both substantive and procedural criminal law as well as international cooperation.

The most significant contents of the substantive criminal law part concern in particular the offenses subject to the obligations of prosecution by the national legal systems. In fact, they went beyond the fundamental triad of legal assets constituted by confidentiality, integrity and the availability of data and systems (confidentiality, integrity and availability: the so-called CIA) to which the Convention refers in Articles 2, 3, 4, 5 and 6. These articles include unauthorized access and therefore the illegal interception and alteration of data, systems and the new preparatory offense for the abuse of devices. In the following articles, in addition to the two classic computer crimes of computer forgery (Article 7) and computer fraud (Article 8), the prosecution of crimes concerning "contents" not necessarily conveyed by data or systems is also envisaged, such as child pornography crimes (Article 9) and serious violations of copyright and related rights (Article 10).

Therefore, the Convention naturally includes crimes that can be defined sensu stricto as computer crimes since they include in their essential constitutive elements the typing of well-described technical-IT elements, such as "computer systems," "computer data," "transmission of computer data" and "computer programs," in the absence of which such crimes would not even be conceivable. However, the innovative element is represented by the inclusion of another category of crimes that can be defined as computer crimes, or more appropriately cybercrimes, which we can describe as an "open" category. These crimes, while not necessarily having the technical-IT characteristics typical of the constituent elements of the legal case, also have a particular legal and procedural importance on the level of international cooperation since there is the need to counter them with adequate criminal sanctions and with specific instruments of investigation. Moreover, if committed online, they pose the problem of the "circulation" of evidence, similar to what is required to combat and prosecute computer crimes sensu stricto. In this regard, Article 14, par. 2 of the Cybercrime Convention describes the field of application of Section II of the same Convention that concerns the related procedural law measures. In particular, letter b) includes any crime committed through IT systems in addition to those provided for by the Convention itself (which are referred to in letter a). Furthermore, in letter c), it also includes any other crime that leaves "electronic traces," a concept that is reaffirmed in Article 23, which represents the opening words of Chapter III, dedicated to measures relating to international cooperation obligations.

With the evolution and expansion of cyberspace, the category of cybercrimes has therefore assumed an even greater importance and extension being that it can include any crime that can be committed in cyberspace. It therefore includes all those crimes entailing the "communication" and above all "dissemination"[24] of criminally illegal content on the internet, such as online defamation crimes[25] or child pornography,[26] which are extremely easy to realize and have a harmful effect to the detriment of the individual—immensely greater than that which would occur in the event of commission with traditional means of communication, such as the post, the press, radio, television, photographs or films on physical media.

Technological evolution has also favored the development of many other types of crimes that offend the most varied legal assets and become much more alarming thanks to the facilitation provided by IT tools. If committed in cyberspace, these crimes require adequate and updated responses at both a regulatory and an investigative level. For example, there has been the need to introduce new types of crimes into the regulations dedicated to cyberspace in order to combat terrorism, which increasingly uses the network both as a place for propaganda and proselytism and as a means of "enlistment" and "training" or for financing criminal activities through online fundraising.[27]

Again, in this regard, legal systems have had to consider and introduce regulations to counter new cases or new aggravating circumstances to tackle phenomena more severely, which, passing from the offline dimension to that of cyberspace, have found new possibilities for offending the individual, such as cyberstalking, cyberbullying, revenge porn and cyber violence against women. In particular, the Council of Europe, following the Istanbul Convention, has included these cases in the category of "domestic violence," providing a specific "positive protection obligation" to the signatory States.[28]

---

[24] See L.PICOTTI, *Profili penali delle comunicazioni illecite via internet, in Il diritto dell'informazione e dell'informatica,* 1999, p.283 ss.

[25] See L.PICOTTI, *Profili penali*, p. 303 and also see, F.P.LASALVIA, *La diffamazione via web nell'epoca dei social network*, in A.CADOPPI-S.CANESTRARI-A.MANNA-M.PAPA, *Cybercrime*, Milano, 2019, p.331 ss.

[26] See L.PICOTTI, *I delitti di sfruttamento sessuale dei bambini, la pornografia virtuale e l'offesa dei beni giuridici*, Napoli, 2007, p.1267 ss.; S.DELSIGNORE, *La tutela dei minori e la pedopornografia telematica: i reati dell'articolo 600ter c.p.*, in A.CADOPPI-S.CANESTRARI-A.MANNA-M.PAPA, Cybercrime, Milano, 2019, p. 374 ss.

[27] See also L.PICOTTI, *Terrorismo e Sistema penale: realtà, prospettive*, limiti, in Riv. trim. Dir. Pen. Contemporaneo, 2017, p. 249 ss.

[28] See the 2011 Council of Europe Convention on preventing and combating violence against women and domestic violence; also see ECHR, IV Section, February 2020, Ric. N 56867/15, Buturuga v. Romania.

This new reality, due to the technological development of the last 30 years, therefore requires a change in the approach to cybercrime. It is now clear that not all crimes that takes place within cyberspace are limited to a restricted number of crimes and, therefore, of potential victims being that they embrace a growing multiplicity of offenses and ways of offending legal interests and fundamental rights. In this regard, it is also important to note that technological advancement and the development of a new virtual territory such as cyberspace have generated new types of fundamental rights that international and national legislation must take into account. For example, extortion[29] can constitute a cybercrime in a broad sense if carried out in cyberspace. In fact, it can be committed with the illegal encryption of the data of a computer system owned by others by means of a malware illegally installed remotely. Through this computer intrusion system, the criminal exercises a form of threat or violence[30] as a result of which the victim is forced to pay a ransom to regain the free availability of their data, which is returned by means of a decryption key for the stolen data.

Another example of a common crime that has "new" characteristics if committed online is money laundering.[31] This crime can be carried out with the electronic transfers of funds, investments or "other operations" also via the web or the dark web. This can be done by moving and exchanging virtual currencies, such as bitcoin or ethereum, based on blockchain systems, through operations covered by anonymity and capable of replacing money or even intangible values and therefore hindering the identification of their illicit origin. This is the case in the new type of crime represented by cyberlaundering, which has allowed new possibilities in the commission of the traditional crime of money laundering.[32] Finally, many other types of illicit trafficking, such as drugs, weapons, people and organs, or frauds carried out, such as through phishing techniques, can also be committed in cyberspace using artificial intelligence systems, which make criminal actions faster, safer

---

[29] Article 629 of the Criminal Code.

[30] Violence against things, pursuant to Article 392 of the Criminal Code, is that which occurs when a computer program is altered, modified or canceled in whole or in part or the functioning of the computer or telematics system is prevented or disturbed.

[31] Article 648-*bis* of the Italian Criminal Code, See Chapter 2.

[32] This phenomenon is also object of EU Directive 2018/1673, relating to the fight against cyberlaundering through the criminal system; See also R.M.VADALA', *La disciplina penale degli usi e abusi delle valute virtuali*, in Diritto di Internet, 2020, p. 397 ss.; also L.PICOTTI, *Profili penali del cyberlaundering: le nuove tecniche di riciclaggio,* in Riv.trim.dir.pen.ec., 2018, p. 590 ss.

and more secure and allow the identification of the most advantageous and the most vulnerable victims.[33]

1.3. The Protection of Property and Legal Rights Amid the Rapid Technological Advancements and the Fast Evolution of Cybercrimes

The new and vast area of ICT covers any product that is able to store, retrieve, manipulate or transmit information electronically (i.e., personal computers, digital televisions, email or robots), also making available new methods allowing the connecting, transmitting and processing of data in increasingly large quantities. The fast global development of ICT has profoundly transformed and evolved several key areas of society, including the economy, politics, the management of free time and social and individual relationships. However, in parallel, the techniques of the realization and the modalities of the manifestation of illicit behavior and harmful criminal acts have also evolved, finding new opportunities to expand and develop in the so-called cyberspace. Therefore, alongside the necessary technological advancements, the parallel social dimension of cyberspace appears an essential element in this rapid transformation in the context of the current "cybernetic revolution."[34] It would be wrong to regard this new dimension as just a "virtual" dimension or world, separated from today's society. Instead, it should be considered as a completely new and real dimension in which an essential part of our personal lives takes place on a platform for the enactment of our everyday life, including the various areas of social interaction, such as education, business, free time and more intimate relationships.

For these reasons, the protection of the individual's fundamental rights must be regarded as a good to be safeguarded in general and not only in reference to criminal law implications. For instance, the fundamental right of "privacy" is in great danger due to the risks represented by IT advancements. In fact, the individual's privacy is constantly exposed to a flow of information and data provided intentionally or unintentionally by the users such that the area of privacy extends from the physical dimension to the virtual dimension

[33] Significant also the recent EU Directive 713/2019 on the fight against frauds and forgery of non-cash means of payment; See also R.M.VADALA', *La direttiva UE 2019/713 del 17 aprile 2019 e la tutela penale dell'uso legittimo delle valute virtuali*, in "Osservatorio Cybercrime" (https://sites.les.univr.it/cybercrime/index.php/news-oc-2/).

[34] L. PICOTTI, *Cybercrime e tutela penale dei diritti della persona e della privacy nel web*, AIAF, issue 1, 2020, p 7-15; L. FLORIDI, *The fourth revolution. How the infosphere is transfroming the world*, Milan, 2017.

of cyberspace, in which even the most alarming and serious violations acquire offensive potentials and unprecedented dangerous connotations.[35]

Over 20 years ago, in the early days of the information era, the internet was made accessible to the general public and was initially regarded as a new space of freedom and democracy, potentially unlimited and open to anyone and able to avoid the constraints and restrictions of the real world. However, most recently, the most attentive legal scholars have emphasized the need to consider the development of a new and complete legal regulation aimed at protecting individuals in the "virtual world," starting from the idea of a "Constitution for the Internet." In this regard, in recent years the Italian Parliament established a working group presided over by the jurist and then-Deputy Hon. Stefano Rodotà, which led, in 2015, to the drafting of a text[36] that was in line with similar internationally developed documents and described an essential list of fundamental human rights that must be primarily safeguarded in cyberspace. This important draft was based on consolidated notions, already recognized by international conventions and the constitutions of democratic societies, which were reformulated and integrated with new contents in order to guarantee the basic freedoms and rights on which the modern digital society must be founded. The document elaborated by Rodotà was primarily aimed at safeguarding the fundamental principles of democracy and preserving the tradition of the Italian rule of law.[37] The document, however, was never implemented into law and therefore not even its purpose was pursued. Nevertheless, its principles have been clearly presented and are of great importance as guidance in order to carefully explore the current legislation with the scope of finding, in the existing laws in force, the legal instruments necessary to contrast the illegality and above all the violations of the fundamental rights committed in cyberspace. The ultimate aim, therefore, would be to pursue the provision of a broad and effective legal protection to those who individually or collectively are victims of cybercrimes, particularly in those circumstances where the perpetrator is covered by anonymity.

Therefore, the typical technological and social characteristics of today's globalized world prove how dangerous and deceptive the new forms of cybercrimes are. They are crimes that may remain hidden for a long time and are often not perceived in time by the victims. This is a further negative aspect of these new-generation crimes, which can preclude the victim the possibility

---

[35] I.SALVADORI, *I reati contro la riservatezza informatica*, in A.CADOPPI, *Cybercrime* (a cura di), 2019, p. 656 ss.

[36] S. RODOTÀ. *Il mondo nella rete. Quali i diritti, quali i vincoli,* 2014.

[37] *Ibidem.*

to report the suffered offense. However, the electronic "traces" of said behaviors or facts remain, mostly on the network, and can be found, collected and acquired as evidence that can be used in criminal trials by expert operators (postal police or other investigative bodies and authorities).

Certainly, cybercrimes require an increasingly sophisticated and evolved legal response, progressively adequate in regard to the characteristics and evolution of the technology that conveys it. The convergence of an adequate procedural discipline, in particular relating to investigation and collection activities, also appears essential. The conservation and use of evidence, alongside an innovative and specific discipline of criminal law that would be able to gradually adapt the current unsuitable regulatory formulations or introduce new specific cases—such as the most recent one referred to in Article 612ter of the Criminal Code that incriminates revenge porn—make the punishment of new criminal phenomena safe or easier.

An additional specific aspect is that of a necessary active intervention of independent public authorities, starting with the role of the "authority for the protection of personal data," which, with adequate specific technical and legal competence, can meet the protection needs not only of the collective and public interests but also of the fundamental rights of individuals. This is of particular importance as the parties involved may not be able to fully establish effective protection measures given the asymmetrical position of weakness in which they find themselves with respect to the potential, complexity and difficulty of governing the cyberspace in which they are the main subjects but also the most exposed players.

It is therefore the legislators' task to adapt to the current technical and regulatory knowledge, which must be considered indispensable in order for them to grasp this new dimension, so that an effective protection can be guaranteed to the potential victims. However, it is important to remember that we must not only guarantee the victims' fundamental rights but also those of the people investigated and accused in the related criminal proceedings.

1.4. Understanding Cybersecurity

This introduction aims at assessing the causal relationship between cybercrime and cybersecurity. However, before engaging in this task, it is of primary importance to discuss the definition of cybersecurity and whether a consensus has been reached among the various international legal systems in the legal framework that describes this field. In fact, only by defining the scope and goals of this new legal field can policymakers then adequately and properly examine how lawmakers could improve existing laws.

Although cybersecurity is a commonly used term in legal circles, at present, no scholarship has been actively involved in defining what "cybersecurity law" exactly is and the goals of statutes and regulations that aim to promote cybersecurity. For instance, the availability of a generally accepted definition of cybersecurity would provide the European legislators with a platform on which to develop a commonly recognized legal framework that promotes the confidentiality, integrity and availability of public and private information, systems and networks through the use of forward-looking regulations and incentives, thus protecting individual rights, privacy, economic interests and national security.

Defining cybersecurity may seem prima facie uncomplicated and an easy task to accomplish.[38] Several options are offered by the international legal literature. However, European legal systems, both at the super-national EU level and at the national level, lack a consistent definition of the term "cybersecurity law." Looking at extra-European legislations, the international legal literature shows that legal scholars in the US discuss cybersecurity based on a definition provided by the local judiciary system. In the US, according to Title 18 of the Code of Federal Regulations (CFR) 39.1, cybersecurity incidents are defined as "a malicious act or suspicious event that disrupts, or was an attempt to disrupt, the operation of those programmable electronic devices and communications networks including hardware, software and data that are essential to the Reliable Operation of the Bulk-Power System."[39] In this field, the EU has made commendable efforts toward providing the Member States with a common policy and shared legislation on cybersecurity and its related issues. However, despite its important efforts, at present the EU has not yet adopted any legal acts in the form of one of the typical EU binding legal instruments such as regulations, directives and decisions. Thus, in 2017, the EU expressed its position on this matter using a non-binding instrument such as a resolution, which, similar to statements, does not intend to have legal effects. The European Parliament was, however, unable to reach a consensus

---

[38] A. CATALDO; F. PELUSO: *Cybersecurity, La nuova disciplina italiana ed europea alla luce della direttiva NIS, 2018.*

[39] *US FEDERAL GOVERNMENT, Code of federal regulations*. T*itle 18 -- Conservation Of Power And Water Resources; Chapter I -Federal Energy Regulatory Commission, Department Of Energy; Subchapter B - Regulations Under The Federal Power Act; Part 39 - Rules Concerning Certification of The Electric Reliability Organization; And Procedures For The Establishment, Approval, And Enforcement Of Electric Reliability Standard.*

right from the beginning and so starting with its definition. Nonetheless, the EU is certainly aware of the fast-growing importance of cybersecurity in the present and future world as it has identified the fight against cybercrime as a major priority under the European Agenda on Security of April 28, 2015.[40] According to this principle, European legislators may now base their future acts on the European Parliament resolution of October 3, 2017, on the fight against cybercrime (2017/2068(INI)). Although the EU Parliament was unable to produce a definition of cybersecurity, notably, the resolution recognized such inability by stating, "*the need to streamline common definitions of cybercrime, cyber warfare, cybersecurity, cyber harassment and cyberattacks to ensure that the EU institutions and EU Member States share a common legal definition.*"[41] Most importantly, the resolution seems to unveil the frustration of the EU Members for not having been able to produce a binding legal instrument as the text includes an important introductory section, which de facto provides a legal framework for future documents having legal effects. As a matter of fact, the EU Parliament Resolution states that "the sharp increase in ransomware, botnets and the unauthorized impairment of computer systems has an impact on the security of individuals. Furthermore, on the availability and integrity of their personal data, as well as on the protection of privacy and fundamental freedoms and the integrity of critical infrastructures including, but not limited to, energy and electricity supply and financial structures such as the stock exchange."[42] The resolution also further recalls that in this context, the fight against cybercrime represents a priority under the European Agenda on Security of April 28 2015.

At present, Italian authors do not seem to agree on a generally accepted definition.[43] While the EU Parliament in its resolution 2017/2068[44] introduces

---

[40] *EUROPEAN UNION COMMISSION.* The European Agenda on Security. Communication from the commission to the European parliament, the council, the European economic and social committee and the committee of the regions. EU Edition, Strasbourg, 28.04.2015 – COM(2015) 185final. https://ec.europa.eu/home-affairs/sites/default/files/e-library/documents/basic-documents/docs/eu_agenda_on_security_en.pdf.

[41] *ibidem.*

[42] *Ibidem.*

[43] A. CATALDO; F. PELUSO: *Cybersecurity, La nuova disciplina italiana ed europea alla luce della direttiva NIS, 2018,* L.PICOTTI. *La proposta di una nuova direttiva sulle misure per un elevato livello comune di cybersecurity nell'UE (c.d. NIS 2), in sostituzione della vigente direttiva (UE) 2016/1148, c.d. Direttiva NIS (Network and Information Security). In Diritto di Internet. Newsletter Osservatorio Cybercrime n.12 2020/31 gennaio 2021,* D.LIMONE. *Elementi di diritto dell'informatica, Lecce, Mediterranea ed., (1999).*

[44] See Resolution 2068/2017, https://eur-lex.europa.eu/legal-content/EN/TXT/PDF/?uri=CELEX:52017IP0366&from=EN; European Commission, Directive of the European Parliament and of the Council, Measures for a high common level of cybersecurity across

the important principle that cybersecurity affects and impacts the security of individuals though a breach of their privacy and offense to their freedom, in some local legislative context, the view on cybersecurity seems to be somehow limited by its technological nature. In this respect, cybersecurity is currently largely regarded as the practice of defending computers, servers, mobile devices, electronic systems, networks and data from malicious attacks, and the legal approach mainly involves information technology security or electronic information security. Within the area of information technology, the term cybersecurity applies in a variety of contexts, from business to mobile computing, and can be divided into a few common categories,[45] which include network security, application security, information security, operational security, disasters recovery, business continuity and end-user education.[46]

Recently, the National Cybersecurity Framework defined cybersecurity as a tool of knowledge that allows an entity to protect its physical assets, confidentiality and integrity and the availability of its information from threats caused by cyberspace. From this definition, we can first understand how the

---

the Union, repealing Directive (EU) 2016/1148: Brussels, 16.12.2020 COM(2020) 823 final 2020/0359 (COD); EUROPEAN COMMISSION, High representative of the Union for foreign affairs and security policy, The EU's Cybersecurity Strategy for the Digital Decade, cybersecurity digital transformation in a complex threat environment. Brussels, 16.12.2020 JOIN(2020) 18 final; EUROPEAN COMMISSION. Directive of the European parliament and of the council on the resilience of critical entities. Brussels, 16.12.2020 COM(2020) 829 final 2020/0365 (COD). {SEC(2020) 433 final} - {SWD(2020) 358 final} - {SWD(2020) 359 final}.

[45] N. CHOUCRI, *What is cybersecurity? Explorations in automated knowledge generation*, in political science department working paper, 2012.

[46] *E KASPERSKY. What is cybersecurity?* (https://www.kaspersky.com/resource-center/definitions/what-is-cyber-security). Network security is the practice of securing a computer network from intruders, whether targeted attackers or opportunistic malware. Application security focuses on keeping software and devices free of threats. A compromised application could provide access to the data its designed to protect. Successful security begins in the design stage, well before a program or device is deployed. Information security protects the integrity and privacy of data, both in storage and in transit. Operational security includes the processes and decisions for handling and protecting data assets. The permissions users have when accessing a network and the procedures that determine how and where data may be stored or shared all fall under this umbrella. Disaster recovery and business continuity define how an organization responds to a cyber-security incident or any other event that causes the loss of operations or data. Disaster recovery policies dictate how the organization restores its operations and information to return to the same operating capacity as before the event. Business continuity is the plan the organization falls back on while trying to operate without certain resources. End-user education addresses the most unpredictable cyber-security factor: people. Anyone can accidentally introduce a virus to an otherwise secure system by failing to follow good security practices. Teaching users to delete suspicious email attachments, not plug in unidentified USB drives, and various other important lessons is vital for the security of any organization.

discipline focuses its attention on objective legal bases in order to ensure the protection of tangible and intangible assets, which can be the object of attacks in cyberspace. Moreover, it is also regarded as a discipline that should enable the protection of the integrity and confidentiality of relevant information while at the same time ensuring the governance, assurance and business continuity of all digital infrastructure support.[47] In this respect, the National Cybersecurity Framework also clearly identifies the following three key elements that describe the area of competence for this discipline: technology, policy and people.

From the point of view of the criminal law scholar, this conceptual implant is suggestive of the diversification of the assets to be protected and, therefore, of the offense titles to be considered.

For many, cybersecurity is said to contain two souls: one human and the other computer. An increase in the number of methods and instruments capable of attacking computer systems must inevitably be accompanied by illicit human behavior. Therefore, one cannot exist without the other.

What is also necessary to bear in mind is its transversality. It is in fact possible to identify cybersecurity as a set of complex and sophisticated multidisciplinary activities and skills, many of which are non-informatics and consequently difficult to integrate with existing TCI management practices—practices that, as we have already mentioned, have as their ultimate aim ensuring the protection of tangible and intangible assets considered as possible victims in cyberspace.[48] Any type of preventive and defensive strategy must therefore necessarily be structured according to a multidisciplinary approach that allows collaboration by disclosing information and experience between the different actors involved, creating shared and accessible policies in order to ensure an efficient security of cyberspace not only at national and regional levels but also at supranational level.[49]

The interconnectedness and multidisciplinary nature of law enforcement strategies against so-called cyber threats are not the only consequence of the transversality of cybersecurity. The very people charged with managing this growing phenomenon and its many facets will have to broaden their horizons and eventually merge together elements of the economic, legal and social

[47] Rapporto Clusit 2016 sulla sicurezza ICT in Italia, in www.clusit.it.

[48] Rapporto Clusit 2016 sulla sicurezza ICT in Italia, in www.clusit.it: "*l'espressione Cyber Security indica un gruppo di attività e competenze multidisciplinari, complesse e sofisticate, molte delle quali non informatiche, che sono oggettivamente di difficile integrazione con le prassi esistenti di gestione dell'ICT.*"

[49] GIUSTOZZI, *Nuove norme cybersecurity, tutto ciò che bisogna sapere*, in *Agenda Digitale*, 2017, in www.agendadigitale.eu.

sciences.[50] If we analyze this phenomenon from a more technical point of view, cybersecurity entails the protection of computer systems from various possible threats, such as theft and the corruption of hardware, software[51] or information as well as from the interruption and hijacking of the services they may offer.

1.5. Cyberattacks and Their Characteristics

The main objective of an effective implementation of a cybersecurity strategy is to prevent the occurrence of cybercrimes, especially cyberattacks. It is important to understand that, in some cases, a cyberattack may simultaneously represent a cybercrime; however, it is not possible to assert the contrary. In other words, not all cybercrimes are cyberattacks.

A cyberattack can be defined as an assault launched by cybercriminals against single or multiple computers or networks. A cyberattack can maliciously disable computers in order to steal data. Cybercriminals use various methods to launch a cyberattack, including but not limited to the use of malware, phishing, ransomware, DOS and so on. A cyberattack's main characteristics can be divided into four points: articulated types of attacks, diversified targets, changeability of the specific object and its purposes and variability of ways of conduct.

Cyberattacks are also commonly divided into two main categories: syntactic attacks and semantic attacks. Syntactic attacks are a specific type of attack directed against a specific target in order to neutralize or destroy it. They are carried out by infecting information/computer systems through malicious

---

[50] *Le leve e le sfide per il rilancio del paese. Le frontiere della sicurezza. Sicurezza informatica e prevenzione del Cybercrime*, Cernobbio, 2017.

[51] Definitions: Hardware means any physical device that accepts input, processes input, stores the results of processing and/or provides output. Software means any and all computer programs, including software implementation of algorithms, models and methodologies, whether in source code, object code, human readable form or other form, databases and compilations, including collections of data, screens, user interfaces, report formats, firmware, development tools, templates, menus, buttons and icons and documentation, including user manuals and other training documentation, relating to any of the foregoing, in www.lawinsider.com.

software, such as viruses, worms, Trojan horses;[52] ransomwares[53] A typical example of syntactic attack is malware. Malwares are malicious software designed to access computer systems without the owners' consent for illicit purposes and/or to destroy it. It is a macro-category syntactic cyberattack being that it includes a variety of "attack programs" such as viruses, worms, Trojan horses, spywares, adware and so on. Semantic attacks, on the other hand, entails the spread of false information or requests with the main purpose of covering their tracks and/or directing the enemy in a wrong direction. This may occur being that the systems subject to this type of attack seem to be perfectly functioning. A typical example of a semantic cyberattack is the DDoS attack—a variation of the DoD syntactic attack, which is aimed at rendering a system or service unusable, for example, by flooding a targeted site with a multitude of simultaneous requests until its resources are exhausted. A DDoS attack is very similar, however, it is considered to be more powerful being that it involves a very large number of computers/networks. Through this type of attack, hackers make use of a considerable number of computers distributed over a wide geographical area or through multiple providers. Generally, DDoS attacks are carried out throughout so-called botnets, which are a group of malware-infected computer systems under the hacker's control in order to carry out a DDoS attack against targeted systems. Thanks to the use and presence of these botnets, it is very difficult to trace DDoS attacks being that they are located in different geographic locations.

DoS and DDoS are only two of the many cyberattacks present in our society. Another common cyberattack that we can cite is the "man-in-the-middle" (MitM) attack, which is a type of syntactic attack by which the attacker inserts him/herself between two interconnected communication systems, generally that of a client and a server, pretending to be one of them and intercepting important data. With this attack technique, the attacker can

[52] Definitions: Viruses are an unauthorized, self-replicating program that inserts itself into a computer system and then propagates itself to other computers via networks or disks. When activated it interferes with the operation of the computer self-replicating programs which hide in the most unlikely areas of the computer.

WORM: unlike viruses, it is an independent software which spreads over a network in order to infect different computers (without the need for a user cooperation). The most common vehicle of diffusion is emails.

TROJAN HORSE: a particular typo of malicious file that can infect the victim's computer and take possession of it. Criminals use this type of malware in order to take control of our device and perform almost any type of operation.

[53] Ransomware: malware that renders inaccessible the data of infected computers and demands the payment of a ransom in order to restore them. Technically they are considered to be cryptographic Trojan horses and have and their sole purpose the extortion of money.

be an active participant, impersonating the system, or he/she can be a passive participant, staying in the background of the attack and silently stealing hidden data. MitM techniques are usually used early on in the cyber kill chain. Attackers will often use MitM also to harvest credentials and gather intelligence about their targets. Other important types of semantic cyberattacks can be phishing, pharming, watering hole and so on. Phishing and pharming will be analyzed in depth in the next chapters. For now, we will limit our analysis of these types of attacks by stating that phishing is directed at stealing an individual's digital personal data recorded on the web in order to carry out illicit online criminal activities. They are usually perpetrated through emails that appear to be from a trusted source, but ultimately, with the use of links to illegitimate websites, they are directed at influencing users to do something or to gain personal information. Pharming, on the other hand, is a particular form of phishing through which attackers steal login credentials in order to implement an identity theft. This attack, although being very similar to phishing in its purposes, is a much more insidious and subtler computer fraud technique being that the client's information is diverted to fake sites set up in order to steal sensitive data. This deceptive attack is very dangerous, and it can also affect users equipped with advanced protection tools. It is, in fact, an attack aimed at manipulating the host's names, consequently being able to act both on the distributed domain name system (DNS) servers and directly on end users. One last type of semantic cyberattack that we can analyze is the "watering hole" attack, named this as its operating mode is reminiscent of that of a predator waiting for prey near the water, aware of the fact that they will come there in order to refuel.[54] This type of attack consists of three main steps. Firstly, the attacker must identify and observe the websites and services that the targeted user uses. Secondly, the attacker will infect and attack one of these services with the use of malware and/or malicious codes, and, lastly, the attacker will wait for the target to become infected after using one of these infected services. This form of cyberattack works being that it is based on the surprise factor. These attacks are in fact very difficult to predict and today are more effective that a common phishing attack.

Of great importance is recognizing and analyzing the several aspects related to the targets of cyberattacks as, in most cases, they involve the functioning of national critical infrastructures, with the aim to acquire data and classified information. Critical infrastructures refer to the whole body of

---

[54] See https://www.ncsc.gov.uk/collection/supply-chain-security/watering-hole-attacks; also https://hackerstribe.com/vocabolario/watering-hole/.

digital and non-digital structures, networks and assets that are essential to the functioning and security of a nation. Therefore, to ensure their continuing operation is essential to areas of national security including economic, public health and strategic defense.

Critical infrastructures are generally similar for all nations as they are developed to serve the basic daily operation needs of various countries. However, infrastructures identified as critical may vary among different countries depending on the local resources, needs and strategic plans and programs.

A recent advisory report by Microsoft[55] solicited by the US Government discusses the key aspects of cyber threats and identifies four key cyber threats worldwide: cybercrime, economic espionage, military espionage and cyber conflict. The report emphasizes that such threats may have serious implications for critical infrastructures. The authors also suggest that understanding the complex threat landscape and grappling with the breadth of cyberattackers, especially those affiliated with nation states or organized crime, is a challenging proposition. The commitment of a concerned nation should be to ensure that the most critical threats are addressed and that the best defenses against those threats are enabled. In this regard, the first line of defense for a nation would be to establish a comprehensive and unequivocal legal framework, essential for developing an effective specific legislation.

Therefore, the first step for the legislator would be understanding national threats as the preservation and protection of individual rights will follow and be included as a consequential benefit. However, understanding and managing a national-level threat is an uneasy task, and establishing national cybersecurity priorities is complex. A clear understanding of the motivations and capabilities of threat actors; potential avenues for attacks or exploitation; the key assets, functions or information that could be targeted is necessary. To effectively recognize and assess the potential impact of cybersecurity episodes on critical infrastructures is a key element that complements the full understanding of possible threats in order to develop legislative countermeasures enabling the ideal management of their risks and minimizing their potential impact at the national and individual levels.

The legislator should approach cybersecurity challenges considering both their horizontal and vertical dimensions. Horizontal dimensions include cross-

[55] J. PAUL NICHOLAS, *Developing a Framework to Improve Critical Infrastructure. Cybersecurity. Response of Microsoft Corporation to Request for Information,* Before the United States Department of Commerce National Institute of Standards and Technology. Docket No. 130208119-3119-01- April 8, 2013.

sector aspects of cybersecurity that cover non-critical and critical infrastructures, while vertical dimensions include asset-focused aspects of cybersecurity that may require a specific set of unique risk mitigations. Critical infrastructures are regarded differently between the public and private sectors as governments are inclined to look at them as a monolithic collection of systems and services, while the private sector focuses on core elements within its direct control or on its contractual obligations to deliver services. Therefore, it comes as no surprise that governments usually read threats to critical infrastructures through the lens of a broad upscale perspective that aims at identifying those elements, facts or events that may compromise the national stability and security and the capability of a prompt reaction as well as the assets needing protection due to their importance for economic stability or force projection. However, often, governments are concerned about events having a high impact but low probability, and this attitude may result in requirements and compliance obligations that may not be necessarily useful to improve cybersecurity for critical infrastructures, private sector enterprises and individual citizens in their daily occupations. Different and somehow opposite is the position of the private sector, which is focused on delivering services, ensuring the timeliness of value chains, innovation and building market share. Private sector organizations typically found their risk assessment evaluation on business objectives, such as shareholder value, efficacy and customer service, and their risk management efforts are addressed to support organizational objectives by enhancing the security and resilience of the information technology sector.

However, in this scenario, in between are the rights and interests of the individual citizens that the legislator is called to safeguard and protect. Therefore, the resulting framework, on which the legislator should elaborate, must be flexible enough to balance the goals of both the government and the private sector while also defending the primary interests and rights of citizens.

The Council of the European Union issued a Directive on the Identification and Designation of European Critical Infrastructures (ECI) and the assessment of the need to improve its protection.[56] This Directive defines a critical infrastructure as a particular asset or system located in Member States that are essential for the maintenance of the health, safety, security and economic or social well-being of people. It also states that the eventual

[56] See Directive (EU) 114/08 www.eur-lex.europa.eu.

disruption or destruction of these infrastructures could have a significant impact on at least two Member States.[57]

The main critical infrastructures subject to a cyberattack are especially control systems, energy, telecommunication, transport, water and financial sectors, thus, mainly sectors that are of fundamental importance for the good functioning and stability of a country. It may occur that a failure of a critical infrastructure in one Member State can cause effects in another one. These critical infrastructures with such a trans-national dimension should be identified and designated as ECI. Because of this trans-national dimension, it is required that each Member State identifies potential ECIs that both satisfy the cross-cutting and sectoral criteria and meet the definitions provided.[58] This procedure shall be implemented by each Member State through a series of consecutive steps established by the Council.[59] Following this designation, the operators of ECIs are required to create so-called "operator security plans,"

---

[57] Council Directive 2008/114/EC On the identification of European critical infrastructures and the assessment of the need to improve their protection, art 2 lett. a; b., a) critical infrastructure' means an asset, system or part thereof located in Member States which is essential for the maintenance of vital societal functions, health, safety, security, economic or social well-being of people, and the disruption or destruction of which would have a significant impact in a Member State as a result of the failure to maintain those functions. b) 'European critical infrastructure' or 'ECI' means critical infrastructure located in Member States the disruption or destruction of which would have a significant impact on at least two Member States. The significance of the impact shall be assessed in terms of cross-cutting criteria. This includes effects resulting from cross-sector dependencies on other types of infrastructure.

[58] Article 3 Directive (EU) 114/08: "The cross-cutting criteria having a horizontal application to all critical infrastructure sectors shall be developed taking into account the severity of the effect of the disruption or destruction of a particular infrastructure. They shall be adopted by at the latest. The sectoral criteria shall be developed for priority sectors while taking into account the characteristics of individual critical infrastructure sectors and involving, as appropriate, relevant stakeholders. They shall be adopted for each priority sector at the latest one year following the designation as a priority sector."

[59] The procedure can be found in article 5 of Decision 1999/468/EC. Article 5 establishes the "regulatory procedure," stating that the Commission shall be assisted by regulatory committee composed of the representatives of the Member States and chaired by the representative of the Commission. The representative of the Commission must submit to the committee a draft of the possible measures that must be taken. After receiving this draft, the committee must deliver its opinion within a specific time limit. On its side, if the measures are accepted by the committee, the Commission will proceed to adopt them. If however the measures envisaged are found to be not in accordance to the committee's opinion, the Commission must submit to the Council a new proposal relating to the measures to be taken and must also inform the European Parliament. The Council may act by qualified majority on the proposal, within a determined period which shall never exceed three months from the date of referral to the Council. If, within that specific period of time, the Council opposes itself to the proposal, the Commission shall re-examine it.

which should establish relevant coherent security solutions for their protection.

Necessary for the fight against cyberattacks is also the implementation of adequate countermeasures. Countermeasures consisting of activities, tools, procedures and techniques that reduce a threat or attack by eliminating or preventing it, minimizing the damage that it may cause and consequently enabling corrective actions that must be taken. The main and most effective measure one can take is to project special software's, use tools that guarantee the attributes of a particular system and in the search for means of prevention, detection and response to threats.

1.6. Violence: A Characterizing Element in Cybercrimes

In the previous sub-chapter, we described the two main categories of cyberattacks, syntactic attacks and semantic attacks, and analyzed the major types, methods and technical features by which cybercrimes are perpetrated. In this sub-chapter, we will discuss the important element of "violence," which is mostly and transversally common to the large variety of cybercrimes and relevant to the legislator in order to adequately frame its role within individual circumstances.

Traditionally in criminal law, a distinction is made between "violence against things" and "violence against a person." However, both notions need to be readapted if they are exerted through automatic processing and transmission data systems or elaborated by communication networks able to disseminate messages, images or any other means carrying harmful or dangerous contents.

As emphasized by L. Picotti,[60] the starting point for analyzing the new context in which cybercrimes are committed is the existing symptomatic norm of our positive legal order on the "violence against things," as outlined in Article 392, paragraph 20 and the newly introduced paragraph 30 of the Criminal Code.[61] In fact, Article 392 enables dealing with damages to

---

60 L.PICOTTI, *Cybercrime e tutela penale dei diritti della persona e della privacy nel web*, AIAF, 2020, pp.7-15.

61 Art. 392 of the Criminal Code. "Della tutela arbitraria delle private ragioni." Esercizio arbitrario delle proprie ragioni con violenza sulle cose. "*Chiunque, al fine di esercitare un preteso diritto, potendo ricorrere al giudice, si fa arbitrariamente ragione da sé medesimo, mediante violenza sulle cose, è punito a querela della persona offesa, con la multa fino a euro 516. Agli effetti della legge penale, si ha violenza sulle cose allorché la cosa viene danneggiata o trasformata, o ne è mutata la destinazione. Si ha, altresì, violenza sulle cose*

intangible computer structural elements or assets, such as programs, software, information and data collected by processing systems and automated processing, that occurred with the initial applications and uses of electronic processors. However, the technological advancements forced the legislator to abandon the initial concept limited to "physicality," thought of as closely related and linked to material objects ("things"), and expand such concept to include the various behaviors of alteration, modification and cancellation in the entirety or in part of a computer program or an impeding disturbance of the operation of a computer or ICT system.

In this regard, such behaviors can be considered as violent only in a translated sense, rather representing a method of abusive or unauthorized interference on the correct functioning of IT systems or a breach of availability, integrity and the authenticity of programs, data and information by unauthorized subjects. However, the equivalence introduced by the legislator is still relevant as this notion is an essential constitutive element of many other crimes. For instance, it is at the basis of computer damage crimes (Articles 635bis of the Italian Criminal Code). Therefore, it not only refers to material things (as foreseen by the crime of common damage in Article 635 of the Italian Criminal Code) but also to data, information, programs or IT and telematics systems. This is a very important new legal vision for these circumstances as it also targets the constituent elements of even more serious crimes, such as the "disturbed freedom of industry or commerce" through violence against things. In this regard, Article 513 of the Italian Criminal Code indicates the use of "fraudulent means," an alternative means concurrent with the illicit actions of threats or violence. Similarly, the circumstance of extortion is equally achievable through violence against things (Article 629 of the Criminal Code). In fact, it could be committed by secretly installing malwares in the computer systems of victims (i.e., through a Trojan horse or deceptive emails), blocking their availability, which can only be reacquired, by extortion, upon payment of a sum in exchange for a decryption key.

With specific regard to the fundamental rights of the person, the incidence of similar forms of interference, manipulation or abusive or otherwise unauthorized conduct committed in cyberspace in the context of interpersonal relationships is even more relevant. For instance, in this context, the forms of the unauthorized collection, processing and management of personal information and data including images, videos or voice recordings of

---

allorché un programma informatico viene alterato, modificato o cancellato in tutto o in parte ovvero viene impedito o turbato il funzionamento di un sistema informatico o telematico."

conversations stolen without the knowledge or against the will of the owner that may circulate in order to coerce the victim's will and freedom of self-determination are relevant. These actions can be perpetrated for the purpose of mere retaliation, debasement, humiliation or even simple defamation of the subject, often producing irreparable offenses against his/her image, identity and dignity.

These behaviors cannot be legally qualified sensu stricto as violent in the absence of a defining norm or normative "equivalence," such as the one examined above with reference to the notion of "violence against things." However, recent experience suggests how they can present themselves with a force of aggression and moral pressure on the victim, which can be de facto greater than physical violence, especially considering the characteristics of non-physical violent behaviors and their effects in cyberspace.

As a matter of fact, it is alarming how these behaviors multiply quickly, especially in social networks, due to the easy access and use of these networks and the lack of direct personal contact with the victims, which contributes to reducing inhibitions to commit potentially illegal actions. These circumstances may involve various areas of society; including social and family relationships. For instance, violent behavior realized through the use of IT means typically involves minors as victims of adult perpetrators, but they are also increasingly committed by minors against other minors, as shown by the growing phenomenon of cyberbullying. This circumstance may occur in many forms and in various contexts and generally takes the form of the oppression and degradation of the victim, particularly in relationships between peers, in which the loss of mutual respect and recognition of the other as a person seems to be facilitated by the intermediation of the IT devices. Furthermore, violent behavior realized by the use of IT means may take place in the context of sentimental, marital, interpersonal relationships. In this context, strong frustration and aggressive attitudes are now increasingly often no longer or not only manifested in a real confrontation between people by direct verbal or written communications or though physical actions but more often exclusively through the web and social networks. Considering the large dissemination and permanence of communications, messages, images or videos on the web, these behaviors determine de facto a serious level of humiliation and degradation of the targeted person. This can similarly be likened to violence or at least to moral violence. The absence of a border between physical and non-physical violence is widely accepted, and the risk factor, represented by the interrelatedness of specific types of physical and non-physical violence and the extent to which they expose the victims to non-physical violence, have been well clarified.[62] In this regard, clarifying examples are provided by behaviors that can be qualified as revenge pornography, which were subjects of recent specific criminal charges defined as cyberstalking and considered a new aggravating circumstance of the crime of persecutory acts.[63]

Therefore, online defamation can be exerted in various forms and, especially in social networks, framed by the jurisprudence as aggravating circumstances in paragraph 3, letter c) of Article 595 of the Italian Criminal Code. However, the manipulative use of IT systems and programs frequently proved to trespass on to other forms of potential illegal activities by means of the deformation of identity and digital identity theft of the offended person. The legislator at the moment considers these offences only as a peculiar aggravated hypothesis of computer fraud and included in Article 640ter of the Italian Penal Code as part of the economic crimes. In reality, digital identity theft goes well beyond the scope of economic-based crimes, impacting the essential core of the rights of the person to be protected as such in cyberspace due to its growing importance in real life. Various legal scholars have solicited such observation several times.[64] These are harmful behaviors that certainly require a specific legislative response given their potential for offensiveness on primary legal assets, such as the fundamental rights of the person, similar to those that are recognizable in corresponding common behaviors and are incriminated as common cases conceived for conduct carried out in the physical world outside cyberspace.

The principle that must apply is that what is illegal and deserving of a criminal sanction offline cannot be lawful or tolerated online. Moreover, a repressive intervention, particularly if the prevention of a specific crime proves to be ineffective or insufficient, as in the case of cyberbullying, appears to be indispensable. This is precisely due to the peculiar characteristics of high and potentially unlimited dissemination in the global space of the web, where information is widely and easily accessible to anyone, at any place and at any time, such that data, messages, images, videos, audio and any other illegal or

---

[62] M. L. LANZA, *Non-Physical Violence*, in AAOHN Journal, 2006 Sep; 54(9), p. 397-402.

[63] Art.612 CP, comma 2. Atti persecutori. Aggravante: *"se il fatto è commesso attraverso strumenti informatici o telematici…"*

[64] L.PICOTTI, *Cybercrime e tutela penale dei diritti della persona e della privacy nel web*, AIAF, 2020, pp.7-15; M. MARRAFFINO, *La sostituzione di persona mediante furto di identità digitale*, in A. CADOPPI, *Cybercrime*, 2019, p. 307 ss.; R. FLOR, *Phishing, identity theft e identity abuse. Le prospettive applicative del diritto penale vigente*, in Rivista it. dir. proc. pen., 2007, p. 899; C.CRESCIOLI, *Una sentenza della Cassazione sulla sostituzione della persona online*, in www.penalecontemporaneo.it

harmful content uploaded and distributed in cyberspace remain available for an indefinite period, being very difficult if not technically impossible to intervene with in order to guarantee a definitive and absolute removal from the network. The extremely complex architecture of the internet and telematics transmission techniques has led the European jurisprudence to recognize the impossibility of a complete and total removal of illegal information. For instance, in this regard, the EU legislation limits the obligation to cancel information just by excluding its availability though common browsers and search engines in the versions accessible in the Member States (the so-called "territorial scope of the right to de-index").

Hence, alongside prevention and accountability policies arose the particular need to implement interventions aimed at guaranteeing the possibility of identifying users and the systematic and prompt collaboration of the managers in charge of the web's networks and services, the so-called "internet service providers." This is especially the case if these managers, as in the typical cases of Facebook or Google, hold dominant positions, progressively acquired through concentrations of power and control, that must be balanced by a consistent attribution of responsibility, even criminal, in the event the obligations of crime prevention or the timely removal of illegal or harmful contents referred to users are violated.

The recent EU and national jurisprudence shows the increasing jurisprudential attention aimed at combating this new criminal phenomena, imposed to adapt and improve the existing regulatory, investigative and operational tools in order to ensure an effective intervention able to guarantee the integrity of the common and primary rights and legal assets that are threatened or violated in cyberspace.

In light of the criminal law in force, a basic systematic classification of the various forms of cybercrime remains valid as it distinguishes all the crimes that have been specifically formulated by the legislator. Nevertheless, it would be important to include in our national legislation further new ad hoc cases and better clarify their constituent elements, such as methods of conduct, objects, means and events characterized by technical IT content—elements that would be inconceivable without ICT and that could help define these circumstances as cybercrimes in the strict sense.

It is important to observe that new indictments in this area of law have been recommended or imposed by supranational organizations, such as in particular the Cybercrime Convention of the Council of Europe of 2001 and the EU Directive 2013/40, in order to fill legal gaps that could not have been overcome otherwise. In this regard, the list of crimes characterized by abusive access to a computer system (Article 615ter of the Criminal Code) include computer damage (Articles 63bis, ter, quater, quinquies of the Criminal Code), forgery of public IT documents (pursuant to Article 491bis of the Criminal Code) and computer fraud (Article 640ter of the Italian Criminal Code).

However, there are other types of circumstances described in the existing legislation that, due to their regulatory and technical formulation structure, are already able to subsume these new forms of illegal activities committed in cyberspace.[65] This is without violating the prohibition of analogy in *malam partem*, which has its constitutional basis in the expressed *principle of legality,*[66] oon the basis of which the rules do not apply outside of the cases expressly established by them. In fact, the used normative language is suitable for including these new behaviors or facts within its scope even if they were certainly not conceivable at the time when the specific legislation was established. Therefore, they can be inclusively called "*cybercrimes.*" A good example is provided by the crime of defamation (Article 595 of the Italian Criminal Code), in which the offense to the reputation of others can certainly be committed by communicating with several people in any form and, therefore, also with messages on the web and, furthermore, by the extortion (Article 629 of the Italian Criminal Code) carried out with malware capable of encrypting data and programs of the computer systems of others. In the field of crimes against a person, crimes of private violence (Article 610 of the Italian Criminal Code) and of threats (Article 612 of the Italian Criminal Code) can assume particular importance as messages that include menace or that force the passive subject to do, tolerate or omit something, against his/her will, and could be conveyed by the web.

A most recent circumstance in this area is the crime of persecutory acts or stalking (Article 612bis of the Italian Criminal Code), in which the repeated conduct of threat or harassment can be carried out with computer communications or in cyberspace, similar to what happens when using traditional means of communication, such as letters and telephone calls. The frequency and the magnitude of the phenomenon led the legislator to introduce the aggravating circumstance referred to in the new paragraph 3 to limit with a more severe penalty this possibility, which is considered particularly insidious.[67]

---

[65] L.PICOTTI, *Cybercrime e tutela penale dei diritti della persona e della privacy nel web*, AIAF, 2020, pp.7-15.

[66] Article 25 co. 2 Italian Constitution.

[67] With the decree law 23 February 2009, n. 11 (Urgent measures regarding public safety and combating sexual violence, as well as with regard to persecutory acts), converted with

An important element that must be emphasized is that, in some cases, the moment in which the offense of the legal good and the full violation of the fundamental rights protected by the law materially takes place involving the natural person, victim of the crime, even if the conduct was carried out through an IT means. This is the typical case of cyberstalking, a new-generation crime in which the offensive conduct of harassment or threat, carried out through computerized means, has a real effect on the victim as it causes him/her a state of anxiety or fear or a modification of his/her life habits. Therefore, the impact on the victim's life by the direct means of a computer or an IT device in general unquestionably demonstrates the inseparable connection of this with the real world. Similarly, in other cases, the facts constituting a crime can be entirely committed and consumed in cyberspace. This is, for instance, the case with the illicit dissemination of sexually explicit images or videos (new Article 612ter of the Italian Criminal Code), with online defamation (Article 595, paragraph 30 of the Italian Criminal Code) or with unlawful communication or the dissemination of personal data illegally acquired "on a large scale" (Article 167bis, Legislative Decree no. 196/2003 and subsequent amendments). In these cases, the effects produced in cyberspace determine an offense to the victim's dignity, identity or reputation or the violation of the victim's privacy.

---

amendments into law no. 38, Article 612-bis, which punishes the crime of "Persecutory acts," was introduced in Title XII of the Criminal Code (Crimes against the person), in section III dedicated to crimes against moral freedom. The current text of art. 612-bis, after the changes made with the Decree Law 14 August 2013, n. 93 converted into Law 15 October 2013, n. 119, reads as follows: " *Salvo che il fatto costituisca più grave reato, è punito con la reclusione da sei mesi a cinque anni chiunque, con condotte reiterate, minaccia o molesta taluno in modo da cagionare un perdurante e grave stato di ansia o di paura ovvero da ingenerare un fondato timore per l'incolumita' propria o di un prossimo congiunto o di persona al medesimo legata da relazione affettiva ovvero da costringere lo stesso ad alterare le proprie abitudini di vita.*
La pena è aumentata se il fatto è commesso dal coniuge, anche separato o divorziato, o da persona che è o è stata legata da relazione affettiva alla persona offesa ovvero se il fatto è commesso attraverso strumenti informatici o telematici.
La pena è aumentata fino alla metà se il fatto è commesso a danno di un minore, di una donna in stato di gravidanza o di una persona con disabilità di cui all'articolo 3 della legge 5 febbraio 1992, n. 104, ovvero con armi o da persona travisata.
Il delitto è punito a querela della persona offesa. Il termine per la proposizione della querela è di sei mesi. La remissione della querela può essere soltanto processuale. La querela è comunque irrevocabile se il fatto è stato commesso mediante minacce reiterate nei modi di cui all'articolo 612, secondo comma. Si procede tuttavia d'ufficio se il fatto è commesso nei confronti di un minore o di una persona con disabilità di cui all'articolo 3 della legge 5 febbraio 1992, n. 104, nonché quando il fatto è connesso con altro delitto per il quale si deve procedere d'ufficio."

Violence can therefore be considered largely structural to cybercrimes. However, legal instruments at the EU and national levels exist but seem to somehow still be limited in scope and be insufficient to prevent the violation of individual rights and ensure criminalization of the most pervasive forms of cyber violence—thus, leaving ample room for improvements to the legislators at both the national and supranational levels.

2. Cybersecurity in the Current European Legislative Framework

The multiplicity and non-organic nature of the laws concerning cyberspace has become one of the primary causes of concern for the international community. The main concern is especially the current lack of a global regulation, that is, a general basis of common rules for judging and possibly punishing any criminal activity that takes place in cyberspace.

In recent years, there have been a number of initiatives, both national and international, principally aimed at strengthening safety standards and ensuring adequate levels of cooperation between key sectors of society so as to enable a more effective approach to different issues relating to this subject matter.[68]

The 2000 European Commission's Communication on Cybercrime was one of the first documents to demonstrate an interest in cybersecurity. This paper demonstrates how following the profound changes brought by digitalization and the convergence and continuing globalization of computer networks, there was a need to pursue a common criminal policy aimed at the protection of society against cybercrime by adopting appropriate legislation and fostering international cooperation.

In 2003, the European Council adopted the European Security Strategy (ESS), which established important principles and set a clear objective for advancing the EU's security interests.

Following the 2004 Madrid terrorist attack,[69] it became very clear how the development of a national cybersecurity strategy and cooperation was imperative. It was also deemed necessary to strengthen the capacity of the various computer security incident response teams (CSIRT)[70] as well as study

---

[68] O. POLLICINO, *Internet nella Giurisprudenza delle Corti Europe,*2013, 5.

[69] Which saw as its protagonist a whole series of terrorist attacks of Islamic origin coordinated in order to hit the local public transport system as well as the users of the service.

[70] CSIRT is and IT security intervention team who has the responsibility to monito, intercept, analyze and respond to cyber threats.

the protection of data, privacy and emerging privacy technologies, including but not limited to IT threat landscapes.

The United Nations Congresses on Crime Prevention and Criminal Justice of 2005 recognized the severity of cybercrimes and cyberattacks. It mainly focused on what effective measures could be taken in order to combat international organized crime, especially those crimes that take place within cyberspace. The Bangkok Declaration supported the efforts made to strengthen and intensify existing cooperation aimed at preventing, investigating and prosecuting computer- and technology-related crimes. Consequently, in this regard, in 2010, the UN achieved two very important results. The first was a recommendation that the United Nations Office on Drugs and Crime (UNODC) provide assistance and training to states requesting such in order to improve national laws in the fight against cybercrime. Furthermore, the United Nations Congress on Crime Prevention and Criminal Justice provided a recommendation that the UNODC convene an intergovernmental group of experts to carry out an in-depth study of the problems regarding cybercrime and the possible initiatives already undertaken by Member States, the international community and the private sector.

In April of 2011, the Cybercrime Convention Committee (T-CY)[71] adopted two resolutions concerning the efforts made by the UNODC in regard cybercrime, underscoring its importance. Firstly, RES/20/7 requested that the UNODC continue to provide technical assistance to requesting states for the prevention, detection and investigation of all forms of cybercrime. Moreover, Resolution 33 was drafted on the "*Prevention, protection and international cooperation against the use of new information technologies to abuse and/or exploit children.*"[72] This framework has been further complemented by RES 22/7, "*Strengthening international cooperation to combat cybercrime,*" and by RES 22/8, "*Promoting technical assistance and capacity-building to strengthen national measures and international cooperation against cybercrime,*" both adopted by the Global Programme on Cybercrime.[73]

In 2013, the European Union Strategy was adopted in order to harmonize the European cybersecurity system. With this new strategy, an invitation to all Member States was sent, requesting them to adopt a specific national

[71] *The Cybercrime Convention Committee* (T-CY) represents the State Parties to the Budapest Convention on Cybercrime. Based on article 46 of the Convention, the consultation of the Committee aims at facilitating the effective use and implementation of the Convention, the exchange of information and consideration of any future amendments, *in* www.coe.it.

[72] Resolution 2011/33.

[73] S. MANACORDA, R. FLOR, J.OH JANG, *Cybercriminality,* Milano, 2012, pp 17 ss.

legislation aimed at preventing and responding to the disturbances and attacks affecting European telecommunication systems.[74]

With the development of the EU internal market, many network and information systems have taken a cross-border dimension, meaning that an incident involving the safety of information system networks in one country may have repercussions in other European and non-European countries. The principles contained in this strategy are as follows: a) the protection of fundamental rights, freedom of expression, personal data and privacy; b) guaranteed network access for all; c) democratic and efficient "multi-stakeholder governance and d) shared responsibility among all actors involved. To address these challenges, the strategy outlines five priorities. Firstly, it must achieve so-called cyber-resilience, consequently reducing cybercrime. It must also develop a common security and defense policy (CSDP) as well as both industrial and strategic cybersecurity resources and, lastly, create an international union cyberspace policy.[75]

Cybersecurity is therefore today a global strategy priority for foreign policy and EU's security.[76] This global strategy emphasizes the need to protect not only the EU and its citizens but also underscores the need to strengthen the EU as a security community.[77]

Recently, in July 2020, the European Commission issued a new document[78] containing a specific strategy to be developed over the next five years. This strategy mainly focuses on the creation of skills and capabilities to ensure a security environment that is appropriate for and compatible with future needs.

---

[74] As a natural continuation, the European Parliament approved the 2013 resolution on "the European Union Strategy for Cybersecurity: an open and secure cyberspace, calling on all Member Stated to adopt specific national rules to prevent and respond to disturbances and attacks affecting telecommunications systems in Europe.

[75] Joint communication to the European Parliament, the Council, the European economic and social Committee and the Committee of the regions: Cybersecurity Strategy of the European Union: An Open, Safe and Secure Cyberspace, in www.ec.europa.eu.

[76] See F. SANTORO, *Cooperazione internazionale in materia di criminalità informatica*, Roma, 2011; L. XINGAN, *International actions against cybercrime: Networking legal systems in the networked crime scene,* 2007, in http://www. webology.org/2007/v4n3/a45.html.

[77] E. CARLI, *la politica di sicurezza e difesa comune dell'UE*, Torino, 2019, 28 ss.

[78] Communication from the Commission to the European Parliament, the European Council, the Council, the European Economic and Social Committee and the Committee of the Regions on the EU Security Union Strategy, 2020, in www.ec.europa.eu.

2.1. International Sources: The Journey to the Convention on Cybercrime (CoC)

At the international level, in 1983, the Organization for Economic Co-operation and Development (OECD) conducted a study on the possibility of applying and harmonizing criminal laws at the international level to combat cybercrime. In 1986, the OECD published the "Computer Related Crime: Analysis of Legal Policy" report, in which the existing regulations and reform proposals, drawn up by some Member States, were analyzed, subsequently recommending a series of criminal instruments in the fight against cybercrime.[79]

At the European level, in 1989, the Council of Europe promoted a recommendation on cybercrime,[80] with which it attempted to identify and define what constitutes cybercrimes, dividing them into a "minimum" list and an "optional" list. The "minimum" list included crimes such as computer fraud, the forgery of computer documents, the corruption of data and programs, unauthorized access and so on. The "optional" list, alternatively, invited states to possibly incriminate the unauthorized alteration of data and programs, computer espionage, the unauthorized use of a computer network or even the unauthorized use of a protected IT program.[81]

In 1997, the Committee of Experts on Crime in Cyberspace was established. This Committee was entrusted with the important task of drafting an international convention aimed at suppressing crimes within cyberspace. This was also primarily to facilitate international cooperation in investigation activities. At the end of a four-year work process, on November of 2001, the CoC was adopted, also known as the 2001 Budapest Convention. To date, this Convention constitutes the most important instrument we have on the fight against cybercrime.

Amongst its objectives, there is a need to pursue an international common criminal policy. This is pursued by developing international cooperation that takes into account the profound changes due to the evolution of digital technology and the globalization of computer networks.

---

[79] See M. BRIAT, U. SIEBER, *Computer Related Criminality; Analysis of Legal Policy in the OECD Area,* Parigi, 1989.

[80] Recommendation (EU) 9/89.

[81] The recommendation of 1989 was later updated in 1994, when the Council decided to introduce the trade of illegally obtained access codes and the spread of computer viruses, such as malware.

The CoC includes substantial procedural rules of criminal law and applies not only to the crimes that are defined by it but also to all crimes that can be committed thorough a computer system as well as to any other crime for which "digital evidence" must be collected.[82]

Specifically, the main areas of intervention concern harmonizing substantive criminal law and procedural aspects, especially concerning evidence, strengthening international cooperation and narrowing the number of provided assistance tools, consequently guaranteeing the exchange of information in real time.

Within the Convention, computer crimes are divided into four titles respectively dedicated to crimes against the integrity, confidentiality and availability of data and IT systems; computer-related offences; content-related offences; and crime relating to copyright infringements.

Chapter III of the Convention is entirely dedicated to international cooperation. According to Article 23 of the CoC: "The Parties shall co-operate with each other, in accordance with the provisions of this chapter, and through the application of relevant international instruments on international co-operation in criminal matters, arrangements agreed on the basis of uniform or reciprocal legislation, and domestic laws, to the widest extent possible for the purposes of investigations or proceedings concerning criminal offences related to computer systems and data, or for the collection of evidence in electronic form of a criminal offence."[83]

The Convention therefore mainly aims to discipline some important issues such as extradition, mutual assistance in investigations and the collection of electronic evidence. It also aims to discipline the so-called "spontaneous information," acknowledging that a party may, within the boundaries of its national legislation, transmit to another arty information that has been obtained during the course of an investigation if it considers that such information would help the receiving party in initiating or carrying out its own investigations or proceedings concerning criminal offences established in accordance with this Convention.

Before the final provisions, title III established the so-called "contact points" in order to ensure immediate assistance and cooperation in investigations and also in the gathering of electronic evidence.

---

[82] GERCKER M., *The Convention on Cybercrime*, in MMR, 2004, 728 ss., M.F.MIQUELON, *The Convention on Cybercrime: an Harmonized Implementation of International Penal Law*, in J.M. *Comp. & Info* L., 2005.

[83] Chapter III, Article 23 of the Convention on Cybercrime, 2001.

To date, the Budapest Convention constitutes the most important treaty against cybercrime as well as a fundamental point of reference for the harmonization of different national criminal legislations.

2.2. European Union's Implementation of Common Levels of Cybersecurity and Cyber Strategy through the European Network and Information Security Agency (ENISA)

In 2004, another very important step was taken toward the instauration of a European cybersecurity policy with the institution of the European Network and Information Security Agency" (ENISA), with regulation (EC) No 460/2004.[84] The agency was dedicated to achieving a common level of cybersecurity and cyber strategy across Europe. Its primary scope was to ensure a high and effective level of network and information security for the benefit of the citizens, consumers and enterprises of the EU, also contributing to the functioning of the EU internal market. ENISA therefore originally contributed to the overall objective of not only ensuring a high level of security for communication networks and information systems but also that of combating cybercrime. The Agency thus became an expertise hub for many Member States, to which it provided technical assistance for the development of policies on network and information security, strengthening its capacity to prevent, detect and respond to IT incidents.[85]

Today, ENISA's directive is Regulation (EU) No 881/2019 of the European Parliament and of the EU Council, commonly known as the "Cybersecurity Act,"[86] (CSA), which repealed Regulation (EU) No 526/2013. The CSA forms a key part of the new EU cybersecurity strategy, which aims to strengthen the EU's resilience against cyberattacks, create a single cybersecurity market in terms of products, services and processes and increase consumer confidence in digital technologies.

This new regulation aims at achieving two main objectives: firstly, to strengthen the role of ENISA and, secondly, to achieve a European legislative

---

[84] This regulation has been repealed since 2013 by regulation (EU) No 526/2013 of the European Parliament and of the Council concerning the European Union Agency for Network and Information Security (ENISA).

[85] A. CONTALDO: *ENISA e le competenze comunitarie per la cybersicurezza,* Pisa, 2020, 71 ss.

[86] A.FONSI, *Cybersecurity Act: l'Unione europea costruisce un sistema di sicurezza informatica by design*, in www.iusinitinere,it, 2019.

and regulatory framework for the certification of IT security and of ICT products, services and processes.[87] The CSA, in other words, intends to strengthen ENISA's role by guaranteeing it a permanent mandate and allowing it to carry out not only technical consultancy tasks but also support activities for the operational management of cyber incidents by the Member States. In this way, ENISA will be able to provide more concrete support, including with respect to the implementation of the NIS Directive. ENISA will also play a leading role in the management of the certification system introduced by the CSA. Another key point of the CSA, as mentioned, concerns the introduction of a European certification system for the IT security of digital products and services, also intended to facilitate the exchange of the same within the EU and to increase consumer confidence in them. Lastly, the CSA intends to introduce an overall framework of rules governing the European cybersecurity certification schemes. As you can read in the paper "Bolstering ENISA in the EU Cybersecurity Certification Framework," the agency's mission is to "pro-actively contribute to the emerging EU framework for the ICT certification of products and services and carry out the drawing up of candidate certification schemes in line with the cybersecurity act, and additional services and tasks."[88]

The establishment of a common certification system should favor the so-called "security by design," therefore realizing cyber security starting from its initial stages: the design stage of ICT products. In other words, it should facilitate the inclusion of informatics safety starting with the initial steps in the development of ICT products, including those devices related to the common daily use of the web called the Internet of Things (IoT). IoT represents an interesting part of the opportunities offered by ICT as they can be described as the interconnection via the internet of computing devices embedded in everyday objects, enabling them to send and receive data. Therefore, IoT security should be understood as a security strategy and protection mechanism that specifically safeguards against the possibility of cyberattacks on IoT devices that are connected to the network and purposely built for a fixed set of functionalities.

---

[87] L. TOSONI, *Cybersecurity Act, ecco le nuove norme in arrivo su certificazione dei prodotti e servizi ICT*, in www.agendadigitale.eu, 2019; A. FONSI, *Cybersecurity Act: l'Unione europea costruisce un sistema di sicurezza informatica by design*, in www.iusinitinere,it, 2019.

[88] *ENISA, Bolstering ENISA in the EU Cybersecurity certification framework,* in www.enisa.europa.eu, 2019.

Next to this, the European legislator also refers to "security by default." When designing ICT products, services or processes, companies, organizations and the public sector should implement a configuration that guarantees a higher level of security that would allow the user to receive a default configuration establishing the most secure setting possible. Consequently, it should not be the users' duty to adequately configure an ICT product, service or process.[89]

In June 2019, the EU took an important step forward toward realizing its ambition to significantly reinforce cybersecurity across Europe through the enactment of the CSA and establishing the European Union Agency for Cybersecurity (ENISA), which has become a key instrument for the accomplishment of its goals in this field. The effectiveness of the new expanded and strengthened capabilities of the Agency in the field of operational cooperation soon had its trial by fire in 2020 as the system was put under pressure by the need to ensure adequate cybersecurity throughout the coronavirus disease 2019 (COVID-19) crisis. The CSA also represents an important framework for European cybersecurity certification schemes, which are directed at establishing a digital single market (DSM) for ICT products, services and processes. In the year 2020, the Agency entered into its full functions, particularly by developing candidate schemes for common criteria and cloud services.[90]

2.3. European Cybersecurity Certification Scheme

The innovative result of the CSA was not only the reform of the ENISA but also and especially the introduction of a European certification system for the IT security of digital products, services and processes. The European legislators' original intent was to, on one hand, attain a European

---

[89] This topic has been addressed more specifically in point 13 of the preamble of the CSA, which states: *"Undertakings, organizations and the public sector should configure the ICT products, ICT services or ICT processes designed by them in a way that ensures a higher level of security which should enable the first user to receive a default configuration with the most secure settings possible ('security by default'), thereby reducing the burden on users of having to configure an ICT product, ICT service or ICT process appropriately. Security by default should not require extensive configuration or specific technical understanding or non-intuitive behavior on the part of the user, and should work easily and reliably when implemented. If, on a case-by-case basis, a risk and usability analysis leads to the conclusion that such a setting by default is not feasible, users should be prompted to opt for the most secure setting.*

[90] www.enisa.europa.eu.

cybersecurity certification framework that could implement the functioning of the EU internal market, increasing the level of EU cybersecurity. On the other hand, they wanted to render a harmonized approach to this certification scheme in order to create a DSM for ICT products, services and processes, thus creating a user-consumer trust relationship.

With the creation of a specific European cybersecurity certification scheme, the safeguarding of the authenticity, integrity and confidentiality of stored, transmitted or processed data was made possible as well as the protection of the functions and services that are offered or made accessible to users.

It is also important to specify that the establishment of specific certification schemes is not in itself an innovation considering that numerous certification systems are already present in many Member States. For example, in Italy, we have the "Istituto Superiore delle Comunicazioni e delle Tecnologie dell'Informazione" (ISCOM) operating within the MISE, which deals with the certification of the IT safety of product and ITC systems in compliance with the national policy for the evaluation and certification of security in the information sector.[91] Similar systems can be found, for example, in France, where we have the "Certification de Sécurité de Premier Niveau des Produits des Technologies de l'information" (CSPN), or in Holland, with the "Baseline Security Product Assessment" (BSPA).[92]

Analyzing more specifically the European cybersecurity certification system, we can see that the European Commission recently published the "EU Commission Work Program."[93] This program sets out the priorities and the actions of the future European certification schemes. The major initiative the Commission wants to achieve is that of a new "European Data Strategy," which is said to enable making the most of the value of non-personal data as an ever-expanding and re-usable asset in the digital economy.

The requirements that the European cybersecurity certification schemes must possess can be even better analyzed if we take into consideration Article 51 of the CSA in relation to the security objectives. According to this article, the cybersecurity certification schemes must be designed to provide adequate protection to stored, transmitted or otherwise processed data against accidental

---

[91] This policy was approved with the Decree of the President of the Council of Ministers October 30 2003, "*Approvazione dello schema nazionale per la valutazione e la certificazione nel settore della tecnologia dell'informazione.*"

[92] L. TOSONI, *Cybersecurity Act, ecco le nuove norme in arrivo su certificazione dei prodotti e servizi ICT,* in www.agendadigitale.eu, 2019.

[93] COM(2020) 37, Commission Work Programme 2020.

or unauthorized storage, processing, access, disclosure, destruction, loss or alteration of the ICT product, service or process.[94] Regarding the possibility to access stored data, the CSA states that only those who are authorized persons, programs or machines are holders of access rights regarding specific data, services or functions. In addition, it is stated that it must also record which of these has specifically been accessed or used.

Other objectives that must be achieved entail the identification of the known and unknown vulnerabilities of ICT products, services and processes. It is also stated that these products, services and processes must be secured by default and by design. The last goal that must be achieved, according to Article 51 of the CSA, is to ensure that ICT products, services and processes are provided with up-to-date hardware and software that do not contain publicly known vulnerabilities, and they must also be provided with mechanisms for secure updates.

In addition to these safety objectives, the European cybercrime certification scheme is required to satisfy a second requirement, according to which it must specify and guarantee one or more "assurance levels"[95] for ICT products, services and processes. The assurance levels identified by the CSA can be divided into basic, substantial and high. This tripartition is commensurate with the risk level associated with the auspicated use of the ICT products, services and processes in terms of probability and impact of an incident.[96]

A European cybersecurity certificate or declaration that refers to a "basic" level of assurance must provide the assertion that the specific ICT products, services and process to which they refer meet the corresponding security requirements, including but not limited to security functionalities and the assurance that their evaluation has minimized the possible known risks of incidents and cyberattacks. As to what concerns their evaluation, these shall at least include an appropriate review of the technical documentation.

In contrast, when a certificate refers to the "substantial" assurance level, it is stated that it must provide assurance that the issued certificate for those specific ICT products, ICT services and ICT processes meets the corresponding security requirements. It must also be proven that they have

---

[94] Article 51 a; b Cybersecurity Act 2019.

[95] "*Assurance level*" indicates, on one hand, the basis for the confidence that an ICT product, ICT service or ICT process meets the safety requirements of a specific European cybersecurity certification scheme, it also states the degree to which the ICT products, services or processes have been subject to evaluation, in article 2 point 21, CSA, 2019.

[96] Article 52, Cybersecurity Act, 2019.

been subject to an evaluation in order to minimize the known cybersecurity risks as well as the risks that may be carried out by actors with limited resources and skills. Different from the basic assurance level, the evaluation activities shall include at least a review certifying the absence of publicly known vulnerabilities as well as a "test" demonstrating that the ICT product, service or process correctly implements the necessary security functionalities.

Finally, with reference to a European cybersecurity certificate that refers to a "high" assurance level, Article 52 of the CSA states that the ICT services, products and processes must meet the corresponding security requirements, including security functionalities. It also states that they must be evaluated "at a level intended to minimize the risk of state-of-the-art cyberattacks"[97] committed by actors having significant skills and resources. The evaluation activities that must be undertaken with regard to these certificates entail a review demonstrating the absence of publically known vulnerabilities; a test demonstrating that the ICT products, services and processes correctly implement the necessary security functionalities and an assessment, through so-called penetration testing, of their resistance level against skilled attackers.

Regarding all three assurance levels, in the case that such evaluation activities are not considered appropriate or are considered to be carried out inappropriately, substitute activities delivering an equivalent effect shall be undertaken.

2.4. The European Union Strategy in the Fight against Cybercrime: the Creation of the European Cybercrime Centre (EC3)

Another important consequence of the need for a comprehensive strategy in the fight against cybercrime was the creation, in 2013, of the European Cybercrime Center (EC3), within EUROPOL. This center was established to strengthen and coordinate the cross-border law enforcement response to cybercrime in the European Union and to help protect its citizens, businesses and governments.[98] Therefore, it cooperates with national law enforcement agencies, EU institutions, international organizations and so on, in order to develop and maintain a strong partnership that can help strengthen the EU's ability to respond to cybercrime. The European Cybercrime Center should also act as a center of technical expertise on cybercrime and cyber attacks.

---

[97] Article 52 n. 7, Cybersecurity Act, 2019.
[98] www.europol.europa.eu.

It is primarily designed to focus on three main areas: cyber crimes committed by organized crime groups, especially those that generate large criminal profits; cyber crimes that cause serious harm to their victims; and cyber crimes that affect critical infrastructure and information systems established in the Union.

To support the EC3, the Cyber Intelligence Team (CIT), in which a pool of analysts collects and processes public or private information related to cybercrimes in order to identify possible patterns in their verification and also emerging threats, was created.

The criminal areas of expertise of the European Cybercrime Center cover different types of crimes, from economy-based crimes to terrorism, from cybercrime to child sexual exploitation and drug trafficking, aiding, and abetting illegal immigration.

The agency delivers tangible results, thanks in large part to its cooperation with national law agencies inside and outside the EU. Specifically, with regard to cybercrime, the EC3 works closely with another European agency, the EMPACT (European Multidisciplinary Platform Against Criminal Threats), which is a European multidisciplinary cooperation platform developed in order to combat international organized crime. Together, the two agencies set common priorities and establish an international work team methodology to take down criminal groups that threaten the security of the European Union.

Among the various objectives, there is the fight against business models based on new modes of operation used by international organized crime groups, which have developed an innovative approach to crime called "Crime-as-a-Service." The international organized crime has shown a remarkable capacity to use IT in their illicit activities. In particular, criminal groups have adopted and adapted, to the world of cybercrimes, a business model based on the concept of "Software as a Service" (SaaS). "Crime as a Service," is a sector in which the single hacker, often rudimental in his/her *modus operandi*, has been replaced by real organizations, structured as companies, but with cyber-criminal purposes and able to offer increasingly sophisticated virtualized and outsourced services and ready-to-use criminal solutions.

The close collaboration between the EC3 and EMPACT platforms thus enables a more effective fight against child sexual abuse and exploitation, including the production and dissemination of child pornography and against criminals involved in fraud and counterfeiting of electronic means of payment, including large-scale frauds with payment cards (especially card fraud) and other non-cash means of payment. Another branch that the EC3 has focused on is cyber methodologies that use social engineering in many crime areas as an attack vector. In fact, even from recent data, many cybersecurity firms continually highlight the human factor as the chains weak link. Getting people to act against their own interest or in the interest of an organization is often an easier solution than resorting to malware. Targeted social engineering allows those who are technically gifted to orchestrate mixed attacks by bypassing human lines of defense of hardware or software.

Finally, special attention is paid by the European Cybercrime Center to criminal markets found on the Dark Web. The Dark Web hosts many of the most profitable markets for various criminal organizations and individual illegal businesses in Europe and worldwide. In this regard, it should be mentioned that the Dark Web, due to its structural specificities, such as the possibility to buy and sell anonymously in a digital environment without national borders, is a fertile place for criminals of all kinds. In recent years, several coordinated investigations have been able to break down some of the largest Dark Web markets, undermining the resources exploited by criminals. For example, in 2017, joint operations led by the U.S. FBI and the Dutch European National Police, with support from EUROPOL and other law enforcement partners, shut down Alphabay and Hansa, two of the largest marketplaces responsible for trading more than 350,000 illicit products such as drugs, firearms, and cybercrime tools such as malware and ransomware. In these specific marketplaces, where cryptocurrencies are the dominant payment method, different types of illegal goods and criminal services were sold, although more than two-thirds of the transactions involved illicit drugs and chemicals. Due to the success of these transactions, their volume has decreased and some "traders" have decided to leave the Dark Web platforms for fear of being discovered by international police. One of EUROPOL's initiatives with EC3 is therefore to create a coordinated law enforcement approach to tackling crime on the Dark Web with the participation of law enforcement from all Member States, operational third parties and other partners, such as Eurojust (the European Union's Judicial Cooperation Unit).

In conclusion, the European cybercrime strategy is in full swing and provides member states with a comprehensive and coordinated approach, through information sharing, operational support, expertise in different crime areas and the development of tools, tactics and techniques, to conduct dark web investigations and identify key threats and targets. In addition, a shared commitment across the global community and a coordinated approach by law enforcement has proven its effectiveness in recent years and is an essential tool in making the web an increasingly safe and hazard-free place, especially for fragile users who are more likely to be victims of cybercrime.

2.5. The Network and Information Security (NIS) Directive

As part of the EU's cybersecurity strategy, the European Commission adopted in 2016 one of the first pieces of EU legislation on cybersecurity and the fight against cybercrime: the Network and Information Security Directive (NIS) (EU 2016/114).[99] Many consider the NIS Directive the cornerstone of the cybersecurity strategy, which requires all EU member states to ensure a secure and trusted environment throughout the Union.

According to the directive, "Network and information systems and services play a vital role in society. Their reliability and security are essential for economic and social activities and in particular for the functioning of the internal market. The magnitude, frequency and impact of security incidents are increasing and pose a serious threat to the operation of network and information systems." The directive also states that to better protect ICT products, services and processes; a comprehensive EU-wide approach is needed.[100] Therefore, the NIS Directive aims to put the onus on each Member State to adopt a national cyber security strategy that establishes specific measures aimed at implementing a high common level of network and information system security throughout the Union. To achieve its goals, it must: improve cybersecurity capabilities not only at supranational level but also and especially at national level; increase cooperation at EU level by establishing a cooperation group; and it must oblige Member States to adopt common risk management and incident reporting obligations for operators of essential services and digital service providers. Obligations that will not apply to companies providing publicly available electronic communications networks.

The Network and Information Security Directive provides legal measures to improve the overall level of cyber security in the EU. This directive obliges Member States to adopt national strategies able to ensure the security of networks and information systems and to define the trategic goals and policy actions that should be implemented in the area of cybersecurity throughout the Union. Member States must also establish a cooperation group to support and facilitate strategic cooperation and information exchange. The directive also states that Member States must establish a network of cybersecurity incident

[99] This Directive applies without prejudice to Council Directive 2008/114/EC and Directives 2011/93/EU and 2013/40/EU of the European Parliament and of the Council.

[100] A. CHITARRO, R. SETOLA, *Nuova direttiva per la protezione cibernetica e la sicurezza informatica*, in *Sicurezza e giustizia*, 2017.

response teams,[101] commonly known as a CSIRT network, which helps implement trust, confidence and ultimately cooperation among member states. It also states that member states may request, when deemed necessary, ENISA's assistance in developing national CSIRT's.

This directive applies primarily to Essential Service Operators and Digital Service Providers who must ensure the security of network and information. An Essential Service Operator is primarily an organization that provides a service, which is essential for the maintenance of critical social and/or economic activities. The provisions state that this service depends on the type of network and information system to which it relates and any incident would have a "significant disruptive effect" on that service. Among the obligations imposed on these entities, we can mention the obligation to take appropriate and proportionate technical and organizational measures to manage the risks that network and information systems face. They must also prevent and minimize the impact of incidents that may affect security, network and information systems. These operators must also notify, without any delay, the relevant CSIRT of any incidents,[102] which affect the continuity of the essential service it provides.

Digital Service Providers are those who provide a specific digital service such as e-commerce and cloud computing. A digital service is defined as any service that is normally provided by electronic means and at the request of a service recipient.[103] Some of the obligations imposed on these entities are similar to those imposed on Essential Service Operators. However, its obligations do not apply to micro and small businesses and only apply if those providers have access to the information necessary to assess the impact of an incident. Under the NIS Directive, Digital Service Providers are subject to "light and responsive ex-post supervision activities" that are justified by their nature. This means that the competent authority only needs to carry out light and reactive ex post supervision when it is provided with sufficient evidence.[104]

Article 21 of the NIS Directive states that Member States must determine the possible sanctions applicable in the event of a breach of the adopted

---

[101] Which ultimately replace the national "*Computer Emergency Response Team*" (CERT) and in Italy the CERT-PA.

[102] In order to determine the incidents relevance it must take into account: the number of users affected by the disruption of the essential service, the duration of the incident and its geographical spread.

[103] Directive (EU) 2015/1535.

[104] NIS Directive art 1 par. 60, in www.eur-lex.europa.eu.

provisions and must take all necessary measures to ensure its full implementation.

The European Commission recently adopted a proposal to revise the Network and Information Systems Security Directive (NIS Directive 2), as the original NIS Directive is beginning to show its limitations and obsolescence.

The recent acceleration towards an effective digital transformation of society (driven by the COVID-19 crisis) has increasingly broadened the exposure to threats and revealed new challenges, which require flexibility, the ability to react by adapting to new conditions and innovative solutions. More often than in the past, any unrest or disruption, even if initially limited to narrow areas or sectors, can now have an unpredictable and dangerous domino effect, which can result in complex and lasting negative impacts in the delivery of services to citizens across the nation and turbulence in the internal market.[105]

The document planned by the Commission and currently in its initial proposal form is part of a package of measures aimed at further improving the resilience and incident response capability of public and private entities, relevant authorities, and the Union and its member countries as a whole.

The proposal is thus in line with the Commission's priorities to make Europe capable of responding to the possible new threats posed daily in the digital age.

The Commission's proposals expand not only the scope of the current NIS Directive, but also the powers given to individual Member States. It aims to eliminate the distinction originally made between Essential Service Operators and Digital Service Providers. Therefore, according to the proposal, entities should be classified primarily according to their importance, thus being subject to a different supervisory regime.

The proposal introduces more efficient supervisory measures for national authorities and aims at harmonizing the different sanctioning regimes adopted by individual Member States. It also strengthens the role of the Cooperation Group in defining strategic policy decisions on emerging technologies and increases information sharing and cooperation between Member State authorities. Finally, it strengthens operational cooperation, including collaboration on cyber crisis management.

---

[105] This proposal in fact comes at a delicate moment, a few days after the cyberattack directed against the European Medicine agency (EMA), which caused the exposure of sensitive information related to the COVID Vaccine Pfizer-BioNtech and the Cyberattack against the American giant SolarWinds, which allowed the introduction of state hackers into governmental and private entities around the world.

3. The National Approach to Cybersecurity

The concept of non-territoriality of computer crimes, considered in a broad sense, and the ease with which they can occur in a transnational context inspired Law no. 547 of December 23, 1993 on the "Amendments to the Provisions of the Penal Code and the Code of Criminal Procedure in Relation to Computer Criminality" and the launch of a common action at European level. The national legislator of 1993, in addition to having modified some provisions of the code of procedure, modified a) article 392 of the Italian Penal Code on the "Arbitrary exercise of one's own actions," including computer systems in the category of the "things" on which violence can be exercised; b) article 616 of the Italian Penal Code on the "Violation, removal and theft of computer equipment"; c) article 616 of the Italian Penal Code on "Violation, removal and suppression of correspondence," where "correspondence" now also means computer or telematics correspondence carried out with any other form of remote communication[106] and c) article 621 of the Italian Penal Code on "Revealing the contents of secret documents" extending the notion of "documents" to "computer supports containing data, information or programs."[107]

In addition, the legislator has extended: a) the hypotheses of falsity referred to in Chapter III (Of falsity in deeds) of Title VII (Of offences against public faith) to computer documents; b) the case referred to in art. 420 of the Penal Code (Assault on systems of public utility) to computer or telematics systems of public utility or to the data, information or programs contained in them or pertinent to them.

Finally, the following crimes were introduced:

a) Art. 615-ter (Unauthorized access to a computer or telematics system)
b) Art. 615-quater (Unauthorized possession and dissemination of access codes to computer or telematics systems)
c) Art. 615-quinquies (Dissemination of programs designed to damage or disrupt a computer system)
d) Art. 617-quater (Interception, obstruction or illegal interruption of computer or telematics communications)

---

[106] The reformed art. 623-bis provides that the provisions contained in arts. 616 - 623 of the Criminal Code, relating to telegraphic, telephone, computer or telematics communications and conversations, apply to any other remote transmission of sounds, images or other data.

[107] *Ibidem.*

e) Art. 617-quinquies (Installation of equipment designed to intercept, impede or interrupt computer or telematics communications)
f) Art. 617-sexies (Forgery, alteration or suppression of the content of computer or telematics communications)
g) Art. 635-bis (Damage to computer and telematics systems)
h) Art. 640-ter (Computer fraud)

On the European side, it should be noted that the first European Council entirely dedicated to the field of Justice and Internal Affairs[108] and especially to crimes relating to the use of information technology, was held in Tampere in 1999. The Budapest Convention of 2001 on computer crimes[109] has also required all EU Member States to adopt legislative measures aimed at the criminal repression of new computer crimes, harmonizing the various internal systems and coordinating the forms of collaboration in the deterrence of the phenomenon and the collection of evidence by the police authorities. Finally, with Law no. 48 of March 2008, Italy has ratified the Convention, introducing and/or modifying substantive and procedural laws also pertaining to the administrative responsibility of legal persons and the treatment of personal data.

3.1. Understanding the Effects of the 1993 Law

Italy, compared to other European countries, has lagged behind in the preparation and stipulation of adequate cybersecurity strategies and policies, issuing its first legislative solution only in 2013 with DPCM no. 66.[110] A directive containing specific guidelines for cyber protection and cybersecurity,

[108] The Justice and Internal Affairs (JHA) sector was created in 1992 with the Maastricht Treaty. It constituted the cd. "Third pillar" of the European Union, until the 1999 Amsterdam Treaty transferred some of its competences to the first pillar. Since then it is more correct to speak of "Judicial and police cooperation in criminal matters." Lastly, the adoption of the Lisbon Treaty in 2009 provided for the abolition of the three pillars and the "communitarization" of the JHA sector.

[109] Budapest Convention on Cybercrime, November 23, 2001. The Convention on Cybercrime, also known as the Budapest Convention on Cybercrime or the Budapest Convention, is the first international treaty seeking to address Internet and computer crime (cybercrime) by harmonizing national laws, improving investigative techniques, and increasing cooperation among nations. It was drawn up by the Council of Europe in Strasbourg, France, with the active participation of the Council of Europe's observer states Canada, Japan, Philippines, South Africa and the United States.

[110] DPCM 66/2013 Directive containing the guidelines for cyber protection and national IT security.

defining the institutional architecture of Italy's national security and responsibility in relation to critical information-based infrastructures. Therefore, this national strategic framework for the security and protection of cyberspace and the information it contains establishes the strategic and operational guidelines for securing legal activities conducted in cyberspace, while punishing those that may be considered illegal activities. We can also say that these documents are of fundamental importance in the history of the Italian national legislation in its fight against cybercrime. With these documents, in fact, the main governmental bodies in charge of managing Italy's cybersecurity and a particular strategy dedicated to ensure its protection have been identified.

A retrospective analysis may help to better understand the process that has led Italy to create its own national cybersecurity discipline, based on what has been established not only at a European level but also internationally. Italy took its first steps towards a real regulation of cybercrime only in the '90s with the approval of Law no. 547, which allowed the introduction of new criminal cases within the code and the attribution of protection functions to the telecommunications administration. Starting from the early eighties, a series of frauds, mainly concerning the processing and transmission of bank data, made it extremely evident that the regulations in force at the time and in our legal system were not considered sufficient to guarantee an adequate repression of the phenomenon.[111] Furthermore, the national legislator was driven by the need to adapt the Italian legislation on the subject to the directives issued by supranational bodies to which Italy has adhered.[112]

The ratio of this intervention is to be found in the need to provide protection in case of new forms of attack, today known as *cyberattacks,*[113] aimed at already criminally relevant goods, protected by the criminal code. The choice of the legislator was therefore to extend the provisions of the code, in force at the time, to these new emerging criminal figures. A choice that led to the introduction of new criminal conducts in the Italian Penal Code, such as computer fraud or the crime of "*damaging a computer system.*"[114] The legislator was mainly oriented to place these new criminal cases close to

---

[111] On this point, doctrine and jurisprudence had expressed contrasting opinions, highlighting the difficulty of the Italian regulatory system in dealing with computer-related crimes. L.PICOTTI, *Commento alla sentenza del tribunale di Firenze,* January 27 1986, in Dir. Dell'informatica, 1986, p. 962.

[112] Report to the bill n. 2773, in www.penale.it.

[113] See § 1.1.4.

[114] With law n. 547 of 1993, "*Modificazioni ed integrazioni alle norme del Codice Penale e del codice di procedura penale in tema di criminalità informatica.*"

similar and already sanctioned criminal cases. According to the Doctrine, the various manifestations of these phenomena, commonly defined as computer crimes, constitute new forms of aggression characterized by means, material objects and juridical goods that are already object of protection in the various parts of the Penal Code.[115]

Some of the areas introduced, reformed or redesigned by the Law of 1993 are:

- computer fraud, which was introduced by article 640-ter of the Penal Code in relation to the types of adjoining frauds;
- falsification of electronic documents, which was introduced into the Penal Code by a new clause, added to article 491-bis, that is mainly aimed at extending the provisions relating to the falsity of public or private documents to electronic documents;
- alteration of computer systems, which is now regulated by the addition of article 617-sexies

We can also highlight that the legislator has introduced a new discipline aimed at protecting the confidentiality of data and computer communications, incriminating not only the unauthorized access to a computer system but also the illicit diffusion of access codes.[116]

From this analysis of Law no. 547 of 1993, we can see how the ratio at its base is perfectly integrated into the logic that led, in 2001, to the signing of the Budapest Convention on computer crimes.[117] A convention that, as we know, constitutes the first attempt at harmonizing the fundamental elements of the crimes perpetrated by the provisions of each single country and that is also aimed at providing individual countries with effective legislation to investigate and prosecute crimes related to the computer area.

The interest of national legislators in adopting appropriate strategies to fight cybercrimes has further intensified in the new millennium. Since the beginning of the 2000's, the legislator's attention has focused on the protection of digital information. In particular, the emphasis of legislators was put on the importance for the public administration to develop basic computer security systems able to avoid that sensitive information is stolen and spread outside

---

115 See Chamber of Deputies, 11th legislature, bill n. 2773.

116 See law n. 547 of 1993, "*Modificazioni ed integrazioni alle norme del Codice Penale e del codice di procedura penale in tema di criminalità informatica.*"

117 P.SCOGNAMIGLIO, *Criminalità informatica. Commento organico alla Legge 18 marzo 2008, n. 48*, Napoli, 2008, 8.

the restricted circle of employees authorized to have access to administratively controlled material.

Following the ratification of the Convention on Cybercrime, Italy has greatly intensified its interest in countering cyber-related criminal phenomena by issuing the Code on Personal Data Protection[118] and the first Electronic Communications Code,[119] which marks the convergence of the telecommunications and information technology sectors, thus harmonizing all transmission networks and related services into a single regulatory framework. In addition, the code establishes a National Regulatory Authority (NRA) responsible for achieving the document's objectives and a national CERT to address any violations.[120] Not long after, it approved the "e-Gov Plan 2012," aimed at the digitization of national infrastructures and services, to reduce the gap between our country and other EU Member States in terms of system computerization.

The evolution of information technologies and the consequent evolution of computer crimes has led to the emergence of new negative phenomena such as child pornography crimes. In order to repress this horrible and inhuman crime, Italy has issued the National Center for the fight against child pornography on the web (Centro Nazionale per il Contrasto della Pedopornografia sulla rete Internet). A special governmental body that aims to limit the possible threats posed to children within cyberspace.

During the end of the 2010s, several reform measures were put in place, regarding cybersecurity, which led first to the establishment of an International Committee whose goal was to design a new national strategy for cybersecurity and implement the European Data Protection Directive. Secondly, we have the establishment of the AgID, the Agency for Digital Italy, whose main objectives are to provide an adequate digital culture throughout the country, promote state-region collaboration and guide its coordination, develop guidelines and disseminate operational standards aimed at reducing costs and, finally, ensure the uniformity and efficiency of the offered IT services. Moreover, through international dialogue, it aims to ensure compliance with the minimum standards of digitalization, required at European level, also promoting digital education of individuals and businesses.[121]

---

[118] See Legislative Decree 196/2003.

[119] See Legislative Decree 259/2003.

[120] C. CENCETTI, *Cybersecurity: Unione Europea e Italia, prospettive a confronto*, 2014, Roma, p. 63 ss.

[121] See the Statute of the AgID in www.agid.gov.it.

In analyzing the Italian path in regulating cyberspace, we can see how the Italian government's awareness of the urgency to better regulate the national cyberspace led to the approval of the 2013 Decree of the President of the Council of Ministers. This decree not only established what can be considered the guidelines for ensuring national cybersecurity and cyber protection. It also provides for a basic model used to ensure the cybersecurity of Italian operators and identifies the national structures responsible for managing crisis generated by cyber attacks.

In the same year, the National Strategic Framework for Cyberspace Security[122] was approved, which defines with greater specificity the issues related to the security of information systems and identifies the specific tools to be used to counter cyber threats. The Framework aims to outline a comprehensive overview of cyber threats and to implement a coordinated and effective fight against these crimes with specifically designed means of prevention and response. It also highlights the need for states to outline an appropriate national cybersecurity policy and ensure its proper implementation.

In 2017, a new National Plan for the Protection of Cybersecurity and IT security was issued, which aimed to identify the strategic lines to put into practice in order to satisfactorily achieve the goal prescribed by the National Strategic Framework.[123]

In recent years, the Cybersecurity Decree has been implemented at national level with Law no. 133/2019.[124] This Decree is mainly concerned with the main aspects of cybersecurity at national level, in order to ensure a high level of security and protection of networks, information systems and IT services, public administrations and public and private operators based within the national territory, which perform an essential state function. There is a need to protect these systems from possible cyber threats since their malfunction, interruption or misuse may result in a harm to national security. In order to ensure this fundamental protection, the "Perimeter of National Cyber Security" was adopted.[125] Thus, with this decree, the national legislator identifies which computer systems, individuals and public entities are most likely at risk of a possible cyber incident and, therefore, require a high level

[122] See www.sicurezzanazionale.gov.it

[123] See www.cybersecurityframework.it.

[124] Law n. 133/2019, Conversion into law, with amendments, of the decree-law 21 September 2019, n. 105, containing urgent provisions on the perimeter of cyber national security, which entered into force on November 5th 2020.

[125] Article 1 law n. 133/2019.

of security and protection. Their identification is made on the basis of specific criteria that the administrations referred to in article 3 of the Decree must follow. Firstly, it is necessary that the entity exercises an essential function of the State or ensures an essential service for the maintenance of civil, social or economic activities that are of fundamental interest to the State. Second, the exercise of this function or the performance of this service must depend on networks, information systems and computer services. It is also of the utmost importance to emphasize that the identification of computer systems, individuals and public entities at risk for possible cyber incident must be done gradually and taking into account the extent of the prejudice to national security. In relation to the specific nature of the various sectors of activity, prejudices to national security may derive from malfunctions, interruptions or the improper use of networks, information systems and IT services.[126] The decree in question also establishes that public or private subjects, who, due to their strategic role and their use of ICT goods, instruments and/or services, fall within the national cybersecurity perimeter, will be required to comply with certain obligations, mainly of an informative nature towards the competent authorities. If complied with, these obligations allow the state to effectively exercise its powers of control and intervention when and if necessary.[127]

The 2020 Clusit Report shows that 2019 was the worst year possible considering the huge evolution of cyber threats and their impact, both from a quantitative and qualitative point of view, highlighting a persistent growth of cyber attack trends, their severity and the consequent damage they create.[128] Attacks on online services grew by 91.5%. Between January and December 2019, there were an average of 139 attacks recorded monthly worldwide with systemic impact on every aspect of society, politics, economics and geopolitics. This is 47.8% higher than the average of 94 monthly attacks recorded over the five-year period 2014-2018. On a qualitative level, this report shows that Critical Infrastructure and the Public Sector, along with Banking and Finance, experienced the most attacks with a critical impact in 2019. While the categories with the highest number of attacks with "High Level Impacts" were healthcare, software and hardware vendors.[129] This is primarily due to the 2020 global pandemic. Since the onset of the pandemic, there has been a huge the negative record of cyber attacks: globally there were 1,871 serious attacks in the public domain detected in 2020, or systemically

---

[126] Article 4 Law n. 133/2017.

[127] Article 11 Law n. 133/2017.

[128] See the 2020 Clusit Report.

[129] *Ibidem.*

affecting every aspect of society, politics, economics and geopolitics. In fact, cybercriminals have exploited the situation of collective unease to target their victims.

The first six months of 2021 showed a significant worsening of cybersecurity violations in Europe compared to the U.S. and Asia. During the first half of 2021, 1.053 serious cyber attacks with a systemic impact on different aspects of society, politics, economy and geopolitics were recorded in Europe. Cyber attacks grew by 24%, showing a monthly average of 170 serious attacks, compared to the 156 recorded in 2020. Clusit experts are now calling this phenomenon "a global emergency." Estimated losses from cybersecurity flaws are $6 trillion in 2021 and account for a significant percentage of global GDP, with a 2-digit annual rate of deterioration and a value equal to 3 times Italy's GDP. Reducing damages and preventing risks, thanks to business continuity plans and specific cyber risk policies, must therefore be a priority for companies of all sizes and sectors. In spite of all the economic difficulties characterizing the year 2021, the global spending on cyber security during this year grew by 4%, which is a sign of the growing general awareness of the risks of this sector.

The Clusit steering committee emphasizes that we are facing a real epochal change in global cyber-insecurity levels. Change caused by the very rapid evolution of actors, methods, pervasiveness and effectiveness of attacks. This underlines the continuous need for the Italian legislator to update the current legislation on cybersecurity in order to better repress cyber attacks and cybercrimes.

4. The Issue of Data Protection

The continuous evolution and innovation of technology has brought to the legislator's attention the need to better protect the storage and exchange of personal data that can be found within the "web" or more simply within one's own computer system. The progressive digitalization of society and the extension of the collection and sharing of personal data has increased. This evolution has necessitated the need for a robust, consistent and effective framework for protecting data collected and stored in the Union.

Computers and smart devices today have not only become our so-called "digital home,"[130] but are increasingly becoming the centerpiece of a significant portion of our society and especially our social relationships. However, they must be considered as "crystal houses," so fragile that they are unable to fully protect our family and social lives.[131]

Putting aside the possible damage that can be physically caused to individual computer systems or the possible consequences related to the mismanagement of the suffered attack, it can be said that, in recent years, cases of identity theft or the partial or total loss of personal data, are occurring more and more frequently. These attacks are extremely dangerous as they can seriously endanger companies private information and/or the personal data of customers, suppliers or employees.[132] In particular, data protection has taken on a more technological dimension, hence the frequent overlaps between the concepts of privacy, data protection and cybersecurity.

This has created the need to protect not only cybersecurity, understood as network security or technological information security,[133] but also digital privacy, meaning the right to the protection of one's digital data located within ICT systems or programs.

In order to harmonize national legal systems, the European legislator issued Directive 95/46/EC of the European Parliament and of the Council on the protection of individuals with regard to the processing of personal data and on the free movement of such data, also commonly referred to as the "Mother Directive." With this Directive, the European legislator established EU principles and standards for personal data protection. The Directive also requires Member States to ensure the protection of the fundamental rights and freedoms of individuals and in particular their right to privacy, especially with regard to the processing of personal data.[134] The directive in question, taking into account the established relevance of data protection, also introduces principles and tools aimed primarily at reducing information asymmetries

---

[130] R. GENGHINI, *La ricerca di un diritto naturale per una società digitale*, in codice e altre leggi del cyberspazio, 2021.

[131] *Ibidem.*

[132] See S.F. GIOVANNANGELI, *la violazione dei dati o data breach*, in Circolazione e protezione dei dati tra libertà e regole del mercato, Commentario al regolamento UE n.679/2016 e al d.lgs. 101/2018, Milano, 2019, p 389.

[133] Security of technological information protects the integrity and privacy of data, both archived and temporary.

[134] Article 1 of Directive 95/46/EC of the European Parliament and of the Council on the Protection of individuals with regards to the processing of personal data and the free movement of such data.

between the data subject and the controller.[135] In this way allowing the latter to use such data only after receiving informed consent, accompanied by detailed information and allowing the owner of such information to control and limit the use of their personal data.[136]

The European Union in 2014 subsequently intervened with Regulation 2014/910/EU of the Commission and Parliament (eIDAS), establishing two fundamental principles: first, the need for certain particularly relevant technological services, known as "trusted e-services," to be transparent and verifiable. Second, it affirmed the need for a "technological neutrality" of laws, which means that the law should always impose the objectives and tools necessary to verify that the objectives of the law are met, however, it should never favor a particular technological solution, in order not to block or slow down technological evolution and business models.

The European Commission and Parliament Regulation 2016/679/EU (GDPR) is the second systemic intervention that has reaffirmed without reservation that our personal sphere is intangible. This regulation essentially takes note of the general dangerousness of the phenomenon in question and aims, on the one hand, to encourage the adoption of appropriate and effective prevention tools and, on the other, to intervene promptly to remove its harmful effects.[137]

Finally, in 2020 the European Commission approved two draft regulations that intend to regulate not only social networks, but also operating systems, browsers and other IT services provided by subjects that act as "gatekeepers" for all of us: the draft regulation on IT services[138] and the draft regulation on the IT market.[139]

Focusing primarily on the protection of personal data within computer systems, it is appropriate to first analyze the general concept of privacy. With the socio-cultural evolution, the boundaries of the notion of privacy have undergone a progressive extension, so that today it is not possible to identify

---

[135] The Data Controller, defined in article 4 of the GDPR, can be defined as the natural or legal persona, public authority body ect. who individually, or in collaboration with other subjects, determines the purposes and means of the processing of personal data. Therefore, it is not he who manages the data, but also he who decides the reason and methods of processing and is legally responsible for compliance with the obligations established by the legislation, both national and international, regarding the protection of personal data.

[136] M.G. STANZIONE, Il nuovo regolamento Europeo sulla protezione dei dati personali: Genesi ed ambito di applicazione, in www.comparazionedirittocivile.it, 2016, p 16-17.

[137] G. MOSCA, *Strategia Europea di cybersecurity, quale impatto sulle PA*, in *Agenda Digitale*, www.agendadigitale.eu.

[138] COM 825/2020.

[139] COM 842/2020.

an internationally accepted definition of "privacy."[140] However, it is possible to identify "Privacy" as the right to protection of all private and family affairs from undue interference by third parties. The first theorization of the right to privacy dates back to 1890, when two famous US jurists[141] identified this particular right as the right to be "left alone," thus extending the concept of "private property," to the intangible sphere of our private lives.[142]

Alongside the right to privacy, the doctrine has theorized a second fundamental right: the "right to data protection." This right can be defined as the right of individuals to restrict the use of their personal data for purposes beyond those for which the data were originally provided. Importantly, "the right to data protection" places an obligation on the so-called "data controller"[143] to comply with the constraints imposed and to protect the data received.

It is clear how the contents of the two rights are extremely different. On the one hand, there is a broad right to prevent disturbances in private life - the "right to privacy" - on the other hand, we have a right according to which the controller must protect the information it receives - the "right to data protection." Another relevant difference between the two fundamental rights is that the right to privacy is recognized by the Charter of Fundamental Rights of the European Union[144] and the legislative systems of the individual Member States. While the right to data protection is governed by the General Data Protection Regulation (GDPR),[145] which precisely regulates the processing of data on the basis of their capital and capitalized value.

In our legal system, the concept of privacy and that of confidentiality are considered equivalent terms, as they both concern the protection of the

---

[140] M. LAMANUZZI, *Diritto penale e trattamento dei dati personali*, 2017, p. 220-221.

[141] S.WARREN-L.BRANDEIS, *The Right to Privacy, in Harvard Law Review*, in www.groups.csail.mit.edu.

[142] This concept was anticipated a few years earlier by Judge Cooley, whom, in analyzing the right to privacy in relation to personal security stated that: *"the right to one's person may be said to be a right of complete immunity; right to be left alone,"* in T. COOLEY, *A Treaties on the Law of Torts. Or the wrongs which Arise Independent of Contract*, Chicago, 1888, 29.

[143] In accordance with article 4, n. 7 of Regulation (EU) 2016/679 (GDPR) a "controller" is the *"natural or legal person, public authority, agency or other body which, alone or jointly with others, determines the purposes and means of the processing of personal data; where the purposes and means of such processing are determined by Union or Member State law, the controller or the specific criteria for its nomination may be provided for by Union or Member State law."*

[144] 2012/C 326/02.

[145] Regulation which repealed the 1995 European Data Protection Directive which established minimum data privacy and security standards.

"private life" sphere and have a purely individualistic meaning. However, the right to the protection of personal data, acquiring within it the further general interest that data be correctly and lawfully processed, cannot be summarized in an "individualistic" right, but deserves to include both a right of the individual and that of the community.[146]

4.1. General Data Protection Regulation (GDPR)

The General Data Protection Regulation (GDPR)[147] was adopted in April 2016 to sufficiently protect the processing of personal data. This regulation is primarily inspired by the need to promote comprehensive privacy regulatory policies and its source of inspiration can be identified within the same principles that characterize today's society: technology and globalization, which bring constant new challenges for the protection of personal data. The GDPR establishes the rules regarding the protection and free movement of personal data. Its main goal is to give people control over their personal data and simplify the regulatory environment for international businesses by unifying the regulation within the EU.

With this Regulation, Directive 95/46/EC, also known as the "Mother Directive" has been repealed. This is a complex body of legislation, consisting of 99 articles and 173 recitals,[148] which provide a remarkably fruitful preamble for understanding the needs that must be met, the objectives, how to implement them and the links to other EU measures.[149] It can be said that this Regulation is a regulatory instrument aimed, on the one hand, at ensuring the protection of individuals and their fundamental rights and freedoms, while on

---

146 M. LAMANUZZI, *Diritto penale e trattamento dei dati personali*, 2017, S. RODOTA, *Tecnologie e diritti*, Bologna, 1995, p 101 ss.

147 Regulation(EU) 2016/679 *on the protection of natural persons with regard to the processing of personal data and on the free movement of such data*, and repealing Directive 95/46/EC (Data Protection Directive).

148 The interpretative function of the Recitals has been repeatedly reiterated by the Court of Justice of the European Union, according to which a legislative act must be interpreted taking into account not only it's literary meaning, but also taking into account the context and the purposes pursued b the legislation to which they belong to. In this sense, the operative part of an EU act is inoperable from its motivation and must therefore be interpreted, if necessary, by taking into account also the reasons which led to its adoption, M.G. STANZIONE, *Il nuovo regolamento Europeo sulla protezione dei dati personali: Genesi ed ambito di applicazione,* in www.comparazionedirittocivile.it, 2016, p. 24.

149 G. NUCCI, *Protezione dei dati personali e GDPR: dai precetti giuridici ai processi organizzativi,* 2018, p. 7.

the other hand it presents provisions aimed at regulating the free movement of personal data within the EU.[150]

From a substantive point of view, through the Regulation in question, the approach to data protection changes enormously: in fact, there is a shift from a formal and authorization-based approach, as stated in the "Mother Directive," to a more substantive approach, based on the principle of accountability.[151] The Regulation therefore requires the need to incorporate respect for the right to data protection into technological and organizational processes.[152]

With the General Data Protection Regulation (GDPR), Directive 2016/680/EU was enacted, laying down specific rules relating to the protection of individuals with regard to the processing of their personal data by competent authorities for the purposes of prevention, investigation and prosecution, including safeguarding against threats to public security.[153]

The timely implementation of the provisions of the regulation has led to profound changes in business and non-business organizations, which have had to reorganize their activities mainly by enhancing the protection of personal data and structuring a real compliance program. Consequently, assigning a prominent role to infrastructure and IT security in order to avoid incurring costs associated with possible sanctions.

Article 1 of the General Data Protection Regulation, in outlining its goals and objectives, states that the Regulation lays down rules relating to the protection of individuals with regard to the processing of their personal data, as well as rules relating to the free movement of such data. It must also aim to protect the fundamental rights and freedoms of individuals, in particular the right to the protection of such personal data. However, it is also clearly stated that the protection of this fundamental right is not "absolute" but rather relative; being that the free movement of data within the Union cannot be restricted or prohibited for reasons relating to the protection of individuals with regard to data processing.[154] This is also stated in Recital 4, which

[150] F. CICLOSI, *La normative europea e italiana in materia di protezione di dati personali*, 2019, p. 46.

[151] C. FARALLI, *Il diritto alla privacy*, Milano, 1982, p.8.

[152] P.COSTANTINI, *Il regolamento UE 679/2016 sulla protezione dei dati personali*, in www.commercialistacostantini.com.

[153] We can see how the Directive (EU) 2016/680 can be considered as a mirror image of the GDPR especially for what concerns its field of application. Many of its rules are in fact similar if not the same to those found in the GDPR. However they are specifically addressed to the competent authorities.

[154] F. CICLOSI, *La normative europea e italiana in materia di protezione di dati personali*, 2019, p. 47.

specifies that, although the processing of personal data must serve individuals, the right to data protection is not an absolute prerogative, but must be considered in the light of its social function and must be reconciled with other fundamental rights, while respecting the principle of proportionality.[155] It is therefore legitimate to say that in European legislation, the protection of personal data is not linked to an individual interest but is instead linked to a more collective interest, as data circulates lawfully and correctly.

In the current framework of European Law on the protection and circulation of personal data, the awareness of the impossibility of controlling and preventing the acquisition and use of personal data by third parties is therefore of fundamental importance. This regulation requires compliance with the obligation to process personal data lawfully, fairly and transparently towards the data subject, to collect them for specific, explicit and legitimate purposes and to process them in a manner that is compatible with the purposes for which they were intended. It also requires compliance with specific storage methods, imposing appropriate data security measures.

Turning to the analysis of its territorial scope and application, in order to standardize the rules relating to privacy and its protection, the GDPR applies to "*the processing of personal data carried out in the course of the activities of an establishment of a controller or processor in the Union, whether or not the processing takes place in the Union.*"[156] Therefore, it seems that the European legislator has significantly broadened the scope of the Data Protection Regulation. In fact, the legislator has devised a mechanism according to which the general applicability of the regulation is always guaranteed in relation to the processing of data of EU citizens, even if such processing takes place outside its territory.[157]

The European legislator outlines, alongside and in addition to the territorial scope of the GDPR, the corresponding mechanism of its material application. To this end, Article 2 of the Regulation provides that it applies to a fully or partially automated and non-automated processing of personal data contained in a filing system. This same article also establishes an important negative limitation of its scope, outlining a number of hypotheses in which it cannot be applied. In particular, it is provided that the discipline is limited to data processing carried out for activities outside the scope of EU law and also

---

155 EU Regulation 679/2016, Recital 4.
156 Article 3 EU Regulation 679/2016.
157 F.PIZZETTI, *Privacy e il diritto europeo alla protezione dei dati personali*, 2016, p. 160 ss.

to data processing carried out by Member States.[158] Second, the limitation covers processing carried out by a natural person for the exercise of activities of a personal or domestic nature executed by competent authorities for the prevention, investigation, detection or prosecution of criminal offences or the execution of criminal penalties, including protection against and prevention of threats to public security. Finally, Article 2 of the Regulation ends by indicating another of its limitations, concerning the processing of data carried out by the institutions, bodies, offices and agencies of the European Union, for which Regulation (EC) 2001/45 applies.[159] Concluding on this point, it is also stated that the Regulation does not affect the application of Directive 2000/31/EC on electronic commerce. In particular, it does not affect the rules on the liability of Intermediary Service Providers operating in this area.[160]

Thus, the GDPR is an effective and valuable tool for the protection of personal data. However, it needs to be constantly updated in order to adapt to modern developments, particularly the complexities that some emerging technologies bring with them, such as artificial intelligence (AI) and blockchain mechanisms.

4.2. Data Protection Facing the Challenge of Emerging Technologies: Blockchain and GDPR

In the modern business environment, traditional transaction mechanisms such as paper money, credit card systems, and internet and mobile technologies have their shortcomings. Including limited transaction sizes, the need for third-party validation, rising transaction costs and a weak model based on trust. In addition, fraud and cyber attacks are inevitable, which also leads to increased payment transaction costs. These challenges prompted the development of a new type of payment system, or rather a network that could establish trust, remove intermediary institutions and allow any two parties to transact directly with each other. The ultimate goal would be to eliminate fraud and provide secure and efficient escrow mechanisms to protect payers and payees. This was the goal pursued with the so-called "Blockchain mechanism," an

---

[158] Which fall within the scope of application of Title V, Chapter 2, TEU (and therefore in the context of activities relating to foreign policy and common security).

[159] Regulation Concerning the protection of individuals in relation to the processing of personal data by Community institutions and bodies, as well as the free circulation of such data.

[160] C. COLAPIETRO, *I principi ispiratori del Regolamento UE 2016/679 sulla protezione dei dati personali e la loro incidenza sul contesto normativo nazionale*, 2018, p.13.

exchange system, developed in 2008, which provides a solution based on a particular type of currency, known as cryptocurrency and a peer-to-peer distributed timestamp server to generate computational evidence of the chronological order of transactions.

One of the most popular uses of the blockchain mechanism is for cryptocurrencies. Cryptocurrencies such as Bitcoin, Litecoin and others are not issued or controlled by any central authority. Decentralization allows these blockchain currencies to take the first steps towards an alternative financial model without intermediaries. Therefore, posing several serious legal issues, which are currently unresolved. Another area revolutionized by blockchain is trading and deal making. Traditional contracts are being replaced by so-called "smart contracts" that are unbreakable, eliminating third parties and work for a wide range of applications: employment contracts, wholesale and retail purchases, property purchase agreements, agreements that secure intellectual property rights, insurance and even marriage contracts. However, the blockchain mechanism can go far beyond cryptocurrencies and smart contracts, as by the use of this mechanism it is possible to store, track and transfer data on real estate and land objects, property rights and medical history, business transactions, taxes and more. The blockchain mechanism is also capable of disrupting even monopolistic spheres such as energy management, governance and law enforcement.[161]

Thus, this is an example of how a new digital technology poses enormous legal challenges and the urgent need for nations around the world to develop appropriate legislation or adapt their current legislation in order to frame an area of social and economic interactions that, at this moment, seems to be completely uncontrolled from a legal perspective. In the context of blockchain technology, the issue of data protection appears difficult to define given the difficulty of clearly defining and identifying the data to be protected.

Blockchain is a decentralized technology or distributed financial ledger, also known as "the ledgers," on which transactions can be recorded anonymously.[162] This means that transaction records are hosted simultaneously across a network of unrelated computers or servers called "nodes," similar to a spreadsheet that is duplicated several hundred times

[161] See S.TANWAR- Q.BHATIA-P.PATEL-A. KUMARI A-P.K.SINGH- WC. HONG; *Machine learning adoption in blockchain-based smart applications: the challenges, and a way forward.* IEEE Access 2020; 8: 474-488; S.DE ANGELIS-L.ANIELLO-R.BALDONI-F.LOMBARDI-A.MARGHERI-V.SASSONE. *PBFT vs proof-of-authority: applying the CAP theorem to permissioned blockchain*, 2017 in www.eprints.soton.ac.uk.

[162] See Buterin V. Ethereum *white paper: a next generation smart contract and decentralized application platform,* 2013, in www.ethereum.org.

across a computer network. The repository contains continuously updated and complete records of all transactions made (the so-called "chain") which are then grouped into blocks. In this record system, a block is added to the chain only if the nodes, which are members of the blockchain network with high computing power capacity, reach a consensus that allows the new block to be added to the chain. Therefore, a transaction can only be validated and be part of a candidate block if all nodes in the network confirm that the transaction is valid. More importantly, regarding the issue of data protection in this complex system, in order to determine the validity of a candidate block, the system includes so-called "miner" nodes (or miner pools) that have the function of competing to solve a highly complex algorithm in order to verify it.[163] For example, on Bitcoin's Blockchain, this procedure is known as "Proof of Work." The first node that solves the algorithm and validates the block should be rewarded, such reward takes the form of a Bitcoin. This mechanism is also referred to as the "mining for Bitcoins."

Applications based on Blockchain technology raise some questions about their compliance with data protection legislation. This issue is much discussed at the European level even among the institutions themselves. Evidence of this are the numerous documents published by research centers, EU authorities and scholars on the topic that analyze the relationship between Blockchain technology and GDPR. In particular, the most comprehensive document has been published by EPRS (European Parliamentary Research Service). In this regard, the discussion mainly revolves around three points: the type of data processed, the identification of roles under the GDPR and the right to be forgotten.

First, it is important to determine whether data protection regulations apply to a given technological solution. To do this, it is necessary to assess whether those passing on blockchain technology are to be considered as "personal data." In light of the provisions of the GDPR, "personal data" is defined as "any information relating to an identified or identifiable natural person. Data that makes a person identifiable, directly or indirectly, may be a name, an identification number, location data, an online identifier, or one or more features of his or her physical, physiological, genetic, psychological, economic, cultural or social identity."[164]

Thus, data protection principles do not apply to anonymous information, (i.e., information that does not relate to an identified or identifiable natural

---

[163] G.NAVA, Blockchain*: tassonomia di un "hype" o "it's here to stay"?*, in Associazione Italiana di Diritto e dell'Energia (AIDEN), 2019, pp. 1-31.

[164] Article 4 paragraph 1 of the General Data Protection Regulation (GDPR).

person) and to personal data rendered sufficiently anonymous to prevent or no longer allow the identification of the data subject.

Blockchain technology allows for transactions between parties without having to directly reveal one's identity; however, each transaction that is executed is published and linked to a public key, which then represents an alias of a particular user. Although the public key does not contain information that can be directly attributed to the user, using the same key for several transactions and cross-referencing it with other information could allow the authors of a given transaction to be identified.

It follows that the public key, if associated with a person, may possibly qualify as personal data for the purposes of European data protection legislation. Indeed, when the public key is traced back to an identified individual, it is possible to obtain information about all transactions that the individual has made on the blockchain. As a result, data protection rules may be applicable to at least some of the data involved in Blockchain solutions.

If we assume that personal data is processed in the Blockchain, it is therefore necessary, according to the GDPR, to identify the controller and define whether this role is held by a single entity or jointly by several entities. The correct identification of this role is an important exercise as it allows to identify the person or entity to whom the data subject must address to enforce their rights under the GDPR. In this regard, Blockchain technology presents a peculiar problem in that it does not rely on a single provider of storage or processing resources, but instead leads to the creation of decentralized and distributed solutions. Because Blockchain and Distributed Ledger platforms are designed to be managed by multiple parties, many actors can potentially influence the determination of the purposes and means of data processing.

Determining roles will therefore also depend on the type of solution used. The access to the network of Distributed Ledger Permissioned platforms requires registration, identification, and then authorization from a central entity or the network itself. With respect to permissioned platforms, generally a specific legal entity (such as a company or consortium) determines the means and in many cases the purposes of processing personal data. In its 2018 guidance on Blockchains and GDPR, the CNIL (French Data Protection Authority) considered that in case a group collectively decides to use a DLT for its own purposes, the controller should be defined *ab initio*.

Distributed Ledger Permissionless platform: in which anyone can participate, freely performing any kind of activity, where the content of the ledger is public and available to all. With respect to permissionless platforms, governance arrangements can influence the means of processing. Importantly, the identity of the controller depends on the perspective one takes.

Seen from a "macro perspective," the purpose of processing is to "provide the transactional service" while the medium refers to the software used by nodes and miners. From a "micro perspective" (e.g., the individual transaction), the purpose of processing is to "record a specific transaction on a blockchain" while the medium refers to the "choice of blockchain platform."

According to the paper published by the EPRS, the "micro perspective" is probably the most appropriate approach since the Data Protection Act deals with specific personal data. For this reason, users of a permissionless platform should be considered as data controllers when a transaction is made directly by them. The technical construction of the blockchain leads to the fact that only the user making the transaction can determine the purposes and means of data processing; as a result, there is broad agreement that DLT users will be considered, at least in some circumstances, as data controllers under the GDPR.

On the other hand, again according to the EPRS, when a legal entity, such as a company, decides to rely on a decentralized platform over another form of database, it has made a decision regarding how to process personal data, thus creating a strong indication that it qualifies as a data controller. Therefore, anyone who chooses a particular technical infrastructure, such as a Blockchain or a Distributed Ledger, to process data can be considered a co-owner of the processing related to that system, even though they may have only limited control over the purposes and no meaningful control over the means of processing.

Among the serious issues that the Blockchain mechanism has raised from a legal perspective is the right to be forgotten, which is now governed by Article 17 of the GDPR,[165] which sets out a number of general criteria and

[165] Article 17 of EU Regulation no.679/2016 on the protection of personal data states the "Right to erasure": "The data subject shall have the right to obtain from the controller the erasure of personal data concerning him or her without undue delay and the controller shall have the obligation to erase personal data without undue delay where one of the following grounds applies:
the personal data are no longer necessary in relation to the purposes for which they were collected or otherwise processed:the data subject withdraws consent on which the processing is based according to point (a) of Article 6, or point (a) of Article 9, and where there is no other legal ground for the processing; the data subject objects to the processing pursuant to Article 21 and there are no overriding legitimate grounds for the processing, or the data subject objects to the processing pursuant to Article 21; the personal data have been unlawfully processed; the personal data have to be erased for compliance with a legal obligation in Union or Member State law to which the controller is subject; the personal

exceptions. The application of the GDPR can also prove to be binding with regard to the right to erasure or the so-called "right to be forgotten," particularly when referring to a "Permissionless Blockchain." Indeed, the fact that the information entered on these platforms is inherently tamper-proof and erasure-proof can be a potential problem.

After identifying a public key and associated transactions, even if the user requested it, there would be no way to delete the information, which would therefore become part of the Blockchain. Technology's unique design of maintaining the history of all transactions that have occurred makes the right to be forgotten very complicated to exercise.

While research into mechanisms for managing data within a Blockchain is ongoing, the idea that data controllers can delete personal data does not seem straightforward: a fundamental incompatibility could arise from the ability to modify data records while maintaining their authenticity requires the appointment of "trusted administrators" who can modify the Blockchain's record according to a set of predefined rules. This would consequently be at odds with the essential characteristics of Blockchain technology, which is inherently decentralized and unmodifiable. For this reason, existing projects seek to manage any personal data outside of the platforms themselves, publishing only references to information held through more traditional databases.

The important question about Blockchain is whether compatibility between GDPR and Blockchain is possible. In this regard, it should be considered that the rules provided by the GDPR are mainly designed to identify a subject (precisely the owner) responsible for the collection, storage and processing of data. While Blockchain and Distributed Ledger technologies are intended as peer-to-peer databases that do not rely on "central authorities" but make decentralization one of their strengths. The data protection challenges posed by Blockchain will therefore vary depending on the specific characteristics of the solution used.

Given the huge diversity of the cases, there is no single solution when it comes to GDPR compliance. In fact, this will be evaluated on a case-by-case basis considering the actual implementation of the technology through which

---

data have been collected in relation to the offer of information society services referred to in Article 8.
Where the controller has made the personal data public and is obliged pursuant to paragraph 1 to erase the personal data, the controller, taking account of available technology and the cost of implementation, shall take reasonable steps, including technical measures, to inform controllers which are processing the personal data that the data subject has requested the erasure by such controllers of any links to, or copy or replication of, those personal data."

personal data is carried. In some cases, the link to personal data may be so remote that only minimal data governance mechanisms will be required, while on the contrary, other projects may involve high-impact data processing and, for this reason, may require a full data protection impact assessment.

Therefore, nowadays it is not possible to generalize the compliance of Blockchain and Distributed Ledger technologies with the GDPR. This mainly depends on how the solutions are configured and because there are many IT techniques that potentially allow the reduction of the conflicts between these technologies and the European regulation. Understandably, the legal issues imposed by new digital technologies, such as Blockchain, remain wide open and challenges to our legal system and must be promptly and appropriately addressed.

4.3. Data Breach

As mentioned above, according to the European legislator and the General Data Protection Regulation (GDPR), nowadays, the protection of privacy and personal data stored within an ICT program or system is of paramount importance. In fact, it has become an important issue not only in the professional life of companies, but it is also a fundamental threat to individuals. With this new knowledge, a new term has entered our daily vocabulary: "Data Breach." A data breach can be defined as a security breach aimed at illegally destroying, altering or disclosing personal data that has been transmitted, stored, or otherwise processed.[166] In essence, it can be said to be a type of breach of the confidentiality and integrity of data stored and made available within ICT programs or systems. Often the violation derives from the malicious behavior perpetrated by individuals authorized to access the subtracted data that is then publicly released. However, nowadays, unauthorized individuals through notorious cyber attacks are frequently perpetrating this type of crime. Typically, it is common for these actors to use malwares aimed at seizing the computer system and preventing the owner from accessing his data until, for example, a ransom is paid.

We can distinguish different types of personal data: "special data" and "judicial and procedural data." Special data is information regarding a particular category of personal data that reveals racial or ethnic origin, political opinions, religious or philosophical beliefs, trade union membership, and so

---

[166] Article 4, n. 12, GDPR.

on. The peculiarity of such data is that they cannot be processed unless there is official consent or an explicit provision in the law allowing access and processing of this information.[167] Another type of personal data that, in certain cases, can be processed is "Judicial Data." Judicial data is a collection of electronically available personal data on legal and law-related topics, for example, data on criminal convictions and offenses. Their processing is only permitted under the control of the public authority or if officially authorized by national state law.

If we once again consider the definition of data breach, previously set out, we can see that it must necessarily be coordinated with the provisions of Article 5 paragraph 1 letter f) of the same legislative text, where the European legislator emphasizes that data must be "processed in such a way as to ensure adequate security [...] including protection, by appropriate technical and organizational measures, from unauthorized or unlawful processing and from accidental loss, destruction or damage."[168]

According to the GDPR, data processing is lawful only if and to the extent that at least one of the explicitly stated conditions is met. Some of the most important conditions stated in the Regulation are, for example, that the data subject must give explicit consent to the processing of their personal data for one or more specific purposes. The processing will be considered necessary for the performance of a contract to which the data subject is a party or to take measures at the request of the data subject prior to entering into a contract. The processing will be considered lawful if it appears necessary to comply with a legal obligation to which the controller is subject. It will be considered lawful if it is considered necessary to protect the vital interests of the data subject or another natural person. It will be considered lawful if it is necessary for the performance of a task carried out in the public interest or in the exercise of public powers vested in the controller. Finally, for data processing to be considered lawful it must be necessary for the purposes of the legitimate interests pursued by the data controller or a third party.

---

[167] With the phrase "Processing information" we intend the operation or set of operations, carried out with or without the aid of automated processes, applied to personal data or sets of personal data, such as the collection, registration, organization, storage , the adaptation or modification, extraction, use, dissemination , destruction and so on. This treatment of data must necessarily be carried out under the conditions of lawfulness provided by the regulation (GDPR) itself.

[168] Article 5 paragraph 1 lett. f) of the GDPR.

In essence, the event of a data breach will therefore correspond to the data controller's failure to comply with the general principles guiding the processing of personal data.[169]

Being that these types of attacks are becoming more and more common in our daily "online life," one might wonder how to act in case you are a victim of a "data breach." According to Article 33 of the GDPR, in the event of a personal data breach, the controller must notify this breach to the competent supervisory authority, unless the personal data breach is "unlikely to result in a risk to the rights and freedoms of natural persons." If this breach is likely to present a high risk to the fundamental rights and freedoms of natural persons, controllers must notify the data subject of this breach immediately.

Article 33 of the GDPR also states that it is mandatory for the data controller to notify the competent supervisory authority in each Member State[170] without undue delay, or within 72 hours of receiving knowledge, unless "the personal data breach is unlikely to present a risk to the rights and freedoms of natural persons."[171] The same task is incumbent, albeit with some adaptations, on the data controller, who, if appointed, is responsible for notifying the personal data breach without delay. Note, however, that this particular obligation does not entail a direct notification to the supervisory authority, but to the controller itself, who will therefore still be required to proceed on the basis of the requirements of Article 33.

4.3.1. Threats Posed by Data Breach

Different types of data are more or less valuable and only become a target when they have value to a third party. Therefore, they can pose different levels of risk to individuals or businesses, which must be assessed in order to legally safeguard potential victims. According to Bloomberg,[172] data breaches in 2016 were up 40% from 2015, and recent data from Risk Based Security[173] revealed that the number of exposed records has increased to a staggering 36 billion in 2020. The costs associated with such incidents for individuals and businesses can be very high. It can threaten individuals financially and compromise a

---

169 S.F. GIOVANNANGELI, *La violazione dei dati o data breach*, 2019, p.407.

170 In Italy the "Privacy Guarantor" (Garante della Privacy).

171 EU Regulation 679/2016 article 33.

172 O.KARIF, *Bloomberg News, Cybersecurity: 2016 was a record year for data breaches*, in https://www.bloomberg.com/news/articles/2017-01-19/data-breaches-hit-record-in-2016-as-dnc-wendy-s-co-hacked.

173 I.GOTTIJNG, *Risk Based Security. 2020 Q3 Report - Data Breach QuickView*, 2020, in https://pages.riskbasedsecurity.com/hubfs/Reports/2020/2020%20Q3%20Data%20Breach%20QuickView%20Report.pdf.

company's ability to continue operating. As a result, it becomes extremely important to identify threats and reduce their exposure.[174]

A variety of data can be exposed due to an IT systems breach, including:

a) Personally identifiable information. This includes data such as social security numbers, contact information, dates of birth, education and other personal information.
b) Financial information. This includes credit card numbers and expiration dates, bank accounts, investment details, and similar data.
c) Health Information. This includes details about health conditions, prescription drugs, treatments, and medical records.
d) Intellectual Property. This includes product designs and manuals, specifications, scientific formulas, marketing text and symbols, proprietary software, and other material the company has developed.
e) Competitor information. This includes competitor data, market studies, pricing information, and business plans.
f) Legal Information. This includes documentation about court cases the company may pursue, legal opinions about business practices, details about mergers and acquisitions, and regulatory decisions.
g) IT security data. This includes lists of usernames and passwords, encryption keys, security strategies, and network structure.

Typically, these types of information attract the attention of third parties for whom the data has value. Personal, financial and health information can be sold and used for marketing, fraud and identity theft. Intellectual property can be sold and used for various illegal purposes. For example, as it relates to businesses, intellectual property can be used to develop products and services that are similar to the originals, and competitive information can be sold and used to block strategic plans and leaked legal information that can damage the legal standing of targeted companies. Cybersecurity data itself is a valuable target because it allows unauthorized parties to gain access to all sorts of other information about the victims' systems.[175]

Threats targeting different types of data can come from employees in various offices with whom victims have a relationship with and from vendors

---

[174] D. PADOVAN, *Data breach e GDPR: gestire la crisi con procedure corrette*, in Network Cybersecurity360, https://www.cybersecurity360.it/legal/data-breach-le-procedure-corrette-per-gestire-la-crisi/.

[175] See A.GUZZO, *Data breach nel GDPR: cos'è e come fare segnalazione e prevenzione*, P4 Hub Innovation Editor, 2021.

and consultants who have access to the victims' network, whether they are individuals or a company. They can access data from within the victim's network, through external email accounts, through mobile devices and through the cloud if the data is stored in this common type of data storage system. Thus, the traditional perimeter protection is no longer sufficient to keep data safe from these threats.

Data protection can fail against insiders if the victim is a company, and in the case of individuals, data breaches can be exercised by perpetrators using malicious emails or websites to install malware on computers and thereby obtain usernames and passwords. Often, criminal incidents involving businesses are perpetrated by employees of cloud service providers who have access to cloud data and email accounts, so that mobile devices can be lost, hacked or compromised. In the face of these threats, companies must identify the consequences of corresponding data breaches and find solutions that reduce their risks.

The consequences for companies experiencing data breaches are severe and increasing. This is primarily due to the increased regulatory burden of notifying individuals whose data has been compromised. Notification requirements and penalties for companies that suffer a data breach differ by jurisdiction, which in the globalized world presents a serious legal challenge to effectively prosecute perpetrators and safeguard victims.

Examples of cyber-attacks perpetrated against commercial enterprises or individuals are provided by recent public hacking incidents: the data system breach suffered by the Italian pharmaceutical company Zambon, and the disastrous database system breach suffered by Facebook.

4.3.1.1. The Zambon Case

Large Italian industries have long been in the crosshairs of web pirates. In April 2021, a maxi-attack from China hit many Italian industrial companies, exploiting a bug active on a widely used management software. Among the victims are also companies in the healthcare sector, already hit hard in the year marked by the pandemic. In particular, the Italian pharmaceutical company Zambon, suffered a major cyberattack that led to a precautionary stop of industrial production lines. According to reports from Edoardo Limone, security expert,[176] hackers entered the Zambon network for about 7 months.

---

[176] E.LIMONE, *DataBreach: Zambon farmaceutica, 2021, "ICT, cybersecurity,"* in https://www.edoardolimone.com/2021/04/23/databreach-zambon-farmaceutica.

DataBreaches.net[177] reports that the threat actors behind the attack belong to the international organization known as Babuk, a new and notorious criminal group, which claims to have exfiltrated about 10 TB of data from zambongroup.com. The company was asked to contact the criminals through an encrypted system in order to prevent the company's sensitive data from being leaked, and was most likely asked to pay a reactivation fee to avoid consequences. As a result of the cyber-attack, the company halted production and operations of 217 employees at the attacked manufacturing facility for 1 week, with obvious severe financial damage. After an internal investigation by the company's cyber experts, operations resumed. It is not known whether a ransom was paid. In any case, the possibility that the data could be sold to a competitor remains open.

4.3.1.2. The Facebook Case

During the month of April 2021, the news appeared in all newspapers around the world that the data of more than 533 million users of the well-known social network Facebook was made available on numerous online sites. Of these users, almost 36 million are Italian citizens. According to what emerged from the same American platform, the data would have been stolen between 2017 and 2018, due to a flaw in computer security systems. However, this flaw would have allowed hackers to steal an impressive amount of data related to almost half a billion people.[178] The personal data that was stolen was of different types: in particular, it would involve the user's name, phone number, email address, information about the user's gender, where they live, their sentimental status, job position, and many other personal information of the individuals concerned. In addition, this data - which for a first period after the theft had been stored in servers on the Dark Web, thus accessible with greater difficulty - since May 2021 has been located on servers that can be reached by any Internet user.[179]

The data breach has alarmed stakeholders and governments around the world for the serious consequences that could result from the dissemination of the information of those involved, which for Italy represent more than half of

---

[177] F.BIGNARDI, DataBreaches.net. IT: Hacker attack on pharmaceutical company Zambon, 2021, in https://www.databreaches.net/?s=zambon.

[178] EMMA GRAHAM-HARRISON, *50 million Facebook profiles harvested for Cambridge Analytica in major data breach* in The Guardian, 17 march 2018.

[179] See A.HOLMES. *Facebook users' phone numbers and personal data have been leaked online. Insider*, 3 April, 2021. https://www.businessinsider.com/stolen-data-of-533-million-facebook-users-leaked-online-2021-4?IR=T.

the population of the entire nation. The data in question can certainly be used by numerous subjects who have an interest in having this type of personal information: such as, for example, companies and agencies that carry out telemarketing activities in order to propose the sale of products and services to the subjects in question. So for minor relevant activities.

However, the most important thing is the legal relevance of this episode, as such data could also be used for fraudulent computer activities and online crime episodes. For example, the use of the cell phone number of the interested parties (which is often used as a second authentication factor, in order to access home banking services or for digital identity or certified e-mail). In fact, malicious subjects can pursue the crime of Identity Theft, using phone numbers to create a copy of the SIM card of the interested party and thus replace the latter in his digital relationships with subjects (such as banks) that rely on the phone number of the interested party to be able to provide their services. In general, the falsification of a citizen's identity can be used as a means of committing illegal and criminal acts.[180]

The Guarantor for the protection of personal data (Italian Data Protection Authority) was well aware of the serious consequences that could result from the dissemination of such personal data and intervened immediately to try to inform citizens of the possible risks of data breaches. The Authority invited citizens to pay attention to all the possible anomalies they could find on their cell phones and, above all, to warn all subjects of the illicit use of data from the database of the Facebook platform.

The two cases clearly show that data breaches and their consequences can hit the two different dimensions of commercial enterprises and private citizens hard. They also show that current legal systems need to be updated and adapted to effectively respond to events made possible by advancing cyber knowledge. Finally, it somehow suggests that cybercrimes should certainly not be confined only to the area of pure economic crimes, but considered as circumstances involving various aspects of private citizens' lives and consider the possibility that they may be victims of various types of criminal activities.

The Data Protection Working Party, which adopted the "Guidelines on Personal data breach notification" under Regulation 2016/679, distinguished three different hypotheses of data breach. First, it outlined the so-called "confidentiality breach," which is when there is an accidental or abusive access to personal data; second, the "availability breach," which occurs when

---

[180] See C.WYLIE, *Il mercato del consenso: come ho creato e poi distrutto Cambridge Analytica*, Milano, 2020; also N.TIRINO, *Cambridge Analytica. Il potere segreto, la gestione del consenso e la fine della propaganda*, Lecce, 2019.

there is an accidental or unauthorized loss or destruction of data; and finally, the "integrity breach," in cases where there is an accidental or unauthorized alteration.[181]

More recently, the European Data Protection Board (EDPB) published its work program for 2021-2022[182] on March 2020, identifying four macro-areas on which it must focus to improve. First, it should aim to simplify compliance processes and harmonize the GDPR. Second, improve cooperation between different data protection authorities to ensure more effective enforcement of the rules and objectives stated within the GDPR. Third, to analyze possible threats to fundamental rights in association with new and emerging technologies and finally to promote EU standards globally. Therefore, the European Data Protection Board is committed to developing and promoting tools to simplify the implementation of data protection rules, especially during the processing phase. Efforts will also go towards making the consistency mechanism more effective,[183] as well as other useful tools in order to smooth out potential differences in the application of the GDPR between individual legislations. With this in mind, the Committee intends to ensure and monitor the consistency and uniformity of the jurisprudence of the various national Guarantors, confirming its role as a body capable of resolving disputes.

There is also talk of the implementation of a Coordinated Enforcement Framework (CEF). This framework is intended to provide a structure for organizing the annual recurring activities of the Committee's supervisors. The annual coordinated action focuses on a predefined topic and allows supervisors in different countries to address the issue by implementing a predefined methodology.

The EDPB also states that it intends to monitor the progress of the development of new and emerging technologies and their potential impact on the fundamental rights and daily lives of individuals, not without strengthening data protection by design and by default.[184]

The EDPB is determined to establish and promote high European but especially global standards for international data transfers to third countries

---

181 Article 29 Data Protection Working Party, opinion 3/2014 on personal data breach notification, 2014.

182 See https://edpb.europa.eu/our-work-tools/our-documents/strategy-work-programme/edpb-work-programme-20212022_en.

183 Article 63 GDPR states that "In order to contribute to the consistent application of this Regulation throughout the Union, the supervisory authorities shall cooperate with each other and, where relevant, with the Commission, through the consistency mechanism as set out in this Section."

184 *Ibidem.*

and to strengthen its engagement with the international community to promote the European data protection system as a global reference model in the field. From this point of view, collaboration and dialogue with international organizations and institutions appears crucial to support a sufficient level of cooperation between the EDPB and third country supervisory authorities. For now, the most interesting country in this sense is the United States, a key country for the European digital economy that is not considered to have a sufficient level of data protection, making it very difficult to cooperate and transfer data in a GDPR-compliant manner.[185]

However, the EDPB seems to have the necessary awareness of the criticality and fragility of the current system and, from what emerges from the analysis of the Work Program 2021-2022, appears intent on acting proactively to mitigate and prevent possible future risks.

4.3.2. Directions of the Italian Data Protection Authority in Case of a Data Breach

In Italy, the Authority for the Protection of Personal Data is an independent administrative authority established by the so-called Privacy Law,[186] subsequently governed by the Personal Data Protection Code[187] as amended by Legislative Decree No. 101 of August 2018. The latter confirmed that the Guarantor is the designated supervisory authority also for the purposes of implementing the General Data Protection Regulation.[188]

In the event of a Data Breach, the data controller (public body, company, association, party, professional) without undue delay and, where possible, within 72 hours of becoming aware of the breach, must notify the Authority for the Protection of Personal Data. Unless the personal data breach is unlikely to result in a risk to the rights and freedoms of individuals. A data controller who becomes aware of a possible breach is required to promptly notify the owner so that it can take action.

Notifications to the Authority made after the 72-hour deadline must be accompanied by the reasons for the delay. In addition, if the breach poses a high risk to the rights of individuals, the data controller must communicate this to all relevant parties, using the most appropriate channels, unless it has already taken measures to reduce the impact. The data controller, regardless of the communication to the Authority, must document all personal data

---

[185] *Ibidem.*
[186] Law n. 675 of December 31 1996.
[187] Legislative Decree n. 196 of June 30 2003.
[188] Article 51 EU/2016/697.

breaches, for example, by preparing a special register. This documentation allows the Authority to conduct any compliance checks.

Only personal data breaches that are likely to have significant adverse effects on individuals, resulting in physical, tangible or intangible harm, should be reported. This may include, for example, loss of control over one's personal data, limitation of certain rights, discrimination, identity theft or risk of fraud, loss of confidentiality of personal data protected by professional secrecy, financial loss, reputational damage, and any other significant economic or social disadvantage.

Finally, the notification must contain the information required by Article 33 par. 3 of Regulation (EU) 2016/679 and indicated in the Annex to the Provision of the Guarantor of July 30, 2019 on the notification of personal data breaches.[189] The notification must be formalized through the use of an official template made available on the official website of the Authority and sent to the Guarantor by certified e-mail at *Protocol@pec.gpdp.it* or by ordinary e-mail at *Protocol@gpdp.it* and must be digitally signed[190] (with qualified electronic signature/digital signature) or signed with a classic handwritten signature. In the latter case, the notification must be submitted together with a copy of the signatory's identity document.

The subject of the message must necessarily contain the words "Notification of personal data breach" and optionally the name of the data controller. In order to simplify the fulfilments foreseen for the data controllers, the Authority has designed and made available a special self-assessment tool that allows to identify the actions to be taken following a personal data breach resulting from a security incident.

Pursuant to Article 58 of EU Regulation 2016/679, the Data Protection Authority may prescribe corrective measures if a breach of the provisions of the Regulation is detected, including with regard to the adequacy of the technical and organizational security measures applied to the breached data. Financial penalties of up to 10 million euros or, in the case of companies, up to 2% of total annual worldwide turnover are envisaged.

---

[189] Web doc. No. 9126951.

[190] For more information on what constitutes a digital signature see Chapter 2.

Chapter 2

Digital Identity Theft

1. The Concept of Identity

The notion of identity, though recurring in our everyday language, remains expansive and ultimately indeterminate. In fact, although several social sciences have attempted to describe its content, we do not have a true comprehensive definition of what identity is. Several meanings can be attributed to the term "personal identity," all of which revolve around a single denominator: personal identity is the formula that sums up what makes a person who he or she is. In this regard, there is a basic consensus that identity is not innate but is the result of a continuous process that shapes and influences it without our knowledge or full awareness. Personal identity is not an immutable and necessary given, something one has "by nature"; rather, it is a cultural and social construct, an object of (more or less conscious) choice, adherence and construction. Therefore, it can be described as the result of a long tumultuous process: the process of identification. The construction of individual identity is thus a process of identification with some of the collective patterns or identities available in our social environment. The definition of identity, therefore, moves between the perception of oneself and the perception of others. Philosophically, every time we say "I am," we implicitly indicate a difference or delimitation with respect to "others.[191]

We can therefore say that with the concept of "personal identity," we are indicating everything we are, our physical, psychological and cultural characteristics, starting from our name and date of birth. It is the expression of the relationship among various personal aspects. Identity is also often defined through membership in a particular group. These "collective identities" are generally formed when several people with shared identity characteristics feel united with each other.

---

[191] L. METTHEY, B. STEINER, *Les associations de migrants et la formation de l'identité: une approche internaliste*, in Nous, mois – les autres, 2009, p. 6.

A final aspect of identity that must be considered is that any statement or claim made in terms of identity involves emphasizing a difference. In other words, highlighting what makes a person himself or herself is also equivalent to highlighting what that person is not. Moreover, if and to the extent that identity is constructed in terms of group membership, highlighting a person's identity means highlighting not only to which group he or she belongs but also to which other groups he or she does not belong, does not want to belong or should not belong.

The construction of identity can thus become, at the same time, a device of inclusion for those who share the same relevant characteristics and of exclusion for those who do not possess, by their own choice or by the decision of others, these characteristics.

The main complexity in analyzing and defining the concept of identity is that it consists of several overlapping layers. Therefore, it cannot be simplified into one specific aspect.

The concept of identity, in sociology, ethno-anthropological sciences and other social sciences is about an individual's idea of him/herself in his/her personal sphere and in society. In this sense, identity is the set of unique characteristics that makes the individual unique and unmistakable and, therefore, what makes a person different from others. Identity is not immutable but transforms with growth and social changes.[192] A more dramaturgical view of the matter is given by Erving Goffman, who, speaking of "representation," affirms that this cannot be considered other than the multiple activities that an individual performs during a period of time in front of a certain group of observers in order to exert a certain influence on them. Social identity is, therefore, recognized and accepted by the individual who actively participates in the construction of this definition.[193]

Identity can be analyzed not only from a sociological perspective but also from a psychological perspective. In psychology, identity can be described as the reality, the truth, the conscious and unconscious characteristic of a subject by which it is distinguished from others.[4]

We can analyze the concept of identity in a final dimension. This dimension is the so-called "legal identity," which includes, in addition to

---

[192] A. MAALOUF, Les identités meurtriéres, Parigi, 1998; P. TERENZI, *Identità*, in S. BELARDINELLI, L. ALLODI, Sociologia della cultura, Milano, p.89-104; for more information on the subject: A. DE BENOIST, *Identità e comunità*, 2015; C. TAYLOR, *Le malaise de la modernité*, 2015.

[193] E. GOFFMAN, *The Presentation of Self in Everyday Life*, 1959, p. 292 ss.

marital status, various contracts (e.g., work, marriage) regulated by law and influenced by the evolution of law and social relations.

Personal identity is therefore a synthesis of who one is. It is constructed on the basis of choices and self-determination.

The construction of one's personal identity often requires identification with a model, which may be an abstract idea or a more or less institutionalized group. Each of these profiles of personal identity is in various ways taken into consideration by the law.[5]

As already clarified, personal data refers to any type of information relating to a natural person who is identified or identifiable even indirectly by reference to any other information.

The need for a specific discipline with reference to the concept of identity arose when this was recognized as a fundamental right of every individual. It was therefore deemed necessary to create geographical boundaries identifying the exact moment from which the person becomes an individual who is entitled to the ownership of rights guaranteed in respect to the sphere of others.

1.1. The Right to Personal Identity

The right to personal identity is the result of a lively jurisprudential activity that began in the mid-70s of the last century,[194] and that culminated in the recognition made by the Italian Supreme Court about 10 years later.[195] Subsequently, the right to personal identity received further jurisprudential refinements by making its entry into some Constitutional Court judgments and finally receiving explicit legislative recognition in Article 1 of Law 675/1996,[196] the first Italian organic law on the protection of personal data, now recast in Legislative Decree no. 196/2003, containing the code regarding the protection of personal data.

The worldwide accepted definition of the "right to personal identity" states that it is anyone's right to the integrity of his/her intellectual, political, social, religious, professional patrimony. According to this definition, such patrimony must not be misinterpreted or altered through the attribution of

[194] The landmark case, which marks the first precise recognition of the new law, is unanimously recognized in Pret. Rome 6.5.1974, GI, I, 2, 514.

[195] Veronesi case, Cass. 22. 6. 1985 n. 3769.

[196] "*La presente legge garantisce che il trattamento dei dati personali si svolga nel rispetto dei diritti, delle libertà fondamentali, nonché della dignità delle persone fisiche, con particolare riferimento alla riservatezza e all'identità personale; garantisce altresì i diritti delle persone giuridiche e di ogni altro ente o associazione.*"

ideas, opinions or behaviors different from those that any individual considers peculiar to himself/herself, as they have been publically manifested. The doctrinal debate and the jurisprudential applications of the right to personal identity confirms the need to provide a definition as precise as possible, which prevents the transformation of this legal position into an elusive and all-encompassing "right to be oneself."

The issue of defining what constitutes the right to personal identity, and its distinction from other rights of the personality, offers the opportunity to mention the additional profile of its constitutional relevance. This is a rather delicate point being that the right to personal identity is not expressly mentioned in the constitutional text, and therefore its traceability to the Constitution can only be justified in an interpretative manner and also because the enucleation of a right of constitutional relevance may reduce the importance of other rights of constitutional relevance possibly having a more direct link to the constitutional text.[197] However, it should be noted that recognizing the constitutional relevance of the right to personal identity is an almost mandatory precondition for the full protection of the right itself.[198]

The constitutional relevance of the right to personal identity has been constantly reaffirmed by the jurisprudence that includes among the individual's "inviolable rights" also the right to personal identity. Such right must be considered as the right of each person to be represented with their own real character and without distorting their own history, own ideas, own conduct, own style of life, own intellectual and ideological professional ethical assets and so on.[199] Although often contested by the doctrine, this important issue was recently clarified by the Constitutional Court stating that Article 2 of the Constitution also recognizes and guarantees the right to personal identity among the rights that make up the untraceable patrimony of the human person. Personal identity therefore constitutes a good in itself regardless of the personal and social condition, the merits and defects of the subject, so that everyone is recognized the right to have their individuality preserved. The constitutional relevance of the right to personal identity now seems to be affirmed, or at least assumed, by the legislator as the "right to be oneself." A right understood as the respect for one's image qualified by the complex of ideas, the religious, ideological and moral convictions that forge the

---

[197] G. PINO, *Il diritto all'identità personale ieri e oggi. Informazione, mercato, dati personali*, in *Libera circolazione e protezione dei dati personali*, edited by R. Panetta, Milano 2006, pg. 261 and so on.

[198] *Ibidem.*

[199] A. TORRENTE-P. SCHLESINGER, *Manuale di Diritto Privato*, Milano, 2015, p. 152.

individual. The right to personal identity is included in the rank of fundamental rights such that regardless of economic or social condition, or one's beliefs, it must be recognized. In this regard, the Court of Cassation stated that each person has an interest, generally considered worthy of legal protection, to be represented in his/her social and relational life with his/her true identity. Moreover, the Court stated that each individual has an interest in not seeing him/herself altered, distorted, obscured or contested his/her own intellectual, political, social, religious, ideological, professional assets, which had manifested itself or appeared on the basis of concrete and unambiguous circumstances, generally expressed in the social environment.[200] This meaning of the right to personal identity protects a rather well-characterized interest: the interest to the correct representation of one's moral, cultural and professional heritage. It is not merely a right to be what one is but rather a right to be represented correctly.[201]

The jurisprudence applied the definition consolidated by the Supreme Court to the most various cases in which it is possible to recognize some deformation of the "social image" of a person or even of a group, a political party, a professional order or a commercial company, mainly by the mass media.

Also at the supranational level, we have the recognition of this now-fundamental right. The Charter of Fundamental Rights of the European Union expressly states, in Article 8, the principle according to which "Every person has the right to the protection of his personal data. Such data must be processed fairly (according to the principle of loyalty) or specific purposes and on the basis of the consent of the person concerned or some other legitimate basis laid down by law."[202] Each person also has the right to access the data collected concerning him/her and to obtain its ratification.

---

[200] Cass. 22.6.1985, n 3769 "Veronesi Case."

[201] RESTA, *Identità personale e identità digitale*, in Dir. Inf., 2007, p. 511-531. Defines this first approach to identity as "essentialistic," but this does not seem an appropriate definition: in fact, nothing in this jurisprudential orientation presupposes an idea of identity as a static and immutable phenomenon - indeed, it is precisely in this orientation that a sub-right of the right to personal identity, a derivation thereof, which is the so-called right to be forgotten: the right that certain events belonging to a person's past existence are not subject to unjustified repetition over time, in order to continue to be associated with a person who perhaps wants to free himself from them. As is evident, the recognition of the right to be forgotten exactly presupposes the possibility that personal identity evolves over time. Perhaps the qualification of "synchronic" meaning of identity would be more appropriate, in the sense that the relevant identity, for these purposes, is the one that is assumed to be deformed at a given moment.

[202] Article 8 Charter of Fundamental Rights.

In the approximately two decades in which the right to personal identity has "inhabited" our legal system as a purely jurisprudential creation, an explicit legislative recognition of the right has taken place in Article 1 of the Law of 31 December 1996, n. 675, the first Italian organic law on the protection of personal data, now recast in the so-called "Code regarding the protection of personal data."[203] It is important to state, however, that this legislative recognition of the right to a personal identity does not include a precise legislative definition of what this right is. The legislator, rather than providing us with an explicit definition, made an implicit reference to those definitions already developed in jurisprudence.[204]

The content of the right to personal identity, as protected by this legislation, entails the interest that one's personal information processed by others is updated, correct and complete—in other words, that the hologram of a person based on their personal data is truthful and, in the absence of particular needs, corresponds exclusively to their current "social image."

An important aspect of the protection of personal identity is that it should give the data subject not only the power of reaction against incorrect representations of their personal identity but also adequate power of control over its circulation and on the construction of the information itself. These powers of control must result from the set of procedural rules including the obligation to inform the interested party of the need for their consent for certain types of processing, the right to rectify data and to update and delete superfluous or useless data and the possibility of opposition to processing for legitimate reasons in compliance with what makes the processing legitimate.[205]

An individual's right to personal identity can be distinguished from other recognized fundamental rights such as the right to privacy and moral integrity. In primis, the right to personal identity is distinguished from the right to privacy in that the latter is the right not to see profiles of one's personality and private life represented externally. It mainly concerns the protection of an intangible sphere of the individual's intimacy and privacy, which must necessarily be protected from intrusions by third parties. Alternatively, that of

[203] Legislative Decree no. 196 of June 2003. A further legislative recognition of the right to personal identity was then found in article 126 of legislative decree 42/2004 "Codice dei beni culturali e del paesaggio."

[204] For some detailed observations on the relationship between the right to personal identity and its legislation, see RESTA, *Identità personale e identità digitale*, referring to the specific protection tools set up by the law itself.

[205] G.PINO, *L'identità Personale*, extract from the volume: *Trattato di Biodiritto, ambito e fonti del biodiritto*, edited by S. RODOTÀ; P. ZATTI, 2010, p. 227-320.

personal identity is the right that the profiles characterizing one's personality and private life, legitimately represented externally, are not infringed. In other words, it relates to the protection of the public image of the person or in any case of the self-image that the subject intends to project in social relations. Therefore, the right to identity aims to protect the way one is projected socially against possible distortions made by third parties, while the right to privacy consists of a sort of ius excludendi alios with respect to facts and circumstances that the third parties have no right to know.[206]

The right to personal identity can also be distinguished, as previously stated, from the right to moral integrity. The latter is the right not to be attributed facts and not to be subject to evaluations that are likely to create a judgment of negative value around the person. Instead, that of personal identity is the right to have the profiles of one's personality disclosed only in compliance with the principle of truth even if not detrimental to the subjects honor, reputation and decorum. The need to protect personal identity is therefore to be considered a fundamental principle; consequentially, it does not cease even in the hypothesis in which the misrepresentation of other personalities is improved by giving the individual traits and characters considered an expression of positive value by the majority of the associates.[207]

We have already had the opportunity to observe[208] that the protection of personal identity is expressly indicated among the purposes established by the legislation for the protection of personal data. Such legislation, inspired by Directive 95/46/EC,[209] was subsequently subjected to numerous modifications and is now merged into the Code regarding the protection of personal data,[210] which in the implementation of the numerous community directives by gradually intervening on the subject dictates a particularly wide and detailed discipline. Article 2 of the Privacy Code provides precisely that the processing of personal data must be carried out in compliance with fundamental rights and freedoms, as well as with the dignity of the interested party, with particular reference, among others, to personal identity, confidentiality and the right to the protection of personal data.[211] In this sense, it can be stated that the

---

206 G.PINO, *Il diritto all'identità personale, ieri e oggi. Informazione, mercato, dati personali*, in *Libera circolazione e protezione dei dati personali*, edited by R. PANETTA, Milano, 2006, p. 257-321.

207 *Ibidem.*

208 Chapter 1.

209 Entered Italy with Law n. 675/1996.

210 Legislative Decree no. 196/2003.

211 G. RASI, *Il nuovo codice sulla protezione dei dati personali tutela la dignità della persona*, in www.garanteprivacy.it, echoing what was stated in article 6 of the Resolution of the

protection of personal data constitutes a constellation of rights with one main purpose: that of protecting the individual's dignity.

The privacy code will not apply to those treatments carried out by natural persons for exclusively personal purposes unless the data processed are intended for a systematic communication to one or more specific subjects or for their dissemination in any form outside indeterminate subjects.

2. Identity Theft and the Related National Jurisdiction

Identity theft is a tricky and unknown crime—tricky in that it is difficult to fight and, in some forms, it is particularly difficult to prevent and unknown because it is in a constant phase of evolution, an evolution directed by the technological evolution we are experiencing, which is transforming the crime's *modus operandi.*[212]

However, identity theft can be described as criminal conduct perpetrated by posing as another person and aimed, in many cases, at unduly obtaining money or advantages. The term is a legal neologism and is not entirely correct: in fact, it is not possible to "steal" an identity; it can only be "used."

In the common and legal language, the interchangeable use of the terms "identity theft" and "identity fraud" has often caused some confusion. In fact, the term identity fraud should be considered as a box that includes a variety of crimes that involve the use of false identification. Therefore, it does not necessarily indicate a method of identification that belongs to a different person. Differently, identity theft is a peculiar kind of "identity fraud" perpetrated by the use of information that personally identifies someone else. However, as previously mentioned, the two circumstances of identity fraud and identity theft are both crimes that are frequently committed in connection with other violations or illegal acts. Furthermore, it must be considered that, in addition to defrauding a third party (i.e., employers, consumers, financial institutions, health care and insurance providers or governments), identity theft may also have a direct impact on the life of the victim whose identity was stolen, therefore with the addition of "victimization" as a further element of this complex crime.

European Parliament of 1989 dedicated to the bundle of rights revolving around the protection of identity and personal privacy.

[212] *Guida al Furto d'Identità, Informativa per il consumatore sui rischi e le tutele da adottare a difesa dei propri dati personali*, in www.adiconsum.it.

As for the concept of "identity theft," we must exclude the possibility of tracing this conduct to Article 624 of the Italian Penal Code,[213] given that identity as such has no material character and therefore cannot be an object of subtraction or possession in the sense accepted by the provision. It seems quite correct to refer to the definition contained in Legislative Decree no. 141/2010 on consumer credit, whose Article 30bis defines identity theft as total or partial impersonation.[214] By total impersonation, we mean the total concealment of one's identity through the improper use of data concerning the identity itself and the income of another person, alive or deceased. Partial impersonation, in contrast, means the partial concealment of one's identity through the use, in combined form, of data relating to one's person and the improper use of data relating to another person.

In general, identity theft occurs whenever individual information relating to a natural person or even a company is obtained in a fraudulent way by a criminal who acts with the intent to assume the identity of others to carry out illegal acts. Identity theft causes the victim both economic and financial damage and moral and psychological damage—the latter relating to the possible emotional stress caused by the feeling of helplessness, which in turn generates anger and fear as well as damage related to the "sacrifice of free time" or the commitment of time and energy necessary to resolve the problems arising from the fraud.

For what concerns businesses, this crime can produce various negative effects and consequences not only form an economic perspective but also reputational (e.g., the possibility that the scammer offers goods and services below the standards of the company whose identity was stolen). The analysis of the crime from the point of view of companies is particularly complex. This is because companies in general have the right and duty to protect, in addition to themselves, their customers, employees and suppliers. Therefore, they are

---

213 Article 624 cp, Fraud: Anyone who takes possession of the movable property of others, taking it away from the holder, in order to profit from it for himself or for others, by introducing it into a building or other place wholly or partly intended for a private residence or appurtenances thereof, is punished with imprisonment from four to seven years and with a fine from € 927 to € 1,500.

214 Article 30bis legislative Decree 141/2010: "Ai fini del presente decreto legislativo per furto d'identità si intende: a) l'impersonificazione totale: occultamento totale della propria identità mediante l'utilizzo indebito di dati relativi all'identità e al reddito di un altro soggetto. L'impersonificazione può riguardare l'utilizzo indebito di dati riferibili sia ad un soggetto in vita sia ad un soggetto deceduto.

b) l'impersonificazione parziale: occultamento parziale della propria identità mediante l'impiego, in forma combinata, di dati relativi alla propria persona e l'utilizzo indebito di dati relativi ad un altro soggetto, nell'ambito di quelli di cui alla lettera a)."

required to adopt particular security measures to protect their company information, primarily through the proper management and archiving of documents. The correct conservation and the destruction of documents that contain personal or third-party sensitive data are also deemed essential. In Italy, companies are liable, both civilly and criminally, for any damage caused to third parties in the event of the incorrect processing of sensitive data. In this regard, it is important to remember that in terms of data processing, the reversal of the burden of proof is envisaged.[215] This means that the data controller must demonstrate that he/she has correctly managed the data in order not to incur possible sanctions. To avoid such risks, the most suitable tool is the provision of proper training of the company's employees to adequately inform them about the possible risks and the ways in which identity theft and other types of fraud may occur as well as about the remedies to be taken.

The following are different types of identity fraud that may be perpetrated:

- Identity cloning: that is, the replacement of a person with the aim of creating a new identity and a new life;
- Financial identity theft: identity theft for the purpose of using the identification data of an individual or company to obtain credit or financial loans or to open current accounts in the victim's name;
- Criminal identity theft: use of the victim's data to carry out, in the victim's place, various kinds of illicit public acts (i.e., activation of new credit cards);
- Synthetic identity theft: use of personal data of different subjects combined to "technically" build "in the laboratory," completely or partially, a new identity according to one's needs;
- Medical identity theft: using the personal data of others to obtain health services;

Ghosting: construction of a new identity, different from the original one, appropriating the data of a deceased person.

The Charter of Fundamental Rights of the European Union states that everyone in the EU has the right to the protection of personal data and has the right to access the collected data and to obtain eventual corrections.

[215] Article 2050 of the Italian Civil Code.

Since May of 2018, with the entry into force of the General Data Protection Regulation (GDPR),[216] all companies operating in the EU are subject, regardless of where they are established, to a single set of rules on the protection of data. The aim of the directive is to protect the right of individuals to the protection of their personal data while ensuring a high level of public security. It applies to the processing of both cross-border and national data by the competent authorities of the Member States for law enforcement purposes in the criminal field. Thanks to the stricter rules introduced by the GDPR, citizens now have greater control over their personal data.[217] The data protection reform package, adopted by the EU in 2016, also includes a directive on the protection of personal data processed for criminal law enforcement purposes.

2.1. Article 494 of the Italian Criminal Code: The Crime of Impersonation

After analyzing the general concept of identity and how it is protected at the European level through the discipline designated by the new privacy code, we can move our focus to the analysis of its protection at national level. Still remaining anchored to the concept of identity understood in a real sense and not as an identity on the web, we can see how in the Italian legal system such concept is protected under Article 494 of the Italian Criminal Code under the term "impersonation"—an unprecedented criminal figure in the Italian criminal legislation prior to the current Code conceived by the legislator to punish conduct far removed from that related to the digital world but which today are fully connected to it. The crime of "impersonation" forges an ad hoc container suitable to include a large number of behaviors, not clearly disciplined, which only apparently seem to incorporate the details of scams or falsification crimes. Furthermore, the aforementioned crime can also represent the background or the prerequisite for the carrying out of further and much more serious crimes.

Article 494 of the Criminal Code, providing that the crime committed does not constitute other disciplined crimes against public faith, punishes anyone who by illegally substituting him/herself for someone else or by attributing him/herself a false name or legal status misleads someone in order

---

[216] For more information regarding the GDPR see Chapter I §4.1 of this Book.

[217] See https://www.consilium.europa.eu/it/policies/data-protection-reform/.

to achieve an "advantage." Such advantage may be obtained not only for personal benefit but also for the benefit of others.[218]

The legal asset protected by Article 494 of the Criminal Code is that of public faith, the notion of which today also includes the indistinct plurality of users. This is a multi-offensive crime since, alongside public faith, the user also undermines the trust of individual victims. For the Court of Cassation, the object legally protected is the interest regarding public faith as this can be altered by deceptions relating to the true essence of a person or his/her identity or social attributes. These are deceptions that can also overcome the restricted circle of a specific recipient, as seen with their recognition as a constant threat to public faith and not only to private faith and the civil protection of the right to a name.[219]

According to this article, therefore, the crime in question, which can be carried out by anyone,[220] entails misleading someone by illegally replacing his/her own person, or attributing to him/herself or others a false name, status or quality that does not belong to him/her, to which the law attributes legal effects.[221]

We can see how this crime, despite its "recent" codification, has always been historically present in our world and in our culture. Just think of Dante's Divine Comedy, where he remembers Gianni Schicchi, who managed to impersonate himself as Buoso Donati in order to falsify his will.[222]

---

[218] Article 494 Italian Penal Code: "Chiunque, al fine di procurare a sé o ad altri un vantaggio o di recare ad altri un danno, induce taluno in errore, sostituendo illegittimamente la propria all'altrui persona, o attribuendo a sé o ad altri un falso nome, o un falso stato, ovvero una qualità a cui la legge attribuisce effetti giuridici, è punito, se il fatto non costituisce un altro delitto contro la fede pubblica, con la reclusione fino ad un anno."

[219] M.MARRAFFINO, *La sostituzione di persona mediante furto di identità digitale*, in A.CADOPPI-S.CANESTRARI-A.MANNA-M.PAPA, *Cybercrime*, 2019, p. 307 ss.

[220] G.FIANDACA-E.MUSCO, *Diritto Penale parte speciale*, vol.1, Torino, 2017, p. 620; PAGLIARO, *Falsità personale*, 647.

[221] Also see: V.JACOVONE, *Il delitto di sostituzione di persona*, Napoli, 1974; PAGLIARO, *Falsità personale*, O. SANTORO, *Sostituzione di persona, in Enciclopedia forense*, v. VII; MANZINI, *Sostituzione di persona*, in Annali 1935; LANZARA, *Osservazioni sul delitto di sostituzione di persona, in Riv. pol., 1970.*

[222] D. ALIGHIERI, *Divine Comedy*, Inferno, Canto XXX, Questa a peccar con esso così venne, falsificando sé in altrui forma, come l'altro che là sen va, sostenne, per guadagnar la donna de la orma, falsificare in sé Buoso Donati, testando e dando al testamento norma. "Questa riuscì a compiere adulterio con lui, fingendosi un'altra persona, come l'altro che se ne va via (Gianni Schicchi) riuscì a spacciarsi per Buoso Donati, al fine di ottenere la regina (giumenta) dell'armento, e a falsificare il testamento per poi registrarlo regolarmente." "She came to sin with him after this manner, by counterfeiting of another's form; as he who goeth yonder undertook, that he might gain the lady of the herd, to counterfeit in himself Buoso Donati, making a will and giving it due form." See also F.ANTOLISEI, *Manuale di Diritto Penale, Parte Speciale, II, Milano, 2003, p.154 ss.*

It can also be argued, in the analysis of this criminal offense, that it can be defined as a "restricted-conduct type of crime" (reato a condotta vincolata) since the false representation, considered the core of the same, in order to be relevant, must be caused by one of the four procedures strictly indicated by the legislator. The first method of misleading entails the illegitimate substitution of one's own person for another. That is, the agent must deceive others about his/her identity, assuming suitable behavior to make his/her person appear different from what he/she really is. This replacement is always to be considered illegitimate, therefore, for many scholars this clarification is deemed superfluous.[223] A second form of misleading conduct entails attributing a false name to oneself or to others. To better understand this second modality, a brief analysis of the definition is required. A false name occurs when one assumes an identity other than one's own. By name we mean that complex of identification marks and, therefore, not only name and surname but also place and date of birth, paternity and maternity and so on. The false name can also belong to another person or be imaginary, while the use of a pseudonym will not constitute a crime.[224] Impersonation is also achievable through the attribution of a false status, which occurs when a "status" different from the real one is attributed.[225] Finally, the offense can be committed by attributing to oneself or to others a quality to which the law attributes legal effects. This is when one claims to possess a quality which according to the law causes certain effects. However, it is necessary that these are qualities to which the law reconnects legal effects in relation to the relationship or the situation in which one declares him/herself to enter.

The article in question also contains an express subsidiarity clause under which the crime of impersonation is not applicable when the fact that integrates it constitutes another crime against public faith.

It appears from the text of Article 494 of the Italian Criminal Code that the fact must be committed in order to procure an advantage for oneself or others or to harm others. Doctrine and jurisprudence in these cases affirm that the advantage or damage does not necessarily have an economic background, assuming, among other things, that the crime in question may be committed with the aim of psychologically and morally misleading someone or in order

[223] G.FIANDACA, E.MUSCO, *Diritto Penale parte speciale*, vol.1, Torino, 2017, p. 620.

[224] For MANZINI, the change of a vowel or consonant of one's name would also be valid to integrate the crime, MANZINI, *Sostituzione di persona*, in Annali 1935.

[225] By status we mean citizenship, ability to act, kinship, marital status, etc. While it will not be considered status for the purposes of the rule in question, neither age, nor residence, nor domicile, as they tell us nothing about the position of the subject in society. PAGLIARO, Falsità personali, 647; see also MANZINI, *Trattato*, p. 978; CRISTIANI, *Falsità,* p.24.

to enter into a relationship with people who otherwise would not have granted their friendship, confidence and so on.

From the tenor of the law, the crime is committed when someone has been misled with the means indicated. Nonetheless, it is not necessary that the advantage pursued by the agent be actually achieved. This is a specific "willful crime" (dolo specifico) entailing the willingness to deceive others on the identity of one's person using one of the methods strictly indicated by the legislator. The punishment of the fact is also subordinated to procure an advantage for oneself or others or to cause damage to others. Being a specific intentional provision, the actual achievement of the advantage is irrelevant as it will be sufficient that the purpose is pursued by the perpetrator at the time the crime is committed. Furthermore, the advantage does not necessarily have to be unfair, meaning that the author's justifications do not apply; what is relevant is the deceptive activity aimed at acquiring any personal interest.[226]

Since the crime pursuant to Article 494 of the Criminal Code has a subsidiary character only with regard to other crimes against public faith, where a fraud is committed by substituting a person, the crime provided for by Article 640 of the Criminal Code materially concurs with the crime contemplated by Article 494 previously quoted. In fact, in this regard, the latter cannot be considered absorbed by Article 640 of the Criminal Code, according to the principle enshrined in Article 84 of the Criminal Code.[227] The Supreme

---

[226] G.FIANDACA-E.MUSCO, *Diritto Penale, Parte speciale, Vol. I, 2017, p. 620 ss.*

[227] G. BETTIOL, L. PETTOELLO MANTOVANI, *Manuale di Diritto Penale*, Padova, 1986, pp 697- 701: According to article 84 of the Italian criminal code: The provisions of the previous articles do not apply when the law considers as constitutive elements, or as aggravating circumstances of a single crime, facts that would constitute, in themselves, a crime. Article 84 of the Italian penal code regulates the so-called complex or compound crime. This crime is configured when the law provides as constitutive elements or as aggravating circumstances of a single crime, facts that in themselves would constitute different crimes. in other words a complex crime, is determined when several behaviors lead to a single legal injury, and therefore a single crime. An example of a complex crime may be the crime of robbery, because the relevant crime is the result of the merger of the crime of theft with that of private violence.

Therefore, in order to have a complex crime, it is necessary that the law considers as a constitutive element or as an aggravating circumstance of a crime, facts which, taken separately, constitute in turn autonomous criminal offenses.

In the complex crime, the conduct taken individually legally have a functional independence, as each of them could give rise to an autonomous crime while linked together they give rise to a unitary and indeed complex crime. In which, however, they do not cease to be multiple. The figure of the complex crime arises when the legislator thus brings together two or more distinct actions in a single criminal fact.

Once it has been ascertained that two or more crimes must be included in the complex case, it does not matter which of the two configurations occurs, as what is relevant is that in no case can these crimes be punished independently.

Court has also, over time, established that there is a formal concurrence of crimes between fraud and impersonation since it is the same conduct that integrates two different and autonomous criminal cases. It follows that the same behavior can bring about the material element of both crimes.[228]

In addition and in conclusion, the crime of impersonation is an offense that, through the use of new information and telematics technologies, is constantly increasing and expanding within the population, so much so that it raises a high level of social alarm in civil society.

3. A New Type of Identity: Digital Identity

The advent of the internet has marked the legislators' need to seek a new set of rules to govern the uniqueness of the phenomenon with respect to the gained experience of traditional systems, which are considered to be completely inadequate with respect to the new requirements of the technique.[229] Amongst the numerous elements that characterize the individual's place and status on the network, the manifestation of one's personality on the internet takes on a considerable social importance. To this regard, it is clear that the digital support of an IT device makes it possible to establish complex dynamic relations between users, which may be difficult to interpret with balance and regulate.[230] To date, the way with which data are processed and entered online, in order to satisfy new communication needs, takes place without having to lose that typical personal connotation that is its traceability to the physical person. The individual's information contained within the processed data leads, directly or through profiling techniques, to a representation of the user's personality. In addition, the close inherence with the person has therefore led

See also: VASSALLI, *Nuove e vecchie incertezze nel reato complesso*, in Riv, It. 1978, p. 407 ss.; G. FIANDACA, E. MUSCO, *Diritto Penale, Parte Generale*, p. 726 ss.; F.ANTOLISEI, *Manuale di Diritto Penale, Parte Generale*, Milano, 2000 p. 535 ss. LOSANA, *Reato complesso e "ne bis in idem" sostanziale*, in Riv. It. dir. proc. pen. 1963, 1189, MANTOVANI, *Concorso e Conflitto*, cit. 262 ss. 299 ss.

228 Criminal Cassation court, Section V, sentence 16 October 1998, n. 10805.

229 S. RODOTÀ, *Tecnopolitica: la democrazia e le nuove tecnologie della comunicazione*, Roma- Bari, 1997, p. 139 ss; See also V.ZENO-ZENCOVICH, *Informatica ed evoluzione del diritto*, in Dir. Inform., 2003, p. 89 ss.; G. PASCUZZI, *Internet*, in Dig. disc. priv., Torino, 2000, p. 225 ss.

230 T. FROSINI, *Telematica e informatica giuridica*, in Enc. dir., XLIV, Milano, 1992, p. 61; G. PASCUZZI, *Internet* (dir. civ.), cit., p. 225 ss.; G. FINOCCHIARO, *Identità personale su internet: il diritto alla contestualizzazione dell'informazione*, in Dir. inform., 2012, p. 389.

authoritative doctrine to consider the data placed online as a part of the user's so-called "digital body."[231]

The expansion of web and ICT technologies has overwhelmingly raised the need to transform an individual's identity in order to better protect it in light of the new technological advancements. Therefore, the evolution of online relationships leads the interpreter to seek a new dimension and new sets of rules of the right to personal identity. As is well known, this is a very personal right that for some time has taken on autonomous connotations and that corresponds to the subject's claim to be represented in life and in his/her social relations with his/her authentic identity characteristics. It is understandable that the connotation and the level of importance characterizing the right to personal identity is relevant in function of the role played by a given individual within his/her community.[232]

The popularity and use of the internet among the public has led to the creation of millions of digital identities, thus giving the possibility to carry out many different activities in this virtual space. It is evident how, within the internet dimension, personal identity has acquired an undoubted importance. The extent of this phenomenon is significant. First, the incorporation of the data into a medium makes the information contained therein transmissible; then, the IT element is characterized by absolute replicability and immanence.[233]

The term "digital identity" continues to lack a specific definition, even today. The legislator has in fact not given any official definition of "digital identity." This has been considered a highly questionable choice being that in addition to creating difficulties for legal practitioners, it also poses serious problems of constitutional legitimacy. Indeed, leaving undetermined a concept or a circumstance is potentially harmful to the principle of determination characterizing criminal law as it is a corollary of the principle of mandatory legality (tassatività) or legal reserve in criminal law. The notion of digital identity, in fact, is not only lacking regulatory evidence, but it also has multiple meanings, thus it is difficult to establish a priori what is forbidden and what is

---

[231] G. ALPA, *L'identità digitale e la tutela della persona. Spunti di riflessione*, in Contr. e impr., 2017, p. 726.

[232] F. OLIVO, *Dati personali e situazioni giuridiche soggettive*, in Giust. civ., 2002, II, 162; G. FINOCCHIARO, *Identità personale* (diritto alla), cit., 723; ID., *Identità personale su internet,* cit., 389.

[233] G. FINOCCHIARO, *Identità personale (*diritto alla), cit., 735-736; ID., *La memoria della Rete*, cit., 392; R. SENIGAGLIA, *Reg. UE 2016/679 e diritto all'oblio nella comunicazione telematica. Identità, informazione e trasparenza nell'ordine della dignità personale,* in Nuove leg. civ. comm., 2017, 1025.

allowed. Part of the doctrine has therefore tried to identify the boundaries of digital identity by searching for definitions proposed in disciplines and areas different from that of criminal law. This attempt has, however, conflicted with the evidence that various definitions have been created ad hoc to serve specific and different provisions, and therefore they were not always able to fully grasp the rationale underlying the introduction of this new provision in the criminal system. This has been particularly true for cases in which digital identity was intended as a process of computer identification simply because the meaning was in reality quite reductive. In fact, in this case, the notion is limited to the moment of the validation of data in order to identify through them whether a user is entitled or not to use certain services.

The Digital Administration Code[234] contemplates and defines only the notions of "electronic identity" (Article 1, letter c and 66 CAD) and that of "digital signature" (Article 1, letter s CAD. Although it lacks specific normative outcomes, it has become part of the everyday vocabulary of jurists and has been represented in two distinct ways. In the first and broader sense, the expression is used as a synonym for "networked" or "virtual" identity. The second and more restrictive meaning of digital identity, generally used by computer scientists, is one that describes digital identity as the set of information and resources granted by computer systems to a user.

Usually this information is protected by an authentication system, which can be carried out through a password, biological characteristics (such as fingerprints, voice detection, face recognition and so on) or also through a specific material object (such as a magnetic card, smart card, digital tokens).[235] From this basic distinction, one might say that digital identity is formed by the combination of two factors. On one hand, the physical subject's identification and, on the other hand, the attribution of a set of electronic codes, which, once introduced into one or more systems, allows the individual's identification.[236] Furthermore, the concept of digital identity is concretized as a personal identity on the internet. In other words, digital identity can be described as the set of information that, within a given computer system, refers to a specific person. The higher the level of complexity within the computer system, the more detailed the information relating to the specific individual will be.

[234] Legislative Decree March 7 2005, n. 82.

[235] The now substantial literature on the subject of "identity theft" commonly refers to this meaning of digital identity.

[236] M.F.COCUCCIO, *Il diritto all'identità personale e l'identità "digitale,"* in Diritto di Famiglia e delle Persone, 2016, 949 ss. See also G.RESTA, *Identità personale e identità digitale*, in Dir. Informaica, 2007, 511-531.

Over the years, many scholars have tried to give a more exhaustive definition of what digital identity is. A study carried out by the Boston Consulting Group defines digital identity as the set of all digital data made available to an individual regardless of their degree of validity, their form or level of accessibility. This type of personal identity may include any, if not all, of the following aspects: intrinsic characteristics (for example, origin, date of birth, nationality, sex), acquired characteristics (for example, the individual's personal history, address, medical data, purchases) and individual preferences (such as interests, hobbies, musical tastes, favorite broadcasts). It is clear how this particular definition of digital identity also includes "sensitive data," which is therefore subject to the new supranational privacy regulations.[237] Another definition of digital identity can be found in the Decree of the President of the Italian Council of Ministers of October 2014, the so-called "SPID Decree," which defines digital identity as the computer representation of the one-to-one correspondence between a user and his/her identification attributes, verified through all the data collected and recorded in digital form.

The Declaration of Internet Rights also defines what can be considered as the right to a digital identity. Article 9 of the Declaration specifically states that each person has the right to the full and updated representation of their identities on the internet. In addition, the definition of identity concerns the free construction of personality and cannot be detached from the intervention and knowledge of the interested party. The article in question also states that the use of algorithms and probabilistic techniques must be brought to the attention of the persons concerned, who in any case may oppose the construction and dissemination of profiles concerning them. Each person has the right to provide only the data strictly necessary for the fulfillment of legal obligations, for the supply of goods and services or for access to platforms operating on the internet. The attribution and management of digital identity by public institutions must be accompanied by adequate guarantees, particularly in terms of security.[238] From the analysis of this Declaration, we can notice how the latter presents a number of interesting aspects. It firstly states the existence of multiple digital identities and the possibility for an individual to assume various different digital identities; however, it also allows the individual to maintain some form of anonymity on the net, if and when requested.

---

[237] A. O. ROVEGNO, *Identità digitale: tra esigenze di condivisione e necessità di tutela, in Cyberspazio e diritto*, in rivista internazionale Giuridica, 2013, 405.

[238] Declaration of the Internet Rights, approved by the Commission for Relative Rights and Duties to the Internet and published on July 28, 2015.

Although the concept may seem at first glance very complex and vast, in reality, digital identity is already a widespread concept practically used by everyone in his or her daily life. This form of identity can have various implications, which may allow certain processes to be improved and simplified. For example, we have the following:

- Digital domicile: protected by the "SPID," which is the public digital identity system. This system guarantees all citizens and businesses unique, safe and secure access to the digital services of the public administration and private entities that join it, also guaranteeing a high degree of usability through the use of multi-platform tools. The system also represents one of the transversal initiatives of the 2014-2020 Digital Growth Strategy.
- PEC: a certified email that uniquely identifies the sender or recipient of a message, which therefore assumes legal value in all respects.
- Digital electronic signature: a new form of signature that presents the same legal value as a handwritten signature; therefore, essentially, it is as if the person had physically signed the given document.

These are just some examples of the "forms" digital identity can take and how this tool can improve and simplify processes and daily tasks.

Among the different possible dimensions relationships can assume on the internet, it is worth underscoring the particular importance of social networks.[239] Their very nature, and wide diffusion, allows considering them the main digital place of expression of one's individual identity. On one hand, this phenomenon involves an exponential increase in the amount of personal data that is shared,[240] and, on the other hand, the non-voluntary or avoidability of the transfer by the user.[241] Nowadays, the digital profile implies a projection of personality rights in the virtual community. The digital profile of the user

---

[239] See also: R. DUCATO, *I social network, in Il diritto dell'era digitale*, directed by G. Pascuzzi, Bologna, 2015, 269 ss. Cfr., also see, A. OTTOLIA, *Privacy e social networks: profili evolutivi della tutela dei dati personali*, in Aida, 2011, 360 ss.; S. SCALZINI, *I servizi di online social network tra privacy, regole di utilizzo e violazione dei diritti dei terzi,* in Giur. mer., 2012, 2569 ss.; F. AGNINO, *Fino a che punto è possibile disporre contrattualmente dei propri diritti?* , in Giur. mer., 2012, 2558; R. COSIO, *Natura del contratto tra utente e social, in Ricerche giuridiche*, 2017, 133 ss.

[240] S. RODOTÀ, *Il mondo della rete. Quali diritti, quali vincoli*, Roma-Bari, 2014, 41.

[241] M. BRUGI, *Dall'identità personale all'identità digitale. Una necessità per il cittadino del terzo millennio, in Informatica e diritto*, 2008, 167 ss.; C. CAMARDI, *L'eredità digitale*, cit., 71.

is in fact a modern form of representation of the individual him/herself, which includes the elements that characterize and identify the user in his/her projection into the digital world.[242]

In light of these reflections, it is important to emphasize how, to date, the right to personal identity, besides being very personal, is changing and evolving over time with the development of the person, connoting their personality. The legal system's response to this change in the perception of the individual's personal sphere, which is no longer to be considered just physical and tangible, was a change in legislative technique. This led to the formulation of rules of principle that can be applied each time a judgment casuistry assesses the merit of the divergent claims.[243] The general structure of the protection system has changed profoundly with the introduction of law 675/1996, which also transformed the overall meaning of personal identity and, with this, its digital sphere. The new discipline of data protection, as issued by the EU, reflects a profound change in the underlying socio-economic conditions, especially in relation to the development of communication technologies and the spread of market logic. For some time, legal culture has retained the awareness that the free construction of identity can be concretely endangered not only in the hypothesis of misrepresentation or de-contextualization by mass media but also when the flow of information concerning the person does not take place through transparent channels and within a well-defined framework of guarantees.[244] The techniques of data collection and individual profiling made possible by new technologies determine the risk that the ego becomes fragmented, without its knowledge, in a multiplicity of databases, therefore offering a partial and potentially harmful representation of the person, which would thus be reduced to the mere sum of its electronic projections.[245] The right to identity, consequently, takes on new connotations as it no longer implies a "correct representation in each context"

---

[242] GAETA, *la protezione dei dati personali nell'internet of things: l'esempio dei veicoli autonomi*, in Dir. informaz, e informatica, 2018, p. 147 ss.

[243] G. ALPA, *Privacy e statuto dell'informazione, in Riv. dir, civ., 1980,* cit., 119; S. RODOTÀ, *Tra diritti fondamentali ed elasticità della normativa: il nuovo codice sulla privacy*, in Eur. dir. priv., 2004, 3 ss.; C.M. BIANCA, *Note introduttive*, cit., XXXIII.

[244] In this regard see S. RODOTA`, *Tecnopolitica. La democrazia e le nuove tecnologie della comunicazione*, Roma-Bari, 2004, 134 ss; ID., *Progresso tecnico e problemi istituzionali nella gestione delle informazioni*, in N. MATTEUCCI, *a cura di, Privacy e banche di dati, Bologna*, 1981, 25 ss.; ID., *La privacy tra individuo e collettività*, in Tecnologie e diritti, Bologna, 1995, 19 ss.

[245] See S. RODOTA`, *Tecnopolitica. La democrazia e le nuove tecnologie della comunicazione*, cit., 148.

but presumes an "integral representation of the person" and moreover "representation not entrusted only to automated tools.[246]

With the evolution of privacy law, we are witnessing an important process of anticipation and qualitative enrichment of protection through the interaction between private and public techniques. The goal is to prepare a series of suitable tools to facilitate, in a preventive way and regardless of the risk of damage, the free construction of one's private sphere.

In light of this evolution, therefore, identity is no longer seen as a pre-existing datum (i.e., as an external projection of an individual heritage already outlined in its distinctive characteristics) but as a process, constantly progressing and evolving, open to a plurality of outcomes and continuously exposed to the widespread and pervasive interference of the various forms of social power. With respect to this process, the legal system is no longer limited to a position of abstention and non-interference but exercises an active role in supervision and control, with the aim of restoring the individual's ability to freely define their own personal identity, removing it from the risk of a heterogeneously imposed normalization.[247]

3.1. The Relationship between Digital Identity and on-Line Personality: The Issue of an Effective Legal Protection of the Citizens' Rights

The protection of digital identity is a widely debated topic, both in jurisprudence and in doctrine, as it is considered a juridical asset-value included in the broader channel of the so-called personality rights. Many still ongoing discussions have taken place in recent years on the extent and limits of this protection, both with reference to natural persons and, albeit to a different and more restrictive extent, in relation to legal persons.

As already discussed in the previous chapters, identity is regarded by the legislator as a juridical asset-value inherent in the social dimension of the individual to which it refers since identity is the result of social interactions, which becomes explicit and well-specified in the public space.[248] A definition

---

[246] S. RODOTA`, *Persona, riservatezza, identità`. Prime note sistematiche sulla protezione dei dati personali*, p. 605- 606.

[247] See S. RODOTA *Tecnopolitica: la democrazia e le nuove tecnologie della comunicazione*, Roma- Bari, 1997.

[248] V. ZENO-ZENCOVICH, *Identità personale*, Dig.disci.priv., sez.civ.,IX,1993,301.

of what constitutes a personal identity can be found in a famous ruling of the Constitutional Court of 1994. In this ruling, it was stated that personal identity constitutes the "right to be oneself," understood as respect for the image projected in associated life, with the acquisitions of ideas and experiences, with the ideological, religious, moral and social convictions that differentiate, and at the same time qualify, the individual."[249] Therefore, identity not only indisputably identifies the subject to which it refers but represents the subject and affirms its individual personality as being different from the others although identical to itself.

Different from personal identity is the new modern digital identity, which refers to a dual concept. This notion generally identifies personal identity "in the network" or as "virtual" as opposed to the "physical" one, while in a more technical and IT-legal sense, digital identity defines the set of information and resources granted by a computer system to a particular user, usually protected by an authentication system.

The notion of personality implies the existence of "personality rights," which refers to a conceptual legal category currently in use in various European civil law systems. For instance, they are known in the French, German, Spanish and Portuguese legal systems as, respectively, "droits de la personnalité," "Persönlichkeitsrechte," "Derechos de la personalidad" and "Dreitos de personalidade," which are aimed at identifying that range of subjective rights that have as their object the attributes of the personality, physical and immaterial, and are characterized by flexibility. The boundaries of this legal notion do not seem to be static as they may include several circumstances such as the right to name,[250] to image,[251] to the confidentiality and control of the circulation of personal data, to the honor and reputation,[252] to personal identity and, finally, also the rights protected by copyright. In this regard, personality rights recognized by the legislator have historically constituted a paradigm shift,[253] particularly directed to protect the intangible assets resulting from the creativity of individuals, recognizing them an exclusive right.[254]

---

[249] Constitutional Court, February 3 1994, n.13, in www.foro.it.

[250] Article 6 of the Italian Civil Code and Article 22 of the Constitution.

[251] Article 10 of the Italian Civil Code and Article 96 of the law of 22 April 1941, n.633.

[252] Articles 594-595 of the Criminal Code.

[253] T. KUHN, *The Structure of Scientific Revolutions*, 1962, pp. 54.

[254] G.RESTA, *Le persone fisiche e i diritti della personalità,* in Tratt. Sacco, Torino, 2006, p. 489 ss; R. PARDOLESI, *I diritti della personalità*, 2005, p. 3 ss.; V. ZENO-ZENCOVICH, *voce Personalità*, in (diritti della), in Dig. Disc. Priv. Sez. civ., vol.XIII, Torino, 1995, p.

Individuals are now holders of personality rights from birth.[255] This category includes the right to identity and, therefore, the protection of their digital identity, particularly their reputational profiles. On this point, there is a very broad jurisprudence given the evolution of the socio-economic context and, most of all, the advent of social media, which have multiplied the possibilities of potential attacks, distortions and risks deriving from the circulation of data, information and, in any case, false offensive if not openly defamatory news.

The violation of digital identity is substantially legally protected, in particular, by the compensation for damages that can be settled on an equitable basis pursuant to Articles 1226 and 2056 of the Italian Civil Code. In the judicial assessment issued in accordance with these articles, factors such as the recognizability of the represented subject and the disclosure of the recipients' image and of the harmful attitude of any accompanying text are taken into consideration.[256] Therefore, the general principle according to which the misrepresentation of personal assets, in its intellectual, political or social profiles, constitutes a violation of the right to personal identity, which rises to constitutional protection pursuant to Article 2 of the Constitution (so-called personalistic principle) applies.

On various occasions, the judges of merit have been called upon to rule on whether the susceptibility of personal identity should have been recognized and protected from potentially defamatory or offensive conducts. However, it is increasingly clear that justices should not disregard the evidence that print media and television dominated the previous historical phase, while the current information context is characterized by the continuous and pervasive use of social media, by a vast and transversal audience, potentially allowing for an unlimited circulation of information in virtually unlimited space and time. With the advent of social media, the possibilities of attacking a natural person's personal identity have multiplied; therefore, the judges of merit have had the opportunity to pronounce, on numerous occasions, on the injury to personal identity and, therefore, to personality rights through social networks. These violations can be realized, concretely, thanks to the functionalities of the online platforms (or, more correctly, hosting service providers, storage service providers) that allow users to create digital content in text, visual and

---

430 ss.; S.BONAVITA – V.POLI; *La tutela civilistica della reputazione online*, in Cyberspazio e diritto, 2017, p. 307-340.

[255] *Ibidem.*

[256] Court of Verona February 26, 1996, in Studium Juris, 1995, p. 752; F. MACIOCE, *Civil protection of the person and personal identity*, Padua, 1984, p. 7 ss.

vocal format (e.g., posts, comments, images, videos, audio) and disseminate it both with a personal account and by creating fake digital profiles.

The issue of the protection of personality rights, which is central to the principles related to the system of civil protection of the personality characterizing the legal model of civil law, continues to remain open and at the center of the current jurisprudential and doctrinal debate. Once distanced from possible rigid dogmatic positions, the paradigm of personality rights, including the protection of personal identity, might be able to adapt to the current socio-economic and civil context although some unresolved questions remain. Thus, with the emergence of new legal situations, such as the protection of a social media account referable to a natural person classified as an "influencer," which is connected to a distinct legal person, the protection of reputation is functional to protect a real intangible asset. The distinctions between natural and legal persons are becoming increasingly blurred, such as in the hypothetical case of influencers, with respect to which it would be interesting to observe the jurisprudential evolution on the possible configuration of the compensable damage in its patrimonial as well as non-patrimonial profiles.

In the background remains the long-debated question of the responsibility of providers who are required, according to some judges of merit, to control the publication of the content created by users and, in any case, to remove the reported content, accepting well-founded requests for de-indexing. As emphasized in the doctrine, the platforms are inclined toward an easy "contractualization" of the non-contractual profiles that are established between the operator and the user. This is in order to prevent, if not completely cancel, the risks and responsibilities deriving from the management of the platform itself and, in particular, content moderation, thus giving rise to an unbalanced structure and burden for the user.[257]

Finally, providing that the individuals' rights not to see their personal identity altered, distorted or misinterpreted remain central and undisputable, it will be important to continuously protect such rights as the judges of merit will deal with the new cases concerning the harms to the rights of the personality. Such harms may result, for instance, from the malevolent use of artificial intelligence and from the spread of new IT means, such as deepfakes and other similar technology suitable for creating highly credible defamatory and untruthful content and, therefore, damaging the identity of the offended

[257] S.SICA-G. GIANNONE CODIGLIONE, *Social network sites and the "labyrinth" of responsibilities*, in Giur. Merit, 2012, p. 2714.

party as well as endangering the legal validity of meetings, documents and contracts.

3.2. Virtual Impersonation through Digital Identity Theft

The laws relating to identity theft include the terms "impersonation" and "criminal impersonation." However, while identity theft involves impersonation, impersonation does not always mean that an identity theft has occurred. In analyzing the correct discipline to apply to digital identity theft, it seems correct and important to point out the differences between identity theft and online impersonation. A preliminary analysis of such terms shows that identity theft is meant to benefit the thief, while online impersonation is meant to harm someone other than the impersonator. In this view, for instance, creating a webpage or sending an email or an instant message on the internet using the name or domain name of another person with the intent to harm, defraud, intimidate or threaten another person or persons defines the circumstance of "online impersonation." Furthermore, identity theft typically involves stealing very specific personal information, such as a tax code number or a credit card number, and it often involves much more than using the name or telephone number of another, usually necessitating some credit report cleanup on the victim's part. While these distinctions do not make identity theft nor online impersonation easier to deal with, there is one more distinct difference between the two crimes that is necessary to emphasize: the ability of consumers to take proactive measures to protect themselves. With identity theft, there are varieties of measures someone can take to secure their personal information and to prevent it from ending up in the wrong hands. Differently, online impersonation is much more difficult to safeguard against since theoretically all someone needs is a name and possibly a phone number to impersonate another person over the internet. On the internet, changing or acquiring a new identity or someone else's identity, even for illegal purposes, is extremely easy. The data on the so-called digital identity theft, now attributable to the broader global phenomenon of cybercrime, are alarming, having also given rise to the existence of real criminal associations that are dedicated to the sale and exchange of the personal data of others illegally obtained.[258]

---

[258] F. CAJANI – G. COSTABILE – G. MAZZARACO, *Phishing e furto d'identità digitale. Indagini informatiche e sicurezza bancaria,* Milano, 2008, p. 188.

Digital identity theft is a criminal phenomenon prodromal to the commission of further offenses, which is divided into the following several phases: obtaining the personal information of the victim; interacting with personal information, which entails the possession and sale of such data; and using personal information unlawfully obtained to commit further crimes, not necessarily against property but also, for example, for defamation or threats. The techniques with which the victims' personal information is stolen are many and have become over time increasingly sophisticated. In addition to the traditional techniques, such as the theft of an identity card, the most widely used and known technique is certainly phishing. This crime entails sending cleverly counterfeited emails that report to the user non-existent problems regarding their banking institution's servers or the need to update their data, with the aim of inducing the user to click on a specific link in which they are asked to provide their identification codes. Many variants are added to this so-called classic phishing, such as malware-based phishing, MitM phishing, smishing and vishing. Another dangerous evolution of phishing, which is now commonly used, is pharming, which merely modifies the conduct through which the perpetrator acquires its victims' personal information. In this case, the victim is in fact invited to provide their personal details with a different and more sophisticated technique based on the cloning of the official website.[259]

In analyzing the crime of digital identity theft, it is important to note how such offence is not currently provided for in Italian law as an autonomous crime. It therefore does not seem doubtful how, at first glance, most of the many forms of modern personal falsification can be easily traced back to the case governed by Article 494 of the Criminal Code, which, according to some, is characterized by an excess of genericity.[260] Considering that the criminal phenomenon of impersonation infringes on the right to privacy and in particular to express the necessary consent regarding the processing of personal data; the first jurisprudential orientation of the Supreme Court regarding identity theft led it back to the crime of unlawful personal data processing, provided for by Article 167 of Legislative Decree of 30 June 2003

---

[259] V. OECD, *Scoping Paper on Online Identity Theft*, op. cit., p. 19: a virus is inserted into the computer of the victim that modifies the list of sites marked as favorites in the browser used by the victim, which is then redirected to a "clone" site of that of the credit institution or institution, and through the login to the latter, his credentials are intercepted.

[260] M. MARRAFFINO, *La sostituzione di persona mediante furto di identità digitale*, in A.CADOPPI-S.CANESTRARI-A.MANNA-M.PAPA, *Cybercrime*, 2019, p. 308 ss.

no. 196.[261] The orientation of the Supreme Court, however, subsequently changed. Using the instrument of extensive interpretation,[262] the Supreme Court has brought back to the case referred to in Article 494 of the Italian Criminal Code[263] the new forms of digital identity aggression, which result in damage to a sphere other than the property of the offended person.

In one of the first rulings on the matter, in 2007, the Supreme Court enunciated the principle of law according to which the juridical good of public faith can well be harmed by deceptions also committed on the internet relating to the true essence of a person, their identity or their social attributes. This jurisprudential orientation has been shared by the doctrine that has correctly held that personal falsehoods are characterized by the content of the representation and not by their form.[264] Another case dealt with by the Supreme Court on the matter of identity theft and person replacement, which deserves to be mentioned, dates back to 2014.[265] In this case, the judges of legitimacy considered Article 494 of the Criminal Code applicable to the conduct of a person who, by creating a false profile on a social network using the image of the offended person, not only provided an offensive description of his/her personal characteristics but also used this false identity to communicate online with other subscribers. Therefore, for our legal system, even just using the image of another person as a photo on your Facebook profile constitutes the crime referred to in Article 494 of the Criminal Code.[266] This is because the legal asset protected by the law is violated by not revealing the alleged "playful" purpose of the agent. The crime of impersonation committed via internet inevitably presents a large obscure figure both for the problems related to the identifiability of the user who creates a false profile and for the habit of those who surf the internet to interface with false identities—a circumstance that in most cases weakens the perception of the offensiveness of the fact.

---

[261] See *Cass pen., sez. III, March 26 2004 n. 28680: the case concerned a man who had posted on an Internet site the images recorded on a videotape containing the striptease of his ex-girlfriend, also publishing his mobile number, thus simulating his availability for sexual encounters.*

[262] See F. ANTOLISEI, *Manuale di diritto penale,* PG, VIII ed. revisioned by L. CONTI, Milano, 1980, p. 66; F. MANTOVANI, *Dir. pen.,* PG, IX ed., Padova, 2015, p. 73.

[263] See P. ASTORINA MARINO, *Sub. art. 494 c.p., in Commentario breve al codice penale,* directed by G. Forti, S. Seminara, G. Zuccalà, VI ed., Padova, 20.

[264] C. FLICK, *Falsa identità su internet e tutela penale della fede pubblica degli utenti e della persona,* in Dir. inf. inf., 2008, n.4-5, p. 526 ss., p. 531 ss.

[265] See Cass. pen., sez. V, 23 aprile 2014, n. 25774.

[266] See Cass. Pen. Sez. V, 10.10.2017, dep. 30.1.2018, n. 4413.

The current jurisprudence easily subsumes all rules established originally as they have remained unchanged since their entry into the criminal code in 1930, including all those deceptive behaviors that are revealed through the use of nicknames or false profiles that conceal people other than those who they claim to be in order to obtain "advantages" of various kinds.[267] As we know from the analysis carried out in the previous paragraphs, this provision penalizes the induction of others into error by means of two forms of falsification,[268] which are the substitution in full of another person and the attribution of a false name, status or non-existent quality. Therefore, this is how modern technologies have changed the possible methods of the execution of the crime de quo. Think of all the cases in which the authentication of the interested party takes place through biometric techniques and/or facial identification. The use of someone else's digital identity can lead to confusions, deceptions and even real violations of the right to a name outside and inside the virtual "community."[269]

Many scholars consider identity theft as a rather complex phenomenon being that it is divided into several phases. It therefore would seem reductive to limit it only to the crime of substitution provided for by Article 494 of the Italian Criminal Code. Nevertheless, several attempts have been made over time to identify further incriminating rules that can be applied in these cases.

In this regard, some perplexity cannot be ignored in reference to an approach related to the circumstance of "using" the human identity of others, which considers it to be similar to that of "stealing" it. Moreover, what really may appear ambiguous in this approach is the legislative attempt to "materialize" the personal identity used on the web (digital identity). By following this line of thinking, the interpreters who apply the law are directed to translate an individual's identity into some defined bounded entity. As a result, elements such as personal data are treated as a simple material constituent and not regarded as a broad privileged form by which the subject projects him/herself, more or less voluntarily, into the digital world. Therefore, such legislative approach may look unclear to many as it seems that to pursue a simplified solution may have overcome the need to provide a clear disambiguating solution.

---

[267] M.MARRAFFINO, *La sostituzione di persona mediante furto di identità digitale,* in CADOPPI A., CANESTRARI S., MANNA A., PAPA M., *Cybercrime,* Utet, 2019, p. 307 ss.

[268] *Ibidem;* "Each of the two conducts, provided by law, is by itself suitable to integrate the case."

[269] LANDINI, Identità digitale tra tutela della persona e proprietà intellettuale, in Riv. Dir. industriale, 2017, p. 180 ss.

Article 9 of Law Decree 93/2013 introduced in paragraph 3 of Article 640 ter of the Italian Criminal Code a new aggravating circumstance with a special effect of the crime of computer fraud, with the declared intention of providing greater criminal protection to cases of digital identity theft. Furthermore, legal theorists and practitioners had already invoked the case in point for some time in order to marginalize the debate around the applicability of the crime of fraud in the IT field. However, this vision was opposed in particular by those who did not believe it in any way assimilable to the induction into error of a man tampering with and/or the fraudulent use of an ICT machine.[270] In this regard, it can be noted that the removal of the latter and the usage of disposable assets draw computer fraud into the sphere of theft by fraudulent means rather than to a spoliation that takes place with the consent of the victim. It therefore seems difficult to explain the jurisprudential statement according to which computer fraud maintains the same structure and the same constituent elements of the scam—to which it differs only because the fraudulent activity of the agent does not directly involve the person since there is no direct induction into error but through the manipulation of a computer system belonging to the victim.[271]

It is therefore quite clear how our legislator wanted to bring this new type of crime closer to the contiguous figures already existing in our legal system. This is because, at the time, it was believed that the particularity of computer science did not deserve a special title but could be classified, albeit with the necessary adjustments, within the classic criminal law sphere and with regard to legal assets already protected. It is therefore a matter of standardization that aims at repressing specific crimes characterized by the use of peculiar means or material objects and to avoid the development of new meta-juridical entities.

The crime referred to in Article 640ter is entitled "IT fraud." This provision punishes anyone who procures for him/herself or others an undue profit with others damage by altering the functioning of an IT or telematics

---

[270] See: ALESSANDRI, *Criminalità informatica*, in Riv. Trim. dir. pen. Economia, 1990; FIANDACA- E. MUSCO, *Diritto penale. Parte special*, vol. II/2, MUCCIARELLI, *Computer (disciplna giuridica del) nel diritto penale*, in Digesto penale, 1988, p.387, PICOTTI, Studi di diritto penale dell'informatica, 1992, p. 87, SARZANA DI SANT'IPPOLITO, *Note sul diritto penale dell'informatica*, in Giustizia penale, 1984; GROTTO, *Reati informatici e convenzione Cybercrime. Oltre la truffa e la frode informatica: la frode del certificatore*, in dir. informaz. e informatica, 2009.

[271] G. FIANDACA-E.MUSCO, *Diritto penale, Parte speciale,* vol. II/2, 2015, p.207.

system or intervening without right with data, information or programs contained in a computer or telematics system or other tool pertinent to it.[272]

It seems therefore mandatory to analyze the circumstance in object with the aim to better understand how to include and regard digital identity theft as an aggravating circumstance within this specific law.

This is a common crime. Nevertheless, paragraph 2 of the case also provides for an aggravating circumstance with a special effect if the perpetrator of the fact is a so-called system operator. This refers to a person who, as a program analyst operator, must necessarily make use of the computer system to carry out the duties of his/her office but uses them unfaithfully to pursue illegitimate purposes, thus betraying the trust relationship that binds him/her to the owner of the violated system.[273]

The objective structure of the punishable conduct only apparently re-proposes the traditional scheme of fraud as indicated in Article 640 of the Criminal Code. In fact, we can see how both the conducts of misleading the person and the artifices or deceptions typical of the fraud case are missing. These requirements are hardly conceivable when operating through a computer as the latter is generally considered to be a machine devoid of the typical characteristics of a human being. However, the double event constituted by the financial damage of others and by the undue profit for the agent or for others is, on the contrary, entirely similar to that provided for in Article 640.

Although the fraudulent productive conduct that causes damage to others and generates an unfair profit can be realized in any way or with any modality, it must necessarily entail an alteration of the functioning of the computer or telematics system or an unauthorized intervention on data, information and programs. With regard to the definition of "computer system," it is now widely accepted that it includes any set of computer devices capable of autonomous processing and necessarily interconnected and able, by recording and storing data, to generate information and data that responds to the logical expectations

[272] Article 640-ter of Italian Criminal Code: "*Chiunque, alterando in qualsiasi modo il funzionamento di un sistema informatico o telematico o intervenendo senza diritto con qualsiasi modalità su dati, informazioni o programmi contenuti in un sistema informatico o telematico o ad esso pertinenti, procura a sé o ad altri un ingiusto profitto con altrui danno, è punito con la reclusione da sei mesi a tre anni e con la multa da euro 51 a euro 1.032.*"

[273] G.MINCUCCI, *Le frodi informatiche*, in A.CADOPPI-S.CANESTRARI-A.MANNA-M.PAPA, *Cybercrime,* 2019, p. 838; PICA, *Reati informatici e telematici,* Digesto pen., 2000, 531.

of the user.[274] This notion is independent of the complexity of the system being that it can also consist of a single personal computer, as suggested by the definition provided for in Article 1 of the 2001 Budapest Convention, according to which any equipment or network of interconnected or connected equipment constitutes a computer system, one or more of which, through the execution of a computer program, perform automatic data processing. By "telematics system," alternatively, we reference any communication network managed by computers.[275]

Passing on to the examination of the modalities with which the crime can be integrated, Article 640ter expressly establishes how the crime can be configured if someone alters in any way the functioning of the computer or telematics system or intervenes without right in any way on data, information or programs. "Alteration of the system" occurs when the manipulative operations of the physical component (hardware) and/or the logical component (software) of the system are involved, resulting in a different IT process that compromises the results produced or that involves distraction from a standard scheme. "Intervention without rights," in contrast, refers to data, information, programs or any file recorded in the computer or telematics systems or any apparatus related to them provided that they are meant to be used in a computer system. Given that it only detects the functional relationship between them and the processing that allows the offender to withdraw the undue profit, it is of no consequence that the data and/or information come from a first processing or an already partially implemented process. In any case, to configure the case in point, the intervention without rights must be abusive and unauthorized.[276]

For some scholars, in relation to the damage, there is a threefold order of reasons that requires choosing the economic-patrimonial conception over the

---

[274] G.MINCUCCI, *Le frodi informatiche, in* A.CADOPPI-S.CANESTRARI-A.MANNA-M.PAPA, *Cybercrime* 2019, p.827 ss.

[275] *Ibidem*, See also L. PICOTTI, *Profili di diritto sostanziale*, in Dir . pen. e processo, 2008, p. 700 ss.

[276] In any case, it seems difficult to distinguish between the notion of "alteration" and that of "intervention." Part of the doctrine recognizes in the latter the preparatory phase for the former, or argues that the former is only a useless specification of the latter. Where others believe that the distinction is justified on the basis of the fact that, while the alteration involves a modification of the physiology of the system, the abusive intervention takes the concrete form of direct interference with the single data/information or program object of the IT procedure, modifying it the content and varying the outcome of the procedure itself. On this point also see G.MINCUCCI, *Le frodi informatiche*, in *Cybercrime*, CADOPPI, 2019, p.827 ss.; FLOR, P*hishing, identity theft e identity abuse: le prospettive applicative del diritto penale vigente*, in Riv. It. Dir. e proc. pen., 2007, p. 909 ss.

juridical one. This is because the juridical conception considers the damaged patrimony as a complex of juridical relationships that undergo an alteration independently from a diminutio patrimonii. Primarily, the economic-patrimonial nature of the damage is considered the only true characteristic of both computer fraud and simple fraud. Given that, in the absence of a real financial loss, the offense would be configured only as endangerment and not as a crime of event that is instead typical of computer fraud and the various forms of scam. Furthermore, decreasing the importance of the pecuniary damage and interpreting the damage only from a legal point of view generates an overlap with the forms of computer damage provided for in Articles 635bis ss. Finally, if the damage occurs in the absence of a causal link, confusion can arise with reference to Article 615quater of the Criminal Code,[277] which punishes those who attribute a direct profit to themselves through the illegitimate use of codes, keywords or other means suitable for accessing a computer or telematics system.[278]

From the point of view of the subjective element, Article 640ter refers to a generic willful misconduct, consisting in the conscience and willingness to engage in the fraudulent conduct mentioned in the law itself so as to cause damage to others and an unjust profit for oneself or for others. However, no willingness to mislead or deceive is required.[279]

Returning to the analysis of the Law Decree no. 93/2013, we can see how there have been many doctrinal discussions on the nature of this crime. If on one hand its systematic doctrinal placement suggests its configuration as an aggravating circumstance having special effects, other elements exist that instead suggest considering it as an autonomous circumstance. In support of this thesis, it should be noted that computer fraud is a legally relevant circumstance established to protect material assets, while the phenomenon of identity theft has a broader connotation as it regards material and non-material assets and is not limited to the reductions in material assets that it may cause. Therefore, it could be considered as an autonomous case aimed at protecting legal assets other than economic-type assets, such as digital identity on the

---

[277] Article 615-*quater*: "Unauthorized possession and dissemination of access codes to IT or telematics systems." The Article states that: *whoever, in order to procure a profit for oneself or others or to cause damage to others, illegally procures, reproduces, disseminates, communicates or delivers codes, keywords or other means suitable for accessing a computer or telematics system, protected by security measures, or in any case providing indications or instructions suitable for the aforementioned purpose, is punished with imprisonment of up to one year and a fine of up to 5,164 euros.*

[278] MARINI, *Truffa*, in Digesto pen. 1999, p. 397.

[279] G.FINADACA-E.MUSCO, *Diritto penale, parte speciale*, vol. II/2, 2015, p. 207.

internet, IT confidentiality and the reliability of IT and telematics systems. Another element suggesting that this may be a new autonomous case is that there is no article in the criminal code that expressly punishes digital identity theft. Nevertheless, the doctrine almost unanimously holds that this provision constitutes an aggravating circumstance of computer fraud.[280]

In any case, the legislative novelty contemplates two different modus operandi regarding the theft or undue use of a digital identity. The mainstream doctrine immediately highlighted that the legislator has not specified what these two conducts consist of. A significant contribution regarding what is meant by "digital identity theft" comes from parliamentary proceedings stating that reference should be made to Article 30bis of Legislative Decree no. 141 of 2010, which recalls the concept of "impersonation," therefore, configuring a different concept than that referred to in Article 624 of the Criminal Code. However, where it is believed that identity theft coincides with impersonation, it is complex to establish the scope of the undue "use" of digital identity given that even the person who uses another's personal digital identity for purposes other than those for which it was apparently authorized impersonates this subject.[281]

Further perplexity manifested in doctrine concerns the fact that the theft or undue use of digital identity appears to have been conceived by the new paragraph 3 of Article 640ter of the Criminal Code as only an aggravating circumstance of IT fraud. Therefore, neither data theft nor the improper use of digital identity can alone integrate the crime of IT fraud given that at least one illegal transfer from one asset to another is required.[282] In the opinion of the doctrine, which has tried to broaden the scope of the case in question, the definition of "damage" can certainly also include "loss of profit," which is the loss of earnings that the victim suffers as a result of computer frauds committed with the theft of his/her digital identity. However, it is clear that this aggravating circumstance is not suitable to compensate the case of

---

[280] See F. MANTOVANI, *Diritto penale*, PS, vol. II, *I delitti contro il patrimonio*, IV ed., Padova, 2016, p. 226.; M. MARGIOCCO, *Frode informatica*, in G. Finocchiaro – F. Delfini , *Diritto dell'informatica,* Assago, 2014, p. 1107 ss., p. 1110; A. DI TULLIO D'ELISIIS, *Frode informatica commessa con sostituzione dell'identità digitale: profili applicativi*, in Altalex.

[281] See G. MALGIERI, *La nuova fattispecie, cit., p. 144;* A. DITULLIO D'ELISIIS, *Frode informatica, cit.*

[282] G. MALGIERI, *Il furto di identità digitale: una tutela patrimoniale della personalità, in La giustizia penale nella rete. Le nuove sfide della società dell'informazione nell'epoca di Internet,* curated by R. FLOR, D. FALCINELLI, S. MARCOLINI, Milano, 2015, p. 37 ss., p. 40 s.

impersonation, which still retains its importance and prevents protection gaps in all cases in which the new provision may encounter application limits.

Legislative Decree no. 93/2013, together with the introduction of paragraph 3 of Article 640ter of the Criminal Code, had also taken steps to insert in Article 24bis of Legislative Decree no. 231/2001 the crime of computer fraud aggravated by the replacement of the digital identity in the list of offenses that include the liability of businesses.[283] However, this provision, inexplicably, was eliminated during the conversion of the Legislative Decree no. 93/2013 into law. This choice is certainly questionable since this provision would have allowed greater protection of digital identity given that in most cases the subjects that manage the personal data of others are entities, such as credit institutions.

3.2.1. The Issue of the "Improper Use" of Digital Identity

As previously discussed, Article 640ter, paragraph 3 of the Criminal Code presents various interpretative and applicative issues as the case of the improper use of digital identity appears problematic for several reasons.[284]

Firstly, Article 9 of the 2013 legislative decree does not in any way refer to the nomen iuris of the aggravating circumstance of Article 640ter, which refers to frauds committed with the replacement of one's digital identity. Therefore, it seems to have no apparent link with the indictment provided for in the Law Decree, which disciplines the replacement of digital identity. Furthermore, the combination of this case with that of identity theft seems to be a very complex matter since they are two apparently heterogeneous behaviors linked by the same judgment of negative value in the aggravating circumstance.[285] In the absence of a precise definition of the "improper use" of digital identity, it seems only right to seek a regulatory reference in our legal system as to the "improper use" of data referring to one's identity.

A first reference can be found in Article 55, paragraph 9 of the Legislative Decree no. 231 of 2007,[286] which punishes those who improperly use credit

---

283 L. PISTORELLI, *Relazione Ufficio del Massimario Cassazione, cit.*

284 See A. DI TULLIO D'ELISIIS, *Frode informatica commessa con sostituzione d'identità digitale: profili applicativi*, in Altalex, 2014.

285 L. PISTORELLI, *Prime note sulla legge di conversione, con modificazioni, del d.l. n. 93 del 2013*, in Dir. pen. cont., 18 ottobre 2013, pp. 6 e 7.

286 Implementation of Directive 2005/60/EC on the prevention of the use of the financial system for the purpose of laundering the proceeds of criminal activities and terrorist financing activities as well as the directive 2006/70/EC which lays down implementing measures." In this regard see U. PIOLETTI, *Possesso o utilizzo abusivo di carte di credito, in* Giur. Merito, 2012.

cards or any other similar document that enables the withdrawal of cash or the purchase of goods or the provision of services that are the property of others. Although this case also affects violations of assets in the IT sector and partially encompasses the conduct of person substitution,[287] it cannot be ignored that the "improper use" refers to concrete objects such as credit cards or other similar documents. For this reason, it is of no real help in correctly defining what constitutes an improper use of digital identity. Perhaps the most significant suggestion is provided for by Article 30bis of Legislative Decree no. 141 of 2010.[288] In defining identity theft, this legislative decree speaks of "impersonation" in terms of total or partial concealment of one's identity through the improper use of data relating to it and to the income of another person. In light of this reference, the improper use of personal data is instrumental to identity theft and is therefore not an alternative conduct as it would appear from the wording of the current Article 9 of the 2013 legislative decree. To support this point of view, it is necessary to mention the definition of identity theft proposed by the OECD, according to which it consists, among other things, in the "use of personal information in an unauthorized manner."[289] Even this definition, in fact, seems to consider "improper use" as a sub-category of identity theft.

Divergent ideas are found in the definitions proposed by common law doctrine[290] and the United Nations study center.[291] According to both definitions, digital identity theft is seen as a mere apprehension of data, while the illegal use of such data is one of the structural elements of identity fraud. According to this paradigm, the improper use of digital identity may well exist as an alternative conduct to theft, therefore, as identity "fraud." Since in this

---

[287] Cass. pen., Sez. V, 6 giugno 2003, n. 24816, Ferruti, Rv. 225945 according to which: the crime of improper use of credit cards and other forms of digital payment, absorbs the crime of substitution of person, pursuant to art. 494 of the Criminal Code, whenever the disputed substitution is carried out with the same material conduct integrating the first offense. And in fact, the criminal hypothesis of the wrongdoing use of the means of payment harms, in addition to assets, also the public faith, while art. 494 c.p. contains a reserve clause destined to operate even beyond the principle of specialty ("if the fact does not constitute another crime against public faith"). On the other hand, there is a material concurrence between the same offenses in the event that the replacement was carried out with a further and different conduct with respect to the one that integrated the other criminal offense. See also U.PIOLETTI *Possesso o utilizzo abusivo di carte di credito*, in Giur. Merito, 2012.

[288] Legislative Decree 141/2010, implementation of EC Directive 48/2008.

[289] OECD, Scoping Paper on Online Identity Theft, June 18 2008, Section I.

[290] Australasian Centre for Policing Research and the Australian Transaction Reports and Analysis Centre, Standardisation of Definition of Identity Crime Terms: A Step towards consistency, Report Series no. 145.3, 2006, 7.

[291] Un Ieg, Results of the second meeting of the Intergovernmental Expert Group to Prepare a Study on Fraud and the Criminal Misuse and Falsification of Identity.

paradigm fraud does not involve an apprehension of the data against the will but only a use of the same against the will of the owner of those data, one could, through this paradigm, understand the structural difference between "identity theft" and "improper use." In the first case, the acquisition of data is already undue; in the second, the offensiveness is detected not in the moment of acquisition but with the subsequent use of the acquired data. In other words, identity theft is revealed in the unlawful apprehension of identity data, while the improper use takes the form of an abusive use of that data regardless of the way in which it was obtained. With this, one might say that the dualism between theft and improper use follows the historical separation, postulated by the most prudent doctrine in the field of cybercrime, between the different forms of unauthorized access (unauthorized access to other people's systems or unauthorized possession of others' data) and unauthorized use (unauthorized use of data lawfully owned by others).[292] In order to better reconcile the provision with its nomen iuris, it could be stated that the new aggravating circumstance always entails a "person's replacement." In regard to "digital identity theft," this is made possible by an "unlawful apprehension of personal data." In the case of "improper use," however, this is accomplished with a "diverted" or "unauthorized" use of lawfully collected data. Only in this way will the two conducts fully be alternative.

Therefore, given the alternation between the conduct of theft and the improper use of digital identity, one may wonder in which concrete conducts an "improper use" of identity data is carried out. To answer this question, it is possible to consider the conduct of the "unlawful processing of personal data" sanctioned by Legislative Decree no. 196/2003 regarding the protection of personal data (also commonly known as the Privacy Code). More precisely, Article 167 sanctions the unlawful processing of personal data given that the definition of the "treatment" object of the legal provision is very broad.[293] In addition, in this case, the "abusive use," with respect to the agreed purposes, of the data obtained with the full consent of the interested party is to be considered relevant. The aforementioned rule punishes any private activity on data contrary to the full and detailed consent of the interested party and any

---

[292] M. WASIK, *Crime and the computer*, Oxford, 1991, pp. 69 ss.

[293] The new definition of treatment, provided for by art. 4 of EU Regulation 679 of 2016, directly applicable from 25.5.2018, is the following: "any operation or set of operations, carried out with or without the aid of automated processes and applied to personal data or sets of personal data, such as the collection , registration, organization, structuring, storage, adaptation or modification, extraction, consultation, use, communication by transmission, dissemination or any other form of making available, comparison or interconnection, limitation, cancellation or destruction."

public activity on personal data that abuses institutional functions if these activities are committed with the will of making a profit or causing damage. The reference to the specific and clearly delimited purposes[294] for which a processing must be carried out is very interesting given that it is precisely the abuse of the agreed purposes that determines the improper use of data.

We may therefore wonder whether this rule of law could represent a solid regulatory reference to the definition of "improper use," or we can regard the fact as the aggravating circumstance referred to in paragraph 3 of Article 640ter of the Criminal Code because it can be regarded as a fact committed by digital identity theft or in conjunction with the crime referred to in Article 167 of the Privacy Code.[295] In reality, the concept of "unlawful processing" seems more restricted compared to that of "improper use" precisely because the former is delimited and confined to the field of application by consolidated and well-delimited and defined legal concepts.

Illicit data processing, pursuant to Article 167 of the Privacy Code, is included in the hypothesis of the "substitution of digital identity committed with theft or improper use of identity data." If the law is considered in reference to the case of computer fraud in its entirety, one cannot help but note that the legal assets remain different (patrimony in the former and confidentiality of personal data in the latter) and that we are faced with a bilateral specialty relationship. This is because in computer fraud the undue profit with the damage of others is a constitutive element, while the illicit treatment requires the specific intent of advantage or damage, and the damage caused is only an objective condition for the punishment.[296] In selected cases, the jurisprudence has considered that the unlawful data processing may be absorbed in fraud in cases where they both aim at protecting the same legal asset.[297] This would create a formal concurrence causing a juridical accumulation of the sentence. However, the doctrine highlights that there can be no univocal correspondence between this case and the new aggravating circumstance referred to in paragraph 3, Article 640ter of the Criminal Code given that the concept of "unlawful processing" is different from that of

---

[294] Art. 13, comma 1, lett. a); art. 23, comma 3, privacy code.

[295] Article 167 Privacy Code (Legislative Decree June 30 2003 n. 196 (updated 02/28/2021).

[296] Cass. pen., Sez. III, July 9 2004, n. 30134, in GDir, 2004, n. 35,; Cass. pen., Sez. III, February 17 11, 1^, Rv. 249991; d Cass. pen., Sez. II, May24 2012, n. 23798, in Diritto & Giustizia, 2012; see also L. Manna, *comment on legislative decree 196/03, DPP*, 2004; V. Destito, *Dati personali* (tutela penale dei), Digesto Online, 2008, D. IELO, V. SAPONARA, in AA.VV., *Codice della privacy,* II, Milano, 2004, 2148 e AA.VV., *Codice in materia di dati personali*, Milano, 2004, 710.

[297] Cass. pen., Sez. II, May 7 2013, n. 36365 (Rv. 256877).

"undue use." The new aggravating circumstance, in fact, only punishes the replacement of a digital person, leaving out other conducts, such as illegal data trafficking for commercial or competitive purposes.

According to some authors, therefore, the only way to describe the conduct of "improper use" and understand its relationship to digital identity theft is to refer to the section of the article "replacement of digital identity." The effect of the two cases is identical, but the methods of execution are different given that in the case of undue use, the possession of such data is considered lawful and only a specific non-agreed use integrates the violation, while in the case of data theft, the violation of the consent already exists at the time of their removal.[298]

3.2.2. The Possible Liabilities of the Internet Service Provider (ISP) in Reference to Identity Theft

Nowadays, many victims of impersonation choose the administrative route as their main form of protection with the aim of obtaining the removal from the digital platforms of one's identity, falsified and/or illicitly used by third parties.

There is no doubt how the controller in such cases plays a vital role especially in light of the system introduced by Directive 95/46, which provides for a series of obligations for the data controller to guarantee the protection of personal data. Primarily, the data processor must ensure within the scope of their responsibilities and competences that the processing of the data in question meets the requirements of the directive. This is so that the guarantees provided by this directive can fully develop their effects, and an effective and complete protection of the data subjects can be achieved, in particular respecting their right to privacy. Amongst these duties, we can see how there is also the obligation to intervene in the event that the data subject reports an abuse of his/her identity or even a replacement of a person, which clearly constitutes a processing of data contrary to European and transnational legislation.

The central issue is precisely the analysis of the responsibility of these ISPs. We have wondered and still wonder whether or not ISPs should be held responsible for any offense committed within their platforms, platforms that are freely accessible by the community.

To date, there is no direct criminal liability of the provider being that it has no obligation to pre-filter illegal content nor does it have direct criminal

---

[298] G. MALGIERI, *La nuova fattispecie, cit., p. 151.*

liability for the offenses committed by its users. This question has occupied the community judges for years. After a longstanding debate, they have finally concluded that the provision of such an obligation would not respect the need to ensure the right balance between the protection of copyright, on one hand, and the freedom of enterprise, the right to the protection of personal data and the freedom to receive and communicate information on the other.

In order to better analyze the issue, it seems appropriate to clarify who the ISP actually is. The ISP is the body that enables access to the internet by providing one or more services, the varying extent of which makes it possible to distinguish three different types of ISPs. Articles 14, 15 and 16 of Legislative Decree no. 70/2003 (in implementation of EC Directive 31/2000) provide for this differentiation.

Article 14 outlines the so-called mere conduit provider, that is, an email provider or a telecommunications company. This ISP transmits information provided by a recipient of the service or provides access to a communication network.

Article 15 outlines the so-called caching provider, such as the Google search engine. Such provider transmits information provided by a recipient of the service, carrying out an automatic, intermediate and temporary storage of such information for the sole purpose of making the subsequent forwarding to other recipients at their request more effective. Through an automatic software called a "crawler" or "spider," the search engine scans the pages of third parties available on the network and, once it reaches a specific web page, scans it and temporarily stores the HTML codes (structured text file according to standardized descriptors) that compose it (so-called "caching" activity).

Finally, Article 16 outlines the hosting provider figure, such as eBay, Facebook and YouTube. A hosting provider typically stores information provided by a recipient of the service at the request of the same.

It should be noted that for each of the categories of ISP listed, specific causes for triggering their liability are envisaged. The rationale that unites them is the need to link the ISP's responsibility to significant choices on the handling of the document, which is symptomatic of their knowledge of its contents. The distinction of functions, operated by the legislator, is made solely in order to distinguish the type of services they may provide in that a provider can in turn cover all three roles. In addition, the combined provisions of Articles 16 and 17 of Legislative Decree 70/2003 unite all categories of ISPs, which establish indiscriminately the fundamental criteria for the attribution of responsibility common to the three categories.

Currently the provider cannot be held responsible for any offences committed within the hosted sites,[299] if it is not aware of the fact that the activity or information is unlawful. However, as soon as it becomes aware of any illicit activities, upon communication by the competent authorities, it must take immediate action to remove the information or to disable access to it. The provision seems to identify two distinct levels of knowledge: criminal offences and civil offences. With relation to criminal offenses, the prosecution will be required to demonstrate the effective knowledge of the provider of the criminal perpetration, while with respect to civil offenses, the injured party will have the burden of proving facts or circumstances that make manifest the unlawfulness of the activity or information.

It is also stated that the ISP must remove the hosted site as soon as it becomes aware of the illicit facts but only upon communication from the competent authorities. It is therefore clear that knowledge of the offense, acquired ex-post, must be not only effective but also qualified in the sense that the information must come only from the competent authorities (so-called public information). With this qualification, therefore, the legislator made private information irrelevant, thereby excessively delimiting the scope of operation of the removal obligation, which, indeed, could also have been subjected only to non-anonymous private information. Effective knowledge of the unlawfulness of the fact is also essential in the sense that it does not appear sufficient for the competent authority to communicate to the manager that the activity could be illegal. Nevertheless, it is necessary to communicate the judicial assessment of the certain illegality of the activity in question, which becomes res judicata, with the effect that the provider will thus be obliged to remove or disable access to the website in question.[300] Such interpretative reading appears to be endorsed by the provision referred to in Article 17 of Legislative Decree no. 70/2003.[301]

In relation to the obligations imposed upon the ISP, some elements give rise to uncertainty. Firstly, the notion of effective knowledge used by the legislator would seem to refer to the expression of actual knowledge, which has a precise meaning in the context of US copyright law.[302] In our legal system, this expression seems to emphasize that it cannot be a question of mere knowledge. Therefore, it will not be sufficient to demonstrate that the provider "could have known" as it is instead the proof of his/her actual knowledge that

---

[299] Article 16 of Legislative Decree 70/2003.
[300] *Ibidem.*
[301] G.STEA, *La responsabilità penale dell'internet provider*, in Giur. Penale, 2016, p.5.
[302] For more on this see www.copyright.gov.

must necessarily be provided. Consequentially, it would seem that the hosting provider has an improper omissive conduct pursuant to Article 40, paragraph 1 of the Italian Criminal Code—especially when, being aware of the illegal activity already perpetrated, it does not prevent the related telematics dissemination, with the effect that the omission represents the concurrent participation in the criminal consumption. To this end, therefore, the hosting provider should have the possibility to intervene, inhibiting or removing the hosted site in order to prevent possible damage resulting from the offense from continuing even after becoming aware of it. However, regardless of any consideration on typicality, some consider that the obligation of removal cannot coincide with the obligation of impediment as, logically, the first arises when the crime has already been committed, while the second is set precisely to prevent the commission of criminal offenses. The non-fulfillment of the removal obligation does not therefore integrate the improper omission referred to in Article 40, paragraphs 1 and 2 of the Criminal Code. Any liability of the provider in the event of a crime involving instant consumption must be excluded since the actual knowledge that would trigger the obligation placed on the provider arises only after the consummation of the crime.

The removal obligation, as outlined by Article 16 of Legislative Decree no. 70/2003, is not useful in configuring the provider's position of control over user activities. This is even more so on the basis of Article 17, Legislative Decree no. 70/2003,[303] which, after stating the discipline regarding provider responsibility, establishes that the intermediary provider is not required to monitor the content of the information transmitted.[304]

When the ISP is made aware of the existence of illegal content and does not intervene for its removal, Article 17, paragraph 2 of Legislative Decree no. 70/2003 expressly provides that the ISP has a specific obligation to inform the judicial authority. More precisely, this article establishes that the provider is required, first and foremost, to inform without delay the judicial or administrative authority having supervisory functions if it is aware of alleged illegal activities or information concerning one of its recipients of the information service. It also has the obligation to provide immediately, at the request of the competent authorities, the information in its possession—information that allows the identification of the recipient of its services, with whom it has data storage agreements, in order to identify and prevent illegal activities. The obligation to provide information on the basis of the provision

303 Article 17, Legislative Decree 70/2003.

304 R. BARTOLI, *Brevi considerazioni sulla responsabilità penale dell'Internet Service Provider*, in Dir. Pen. e Processo, 2013, 5, p. 603.

in question arises as soon as the provider becomes aware of an offence perpetrated through its service, both following the notification by a third party and when the lender itself, browsing on its sites, comes across information deemed illegal. In fact, the prior evaluation by the provider of the actual illegality of the information is not necessary as the obligation to report is imposed even where the offence is only presumed.

Therefore, the provider is obliged to report any presumed illegal activity it becomes aware of in order to allow the competent authority to identify and prevent illegal activities by adopting the most appropriate initiatives, including urgent ones.

The general obligation to report constitutes the only hypothesis of having to take action, at the expense of the provider, in the case of alleged illegal activity perpetrated by a hosted site, thus leaving space for possible exegetical attention. In truth, the obligation in question is obviously aimed at the normal and effective functioning of the institutional activity of the repression and prevention of criminal activities. However, it seems that ensuring a general position of guarantee for the provider does not seem to be sufficient in that such obligation to report does not imply a power to prevent the event in the sense that the timely reporting of the alleged illegal activity cannot become a real power of the provider to interrupt the criminal action of the third party, placing itself, rather, as having a duty to avoid facilitating the criminal activity.

Up to now, the jurisprudence has interpreted this duty as a source of liability only and exclusively of a civil nature.[305] In practice, however, in the event that the user sends a formal warning, such as to a social network, thus formally making it aware of a fact-offense, and the provider subsequently does not intervene, then a possible criminal liability could arise. Seen from this point of view, it would then seem more correct to argue that there is not a liability by way of omission, pursuant to Article 40 of the Criminal Code, but an intentional complicity in the crime committed by third parties. This is because it cannot be argued that the ISP was not aware of the commission of the crime if the user or the judicial authority communicated it.

The position of the provider must be framed in the context of tempered surveillance obligations. This is because the rule in question excludes the operator itself from having to supervise the activities of the users of the service offered while imposing at the same time the obligation to report without delay

---

[305] Tib. Napoli Nord, sez. II, ord. 3.11.2016, n. 9799.

the alleged illegal activity, which obviously means a demand for attention in the exercise of the service and, above all, its use by the community.[306]

Recently, the court of Naples established in 2016[307] some fundamental principles that go in the direction of a gradual accountability of the provider in the event of reports. The court in fact established that if a user sends a request for the removal of a certain content to the provider, it would have to take action to prevent the further dissemination of the link without waiting for the provision of a judicial authority. This is an additional tool in protecting the victim, who will thus have the power to directly contact the provider in order to obtain the removal of the harmful content and therefore ensuring promptness in action.

In the analysis of a possible liability of the ISP, there is also a problem of relationships between different rules. In fact, what can normally be considered a crime in one country cannot necessarily be considered such in another country, especially if we are talking about European and non-European countries. In most cases, collaboration with the provider itself is required in order to identify the user who operates under a false name. Furthermore, for most providers, a motivated decree from the public prosecutor is not enough to have the data acquired by the requesting authority, but it will be necessary to proceed with a rogatory letter, which will only be possible if the fact is considered a crime in both states. It would therefore seem that a transnational effort is needed in order to solve this problem, a problem that is becoming a social emergency of its own, especially due to the unpredictable consequences that an impersonation can trigger. Think, for example, of all those cases of donations of money following the various forms of impersonation and the possible consequential acts of self-harm that follow, which may lead to the extreme of suicide.[308]

During recent years, many scholars have felt the need to create a transnational organization that could meet the users' growing request for a human control over illegal contents and timeliness in the intervention. In an effort to guarantee these two fundamental certainties, in 2017, the EU

---

[306] G.STEA, *La responsabilità penale dell'internet provider*, in Giur. Penale, 2016, p.7.

[307] Order of the Court of Naples North section II civ. November 3, 2016 in which it was stated, that Facebook is not deemed to have a duty to check in advance the content of posts and comments entered by users, the duty to inhibit, in general, an upload on its platform "of each video, images, news or articles referring to the person of the applicant" being, however, possible to prevent, in view of the duty of "subsequent" and "targeted" control, the only new upload specific links communicated.

[308] M.MARRAFFINO, *La sostituzione di persona mediante furto di identità digitale*, in A.CADOPPI-S.CANETRARI-A.MANNA-M.PAPA, *Cybercrime,* 2019, p.325-328.

developed a policy aimed at making ISPs responsible even beyond the provisions of Directive 2000/31/EC, of which Legislative Decree no. 70/2003 had been timely implemented. In fact, the European Commission has aggravated the charges borne by the ISPs in various respects, sanctioning the inactivity of Member States in the so-called cases of "take-down" and "stay-down," where "take-down" defines the need for a detailed regulation of the procedures leading to the effective and timely removal of illegal content and "stay-down" the need to prevent the reappearance of illegal content similar to those already subject to take down.

Still, in the analysis of the possible configuration of a liability of the ISP, a comparative reference to German law seems appropriate and necessary. Recently, a new provision has entered into force in order to improve the application of the law especially in online services. This new legislation is named "Netzwerkdurchsetzungsgesetz,"[309] also known as the "Network Enforcement Act." This law not only imposes providers to adopt rigorous organizational models with important sanctions but also imposes the obligation, especially in the social network area, to submit a bi-yearly (every six months) report on the victims of cyber bullying and on defamatory and slanderous fake news. The other compliance obligation required by German legislation today is to ensure the cancellation or even the blocking of illegal content within 24 hours of reporting. If the case seems to be particularly insidious, the deadline for fulfilling the providers' duties will be increased by another seven days.[310] From this brief comparative analysis, we can see how there is a lack, at the European level, of a commitment to seek a unanimous solution, even shared at the global level.

3.3. Digital Signature

The need to provide adequate protection against specific crime figures of computer forgery committed through IT means derives from the intensification of the use of these tools in daily activities. In view of the increase in various types of public and private virtual relations, in recent years the need for a secure recognition of interconnected subjects, the authenticity of content and the legal value of digital documents has emerged.[311]

---

[309] Long Title: Gesetz zur Verbesserung der Rechtsdurchsetzung in sozialen Netzwerken.

[310] See https://www.gesetze-im-internet.de/netzdg/NetzDG.pdf.

[311] G.FIANDACA-E.MUSCO, *Diritto penale. Parte speciale*, vol. I, Roma, 2017, 624.

In the criminal field, the concept of the IT document (or digital document) has been introduced by Article 491bis, which defines it as any IT medium containing data or information with evidential value or programs specifically intended to process them. This definition of a digital document was subsequently reshaped with Article 1 and following of the "Presidential Decree" (D.P.R) no. 513/1997, issued in implementation of Article 15, paragraph 2, of law no. 59/1997 (Bassanini-uno Law), according to which it must be considered as the computerized representation of legally relevant deeds, facts or data. This implementing regulation is not limited to only establishing a definition of an IT document but goes further, introducing the concept of the digital signature, defining it as the result of the IT validation procedure based on a system of asymmetric keys in pairs, one public and one private, which allows the subscriber, through the private key, and the recipient, through the public key, respectively, to disclose and verify the origin and integrity of an IT document or a set of IT documents.[312]

The concept of electronic signature, like that of certifier, is provided for by Directive no. 1999/93/EC of the European Parliament, implemented in Italy by Legislative Decree no. 82/2005, also commonly known as the Digital Administration Code. This, in Article 1, defines digital signature as that set of data in electronic form, attached or connected by logical association to other electronic data, used as a method of computer identification. In other words, it is nothing more than an identification mark affixed to any document by means of an electronic device.

It should be noted that the Italian legislator has followed a very different path from that followed by the European legislator, entailing many coordination problems between the two legislations. The Italian legislation, in fact, is built on a strict and detailed regulation in terms of the IT procedure, which allows the digital signature to be affixed by subjects responsible for its implementation. Of another opinion was the European legislator, who established a neutral principle on the validity of digital signatures and promoted the free circulation of certification services. In particular, under the first aspect, the directive does not give a single notion of digital signature but distinguishes between a simple electronic signature and an advanced electronic signature, guaranteeing integrity with the latter in addition to the origin of the document.

---

[312] P.LOPRIORE, *Dalla firma digitale alla firma elettronica qualificata, in Firma informatica: dalla firma digitale alla firma elettronica qualificata,* 2012, p. 2.

Both "qualified electronic signature" and "digital signature" are to be considered forms of electronic signatures. The first is defined as an electronic signature obtained through an IT procedure that guarantees the unique connection to the signatory, created with means in which the signatory can retain exclusive control and be linked to the data to which it refers. It allows detection if the data have been subsequently modified, which is based on a qualified certificate and made using a secure device for creating the signature.[313] *Digital signature,* in contrast, can be defined as a particular type of qualified electronic signature based on a system of cryptographic keys, one public and one private, related to each other. This system allows the holder and the recipient, through the private and public key, respectively, to disclose and verify the origin and integrity of an IT document or a set of IT documents.[314]

Digital signatures provide integrity and authenticity to electronic documents. They enable the unequivocal confirmation regarding the identity of the sender by means of unique elements characterizing the sender and the message sent. Digital signatures are certifiable and cannot be rejected. Similar to that, the use of the so-called "digital handshake" among computers in order to exchange digital certificates (Internet ID cards) guarantees that the parties, the actors of the exchange of documents, are who they say they are. Furthermore, it evaluates officially the authenticity of the services provided and whether they have been altered.[315]

From this preliminary analysis of the concept of digital signature, we can now move on to understand its concrete functioning according to the system established by the Italian legislator, which is based on the use of a pair of asymmetric keys, one private, therefore secret, and the other public, which can be found in the appropriate lists.[316] This system must guarantee the following two requirements: the origin of the signed document and the secrecy of the document itself. In order to guarantee these two requirements, it is necessary to simultaneously use the pair of keys of the subjects for both encoding and decoding procedures.

---

[313] Legislative Decree 82/2005 Digital Administration Code.

[314] *Ibidem.*

[315] Green Paper on "Public Procurement in the EU: Exploring the Way Forward," COM(96) 583 final. 27.11.1996.

[316] On the functioning of the digital signature in general see, G. FINOCCHIARO, *Documento informatico e firma digitale,* in Contratto e impresa, 1998, 956; ZAGAMI, *La firma digitale e sicurezza giuridica,* 2000, 62 e ss.; G.CIACCI, *La firma digitale*, Il Sole 24 ore, 1999, 47 e ss.; M. PIZZACALLA, *Firma digitale: le novità legislative e regolamenti, in Impresa* , 2001, 453 e ss.

3.3.1. Article 640quinquies of the Italian Criminal Code: Electronic Signature Certifier IT Fraud

A main crime that emerges in the analysis of digital identity theft and in the illegitimate use of the digital signature is Article 640quinquies of the Criminal Code. This explicitly sanctions the subject who provides electronic signature certification services, who, in order to procure an undue profit for him/herself or others or to cause damage to others, violates the obligations established by law for the issue of a qualified certificate.[317]

The offense in question was introduced by Law no. 48 of 2008, on the ratification and execution of the CoC, in order to fill one of the largest protection gaps left by previous regulatory interventions on the subject.

In an initial analysis, we can note that the crime in question, being devoid of any fraudulent character, misleading conduct or illegal use of others' property, only implies a sanction for the violation of the extra-criminal obligations of the certifier, having a similar structure to that of the case referred to in Article 323 of the Criminal Code, which sanctions the conduct described as "abuse of office."[318]

Since its entry into force, the doctrine has almost unanimously maintained that the offence in question is strategically placed in order to protect the patrimonial sphere of individuals Nevertheless, some scholars still suggest that the protected legal object resides in public faith.[319] especially from its proximity to Article 495bis of the Criminal Code. In fact, we can see how the legislator, in configuring this new case, has used the same model adopted by Article 495bis of the Criminal Code. This article punishes false declarations made to a certifier in the case of affixing an electronic signature. As previously analyzed, when placed on an electronic document, this signature has the power to make the document relevant, from a purely evidential point of view, only if certified by a person in charge of this.

Article 640quinquies can said to be a so-called "blank criminal rule," which is to say, a norm characterized by an indeterminate precept and a

---

317 G.FIANDACA-E.MUSCO, *Diritto penale, parte speciale*, vol. I, Roma 2012, p. 624-626.

318 Article 323 of the Italian Criminal Code states that establishes that, unless the fact constitutes a more serious crime, the public official or the person in charge of a public service is punished who, in carrying out his duties or service, in violation of specific rules of conduct expressly provided for by law or by acts having the force of law and from which there is no margin of discretion, or by failing to abstain in the presence of one's own interest or that of a close relative or in other prescribed cases, intentionally procures for oneself or others an unjust financial advantage or causes others a unfair damage. On this point also see F. MANTOVANI, *Diritto penale. Parte speciale* II, Padova, 2019, p 227.

319 L.PICOTTI, *Ratifica della Convenzione Cybercrime e nuovi strumenti di contrasto contro la cirminalità informatica e non solo*, in Dir. Internet, 2008, p. 440.

specific sanction. Due to this characteristic, the Digital Administration Code, in Article 32, expressly contemplates a series of obligations relating to the provider of the qualified certificate as identified and characterized by Article 28 of the above-mentioned code.

This is a proper crime being that the suppliers of the qualified certifications of electronic signature services can exclusively commit it.[320] However, the certifier should not be confused with the manager of the certified email service, who is exclusively responsible for the transmission of electronic documents via the aforementioned means.

In order to better understand the implication of this article, it of primary importance to define the status, role and responsibilities of certifiers. Certifiers are defined by Legislative Decree 82 of 2005 as those subjects who provide certification services of electronic signatures or that provide other services connected with the latter. Above all, they are given the ability to perform the so-called "certification service," including registration, time validation, repertorization and IT or consulting services relating to electronic signatures. The certifiers therefore play a role of public interest as without their presence and intermediation the citizen would not been able to sign digital documents. In the analysis of the role and duties of a certifier, we can note that, in addition to ensuring the most appropriate organizational and technical measures to avoid damage to third parties, the qualified electronic signature service provider must also ensure a number of guarantees, as follows:

- Provide with certainty the identification of the person requesting certification even if this activity is entrusted to third parties;
- Issue and publish the electronic certificate in the manner and in the cases established by the technical rules referred to in Article 71 and in compliance with the rules on the processing of personal data;
- Specify in the qualified certificate the powers of representation of other titles relating to the professional activity or positions held;
- Inform applicants in a complete way of the certification procedure, particularly whether technical requirements are necessary to access it and on the special limitations relating the use of signatures based on the certification service;
- Proceed with the timely communication that the electronic certificate has been revoked or suspended in the event of a request from the holder or from a third party;

---

[320] FUMO, *La condotta nei reati informatici*, in Arch. Pen., 2013, p. 786 ss.

- Ensure a safe and timely service for the revocation and/or suspension of electronic certificates as well as guaranteeing the efficient punctual and secure functioning of the lists of suspended and revoked signature certificates;
- Ensure the precise determination of the date and time of issue of the revocation and of the suspension of these electronic certificates;
- Keep electronic records of all information relating to the qualified certificate from the moment of its issuing and up to at least 20 years;
- It must not copy nor store the private signature keys of the person to whom the qualified electronic signature service provider has provided the certification service;
- It must use reliable systems for managing the register of certificates in ways that ensure that only authorized persons can make entries and changes;
- It must guarantee the correct functioning and continuity of the system and immediately notify AgID and assistants of any malfunctions that cause service suspension and interruption of the service itself.

It is important to underscore that any violation of these obligations constitutes ipso facto a criminal liability given that its criminal profile is concentrated in the specific purpose of the willful misconduct. In its absence, the rules on the civil liability of the certifier referred to in Article 30 CAD apply.

With regard to the conduct punished pursuant to Article 640quinquies, it mainly entails the violation of the obligations established by law, resulting in omissions given that such obligations very often impose to the qualified certifier a facere. In summary, therefore, the standard incriminates all conducts contrary to the specific obligations introduced by the European Directive intended for the certifier in relation to the issue of qualified certificates. This mere conduct crime, having a pure sanctioning structure, refers in full to the extra-criminal discipline provided for in Article 32 CAD, an article whose content can be summarized in compliance with the technical rules, the identification and communication obligations and the execution and publication of the revocation or suspension of the certificate, including the communication of the date and time of the data storage.

Also seemingly legitimate is the position of those who believe that the violation of Article 32 CAD should be followed by the issuance of the qualified certificate as an implicit event with reference to the certifier's fraud in the absence of legal requirements in order to transform the nature of the fraud committed by certifiers, with respect of the victims' financial integrity, from an anticipated consumption crime into a concrete danger crime.[321]

The offense in question is a specific willful crime as there is the conscience and the will to violate the obligations established by the relevant legislation as well as the purpose of procuring for oneself or others an undue profit by causing damage to others. In particular, it is a specific willful crime of offence anticipating the protection given that the offensive event constitutes nothing more than a purely intentional result and that the conduct, in itself, does not lead to an appreciable criminal penalty. The intentional requisites of damage and profit are envisaged. Alternatively, both must be interpreted in the sense of their effective capitalization imposed by the topographical location of the law and their delimiting function.[322]

3.4. Deepfakes: An Emerging Cybersecurity Risk

The technological evolution has radically changed the way man perceives himself, his identity, his image, as well as his relationships with other human beings and, more generally, the reality that surrounds him. As previously described, if, on the one hand, the tools made available by technological evolution have brought men closer in their equality and have often represented freedom, on the other hand it has led to rather worrying situations. Above all, if we consider that the possibility given to everyone to insert and make public, within the network, the contents they prefer without receiving substantial censorship and without having to be legitimized or authorized, is increasingly perceived by users as a danger. Another worrying factor is represented by the fact that the Internet is conceived as a space without masters and rules, able to read or even "kill" one's own personality or that of others. A space that is often improperly managed by private powers outside the constitutionally established states and their laws. It is in this context that the deepfake phenomenon occurs, perceived by many as a future risk for our society and its freedom.

The term deepfake is a combination of "Deep Learning" and "Fake" and is reminiscent of the more popular term "Deep Web," an area of cyberspace frequently used to conduct illegal activities. As the combination's terminology

[321] GROTTO, *Reati informatici e convenzione Cybercrime. Oltre la truffa e la frode informatica: la frode del certificatore*, in Dir. informaz. e informatica, 2009, p.149 ss.

[322] F. MANTOVANI, Diritto penale. Parte speciale, vol.II, Padova, 2019, p.229.

suggests, deepfakes are created using artificial intelligence technology, specifically machine learning techniques. Algorithms work on massive datasets, which belong to the source to create deepfakes. A fairly convincing deepfake can be made with as little as 300 images. Then, the algorithms swap one face, which is the source, with another face, the target, using a digital face swapping technique. There are three essential techniques used to create Deepfake content: face swap, expression swap and Generative Adversarial Networks ("GANs"). Regardless of which technique is used, the process generally has the same steps including extraction, training and creation and no longer requires the use of massive datasets.

Therefore, this AI technique is able to synthesize the human image from real content (images, videos, and audio) to modify or recreate the features and movements of a face or body or faithfully imitate a specific voice. The result is digital fakes that can seriously compromise a person's image.

Deepfake content was initially used in relation to celebrities. However, currently phone Apps, which can produce deepfake activity, are available and downloadable by ordinary users. Therefore, with the use of readily available software, even ordinary people can create their own deepfake content, and it only takes one photo from a source to do so. With the widespread use of deepfake content, problems such as audience manipulation, personal rights attacks, intellectual property rights violations and personal data protection are becoming more common. Therefore, deepfakes are a truly innovative product in the field of AI, which poses serious legal challenges.

Not all uses of deepfake are considered illegal or pose a problem. For example, it has been used in the healthcare industry to detect cancer. In addition, an outright ban on the tools used to create deepfakes would be impractical as it would stop legitimate uses of these techniques and conflict with free speech regulations. Some examples of deepfakes are created as political satire, while synthetic content has long been created in the entertainment industry as special effects for film and television. Filters are often used in social media to synthesize or alter images - whether to add cat-like features to a face or to reduce a waistline. One possibility for legislation, and particularly any criminal prosecution, might be to require proof of a malicious intent, an intent to deceive, or a limitation that only content that is "inherently humiliating" should be considered illegal. However, such concepts would be difficult, if not impossible, to work into technical/automated solutions to detect and remove deepfake content.

However, deepfakes certainly have several drawbacks as with post-truth politics and harassment of women in the form of revenge porn, manipulation of the public and intervention in state elections. In particular, serious questions and legal implications have been raised at international and national level in relation to violations of data protection rights and intellectual property rights.

An outright ban on deepfakes would be the most effective and simple way to eliminate all of the above problems, however it would be highly controversial and criticized, as it would violate the concept of freedom of expression as a fundamental individual right. This right is documented as a human right under Article 19 of the Universal Declaration of Human Rights (UDHR)[323] and the International Covenant on Civil and Political Rights (ICCPR).[324] In this regard, it is understandable how deepfakes have challenged legislative systems around the world.

At the international level, the World Intellectual Property Organization ("WIPO") published the "Draft Issues Paper on Intellectual Property Policy and Artificial Intelligence" on December 2019.[325] The draft holds deepfake content issues in terms of intellectual property rights. There are two questions specifically addressed to the deepfake issue on the paper. The first question is based on the fact that deepfakes are created based on data that can be copyrighted, and therefore it needs to be clarified who should own the copyright in a deepfake. The second issue is whether there should be a system of equitable remuneration for the people whose likenesses and "performances" are used in a deepfake. WIPO states that deepfakes can cause more serious problems than copyright violations in cases involving human rights violations, privacy rights, data protection rights and other similar circumstances. Therefore, according to this organization, the main concern would be whether copyright should be granted to deep fake images, rather than to whom the copyright in a deep fake should belong. As a response, it states that if the deepfake content is completely incompatible with the victim's life, the deepfake content should not be awarded copyright protection. For the above issues, WIPO also mentions that if deepfakes are subject to copyright, it should belong to the inventor of deepfakes, as for the reason that there is no

---

323 G.A. Res. 217 (III) A, Universal Declaration of Human Rights (Dec. 10, 1948). https://www.ohchr.org/EN/UDHR/Documents/UDHR_Translations/eng.pdf.

324 G.A. Res. 2200 (XXI) A, International Covenant on Civil and Political Rights (Dec. 16, 1966), https://treaties.un.org/doc/publication/unts/volume%20999/volume-999-i-14668-english.pdf.

325 United Nations Agency: World Intellectual Property Organization (WIPO). WIPO Conversation on Intellectual Property (IP) and Artificial Intelligence (AI). Second Session. Issues paper on intellectual property policy and artificial intelligence. WIPO/IP/AI/2/GE/20/1 (Original: English) Date: December 13, 2019.

intervention of the original person whose image, sound or other feature is used during the creation of deepfake but only his consent.

Consequently, the adoption of intellectual property rights does not seem to be the correct "weapon" to use against deepfake problems, since the victim of deepfakes does not possess a copyright interest in their image. On the other hand, the victim of the deepfake crime can invoke the right to protection of personal data in his defense. According to Article 5 of the EU General Data Protection Regulation ("GDPR"),

> "personal data must be accurate and, where necessary, kept up to date; every reasonable step must be taken to ensure that personal data that is inaccurate, having regard to the purposes for which it is processed, is erased or rectified without delay ('accuracy')."[326]

Accordingly, if deepfake content is irrelevant, inaccurate, or false and fabricated, it should be deleted or rectified. Moreover, even if the deepfake content is true or accurate, a data subject, being considered a victim of a deepfake, can exercise the right to be forgotten, granted to European residents by Article 17 of the GDPR as the "right to erasure." Under Article 17, a data subject has the right to obtain from the controller the erasure of personal data concerning him or her without undue delay, and the controller has an obligation to erase such data.[327]

In individual European nations, there is generally a lack of specific laws against deepfakes; however, laws regarding misinformation can limit deepfakes. In Germany, the Network Enforcement Act, which was enacted in 2017 to combat the dissemination of false information, can be invoked to prohibit deepfakes if it is used to circulate fake news.[328] Spain[329] and France[330] have enacted similar laws. The European Commission, when discussing strategies to address online misinformation, noted that deepfakes have been

---

[326] See P.VOIGT- A.VON DEM BUSSCHE, *The EU General Data Protection Regulation (GDPR)*, London, 2017.

[327] G.A. Res. 2200 (XXI) A, International Covenant on Civil and Political Rights (Dec. 16, 1966), https://treaties.un.org/doc/publication/unts/volume%20999/volume-999-i-14668-english.pdf.

[328] Initiatives to Counter Fake News: Germany, LIBR. CONG., https://www.loc.gov/law/help/fake-news/germany.php (last visited July 29, 2020).

[329] TIM CUSHING, Spanish Government Moves Ahead with First 'Fake News' Prosecution, TECHDIRT. (Mar. 3, 2020), https://www.techdirt.com/articles/20200229/16563544010/spanish-government-moves-ahead-with-first-fake-news-prosecution.shtml.

[330] F.MICHAEL-ROSS, France Passes Controversial 'Fake News' Law EURONEWS (Nov. 22, 2018), https://www.euronews.com/2018/11/22/france-passes-controversial-fake-news-law.

used to create misinformation and manipulate public opinion,[331] and provided guidance on how to address online misinformation, including requiring online platforms to take steps to protect users from misinformation.[332] The creation of deepfakes could also violate other European laws, exemplified by an incident in the United Kingdom where a municipal worker was convicted of harassment when he created a gallery of fake pornographic images of a colleague.[333]

At national level, current Italian law offers the possibility of tracing cases with novel elements back to the events that inspired the existing discipline in a given circumstance. This is the case, for example, of the phenomenon known as "Deepnude," through which the faces or bodies of unsuspecting subjects (even minors) are manipulated or grafted onto the bodies of other subjects, nude or engaged in poses or acts of an explicitly sexual nature.

The risk is not abstract and can involve ordinary people, who can become the object of actions that are psychologically and socially very damaging to their personal dignity. Suffice it to think of the crime referred to in Article 612ter of the Penal Code, commonly known as "Revenge porn," a term used to indicate the disclosure by the ex-partner, for purposes of blackmail, denigration or revenge, of photos and videos with sexual or even pornographic content, obviously falsified in cases of deep nudity. The issue acquires importance also if we consider that this form of protection does not seem to be applicable to artificially created images, although the offense to the protected legal good is potentially the same. In fact, the rule mentioned could not be considered applicable to the case in which the images disseminated are artificial. Being that the principle of legality of criminal law contained in article 1 of the Italian Penal Code and 25 of the Italian Constitution, for which no one can be punished for a fact that is not provided for by law as a crime, according to the principle of malam partem, also entails the prohibition of analogy.

Also in this regard, even if one wished to forcefully link this hypothesis to an already existing case, such as the one indicated by article 612ter, the

---

[331] Tackling online disinformation: a European Approach, at 5, COM (2018) 236 final (Apr. 26, 2018), https://eur-lex.europa.eu/legal-content/EN/TXT/PDF/?uri=CELEX:52018DC0236&from=EN.

[332] J. VINCENT, *Deepfakes for Dancing: You Can Now Use Ai to Fake Those Dance Moves You Always Wanted*, 2018, https://www.theverge.com/2018/8/26/17778792/deepfakes-video-dancing-ai-synthesis.

[333] Mei-Ling Huang, *Deepfakes and the Law – What Can You Do If Your Face Appears in a Deepfake Video?,* 2019, https://www.roydswithyking.com/deepfakes-and-the-law-what-can-you-do-if-your-face-appears-in-a-deepfake-video/.

principle of offensiveness of the criminal law would require a qualification in terms of an impossible crime pursuant to paragraph 2 of article 49 c.p.. This is due to the unsuitability of the action or the inexistence of the object of the same, capable of endangering or damaging the protected legal asset.

The considerations on the legal complexities that this case generates, focus the attention of the legislator on the importance of this phenomenon, whose repression currently clashes with an important regulatory vacuum.

In this regard, the Guarantor for the Protection of Personal Data, in 2020, took its first steps by opening an investigation on the famous instant messaging app "Telegram" following the complaint of some girls who found their intimate images used without their consent through one of the channels of the application, which uses artificial intelligence to reconstruct what the body would look like under clothes. In addition to the launch of the investigation, the Guarantor is evaluating further initiatives to counter the illicit use of this type of software and contain the distorting effects of deepfake.

Therefore, the significant scope of this phenomenon, which is continuously expanding, and the potentially devastating impact it can have on people's lives, calls for careful reflection and organic intervention by the legislator. The possible intervention of the legislator must concern in particular the theme of fake news, which is however closely contiguous to that of deepfake. Unfortunately, since the deepfake phenomenon is very recent and therefore not yet fully recognized by the legislator, there is no specific law addressing this issue. However, even its generic placement in the laws regarding fake news is undoubtedly a step towards the development of a specific legal regulation dedicated to deepfake.

Therefore, in 2017, with the aim of endowing the Italian legislative system with a more complete regulation of acts concerning the manipulation of online information and the fight against fake news, Senatorial Act no. 2688,[334] was presented bearing "Provisions to prevent the manipulation of online information, ensure transparency on the web and promote media literacy." This bill, following the guidelines expressed by the Parliamentary Assembly of the Council of Europe on the subject of online media and journalism, proposes the introduction of a new crime in the Penal Code, inserting article 656bis on the "Publication or dissemination of false, exaggerated or tendentious information, likely to disturb public order, through computer platforms." This article is placed immediately after article 656 of the Penal

---

[334] A.S. n. 2688/2017 Disposizioni per prevenire la manipolazione dell'informazione online, garantire la trasparenza sul web e incentivare l'alfabetizzazione mediatica.

Code relating to the crime of publication or dissemination of false, exaggerated or tendentious information aimed at disturbing public order, which substantially follows the case of article 656bis, providing for the specific case of the use of computer platforms.

The same bill also introduced two further offences, through the insertion of articles 265bis and 265ter concerning, respectively, the "Spreading of false news that may cause public alarm or mislead sectors of public opinion" and the "Spreading of hate campaigns aimed at undermining the democratic process." With which an ad hoc sanctioning system was established for cases in which the dissemination of false news affects other more important values such as public opinion, triggering forms of public alarm, and the democratic process.

Another draft law (DDL no. 3001/2017[335]) was submitted to parliamentary approval in the same year, bearing general rules on Social Networks and for the contrast of the spread of illicit content and fake news on the Internet.

The latter initiative, rather than regulating the cases falling under the notion of fake news, aims to provide for a regulation of the phenomenon as a social event, configuring a series of responsibilities in charge of web service providers.

These first attempts to regulate the matter were followed, in 2019, by the first bill, A.C. 2103, presented in Parliament concerning the establishment of a Parliamentary Commission of Inquiry into the "serial and massive dissemination of illicit content and false information through the Internet, telematics social networks and other digital platforms." This last proposal starts from the premise that the publication and diffusion of fake news has become in recent years a pervasive phenomenon, capable of influencing politics and the results of an election, destroying the reputation of public figures but also of private citizens. The increasing importance of social networks in the lives of citizens requires Parliament to provide the legal system as soon as possible with a specific discipline to combat the commission of crimes through social platforms on the Internet.[336]

---

[335] D.D.L S. 3001/2017 Norme generali in materia di social network e per il contrasto della diffusione su internet di contenuti illeciti e delle fake news.

[336] Atto Camera n. 2103/2019 sull'istituzione di una Commissione parlamentare di inchiesta sulla diffusione seriale e massiva di contenuti illeciti e di informazioni false attraverso la rete internet, le reti sociali telematiche e le altre piattaforme digitali. Approvato con il nuovo titolo: "Istituzione di una Commissione parlamentare di inchiesta sulla diffusione massiva di informazioni false."

The aim is to push social network providers to equip themselves with systems, procedures and bodies for self-regulation and control of the content conveyed by their platforms, able to counter the publication of illegal content. Hence the need to establish a parliamentary committee of inquiry to investigate cases of serial and massive dissemination of fake news through social networks. That proposes legislative and administrative solutions in order to achieve the most appropriate prevention and the most adequate contrast to the commission of crimes through digital platforms on the Internet and verify the adequacy of the competent public administrations to carry out activities of prevention and repression of digital platforms of fake news and illegal content.

The legislator has therefore implemented the concept of "Fake." However, it should be noted that, in the panorama of Italian laws, there is still no provision specifically dealing with deepfakes and their consequences.

In conclusion, as discussed in this section, deepfakes are a global phenomenon and a legal solution to the problems they raise is complex and currently seems far from clear. Instead, what is clear is that we need to take some rigorous steps to address the problems created by this recent technological medium. While existing laws may limit the movement of deepfakes under certain circumstances, the need to develop specific legislation that aims to limit the potential harms of deepfakes is highly necessary.

On the other hand, governments should focus on increasing public awareness of the relevant issues, because legislation cannot prevent the circulation of all deepfakes, and legal remedies, however good and efficient they may be, can only be applied after the damage has already been done. In this regard, the role of the Data Protection Authorities (DPA) must be considered central to an effective prevention strategy aimed at raising awareness among stakeholders and the public against the risks of AI in general and emerging techniques in particular, as in the case of Deepfake.

4. Common Scam Techniques Used to Pursue Digital Identity Theft

Cybercriminals can use many different scam techniques to steal someone's digital identity. In fact, identity theft is closely tied to recent and emerging forms of social engineering techniques that are often used to steal sensitive information from the victim.

Public profiles on social networks or other popular online services can also be used as a source of data, helping criminals impersonate their targets. Once identity thieves have collected this information, they can use it to order goods, take control of victims' online accounts or take legal action on their behalf.[337]

In the short term, affected individuals may suffer financial losses due to unauthorized withdrawals and purchases made in their name. In the medium term, victims may be held accountable for the perpetrator's actions and be investigated by law enforcement, as well as face consequences such as legal charges, changes in their credit status, and damage to their good name.

This section explores the most common scam techniques used to prosecute criminal activity, including phishing, vishing and pharming, with the goal of discussing their relationship to crimes covered by current criminal legislation.

4.1. Phishing and Vishing

The widespread use of internet by an increasing number of subjects, often lacking the necessary basic computer knowledge, has made the illegitimate conducts aimed at exploiting their misinformation grow exponentially. In fact, identity theft is constantly increasing. Such theft must be understood as the illegal collection of information about a person or an organization for the purpose of their subsequent use in illegal activities. Identity theft is therefore often the means used to subsequently carry out illegal conducts such as spamming, preparing scams or stealing funds from online accounts. One of the latest expressions of identity theft by cybercriminals is "Phishing."

Phishing is derived from the verb "to fish" and from the slang word "phreaking," which indicates the activity of someone who studies, experiments or exploits telephones, companies and telephone systems for fun, personal gain or curiosity, looking for holes in the technology that allow random discoveries in the system that could be used for various purposes. However, it may simply be a password collection portmanteau.[338]

Phishing is a fraudulent activity, carried out against a large number of individuals, usually by sending e-mail messages, with the aim of acquiring

---

337 On this point see also A.CADOPPI-S.CANETRARI-A.MANNA-M.PAPA, *Cybercrime*, Milano, 2019.

338 G.MINICUCCI, *Le Frodi Informatiche,* in A.CADOPPI-S.CANETRARI-A.MANNA-M.PAPA, *Cybercrime*, Milano, 2019, p.827 ss.

their personal information such as identification codes, credit card numbers, home banking device codes and so on. Such information is subsequently used by the agent (the so-called Phisher) in order to carry out operations (such as banking and access to computer systems) aimed at replacing the legitimate owner to its own advantage. Statistically, Phishing is mainly used to steal information about credit card numbers or device codes in order to take possession of the economic goods of the victims. Obviously, Phishing can harm not only individuals, but also companies if the recovered information is its property. Just think in this sense of the eventuality that an employee becomes the victim of an attack and communicates the company's passwords to access online accounts.

The doctrine generally considers Phishing a technique of social engineering, that is a method of social behavior aimed at stealing the life and personal information of the victim.[339]

Phishing attacks are launched through very similar methodologies and are repeated over time. For example, in the case of illegitimate activities related to the victims' bank accounts, the attack begins by sending an email to an indistinct mass of recipients (whose email address has been obtained illegally) that faithfully reproduces graphics and logos used by a banking institution. With the message sent, the subject is alerted, for example, of some technical or security problems that have occurred with their bank account. In reality, the phisher does not know whether the recipient of the email is or is not a customer of a particular bank, but the more messages sent, the greater the likelihood of reaching their customers. The account holder is then invited with a special link to a website to solve these technical problems related to his bank account (the website is also usually identical in every way to the original website of the bank) and asked to authenticate himself by entering his password and device codes. This data is then stolen by the phisher and subsequently used to perform transactions on the victim's bank account (e.g., money transfers).

As mentioned, Phishing is a fraudulent conduct, therefore punishable under Article 640 of the Criminal Code relating to fraud that punishes anyone who, with artifice or deception, or by misleading someone, procures for himself or others an unfair profit, causing at the same time a damage to others.[340] A Phishing attack contains, in fact, all the elements foreseen by the aforementioned legislation. In particular, the "artifice or deception" consisting

---

[339] *Ibidem.*

[340] Article 640 Italian Criminal Code: *"Chiunque, con artifizi o raggiri, inducendo taluno in errore, procura a sé o ad altri un ingiusto profitto con altrui danno, è punito con la reclusione da sei mesi a tre anni e con la multa da euro 51 a euro 1.032."*

in the reproduction of e-mails and websites belonging to banking institutions; the "induction in error" of the recipient, who believed to provide his bank with the data related to his current account and the undue profit consisting for example in the illicit withdrawal made from the account of the person induced in error.

It is therefore possible to imagine a bipartition of the phenomenon, thus giving rise to a different legal qualification of the same. If the author of the crime has fraudulently operated, through the use of a self-installing software, on the computer or telematics system of the offended person, the crime of computer fraud can take shape.[341] This is due to the alteration of the operation of the user's machine resulting from the aggressive unilateral nature of the illegal act. On the contrary, a simple fraud will take shape, according to article 640 of the Penal Code, in the case in which the author of the crime proceeds by sending fraudulent e-mails and/or links to sites-clone in which to insert his own credentials. Given that such activity does not imply an alteration or an undue intervention on the user's system but, on the contrary, reveals a clear participation of the offender in the crime, just according to the typical scheme of the crime as per article 640 of the Italian Penal Code.[342]

Moreover, the appearance of a new threat to the security of communications made with the aid of internet telephony is very recent. In fact, after Phishing, which alludes to the use of increasingly sophisticated techniques aimed at "fishing" financial data and passwords of unsuspecting network users, is spreading a new behavior, with criminal implications, and commonly called "Vishing," terminological contraction between VoIP (Voice Over Internet Protocol). As the phisher, the visher mainly uses the e-mail as the main means of perpetration, however it does it in a different way and the strategic process followed can be summarized in the following steps: The attacker (called a visher) sends the unfortunate and unsuspecting user an email message that simulates in graphics and content a company or entity known to the recipient (e.g., his bank, an online auction site to which the user is actually

---

[341] Article 640*ter*: *"Chiunque, alterando in qualsiasi modo il funzionamento di un sistema informatico o telematico o intervenendo senza diritto con qualsiasi modalità su dati, informazioni o programmi contenuti in un sistema informatico o telematico o ad esso pertinenti, procura a sé o ad altri un ingiusto profitto con altrui danno, è punito con la reclusione da sei mesi a tre anni e con la multa da euro 51 a euro 1.032."*

[342] G.MINICUCCI, *Le frodi informatiche*, in A.CADOPPI-S.CANESTRARI-A.MANNA-M.PAPA, *Cybercrime*, 2019, p. 827-855; For further information on *Phishing* see also FLOR, *Phishing e profili penali*, 59 ss.; CIPOLLA, *Social network, furto d'identità e reati contro il patrimonio*, in Giur. di Merito, 2012, 2672 ss; CAJANI, *Profili penali del phishing,* in Cass.pen, 2007, 2294 ss; FLOR, *Phishing, identity theft e identity abuse,* 899 ss.

registered). The email generally contains notices of special situations or problems that have occurred with the recipient's bank account, such as a chargeback or account expiration. Then, the typical malicious email invites the recipient to dial a phone number to avoid the charge, or to regularize their position with the institution or company. The subsequent dialing of the phone number doesn't actually allow the recipient to contact the official call center, but a fake receptionist who will ask the victim of this scam to provide personal information, especially the number of the bank account or credit card. In this way, the information collected ends up in the hands of the attacker, the so-called visher, who will use it to purchase goods, transfer sums of money or even just as a tool for further attacks, perhaps using the identity of another individual.

This particular crime differs from Phishing in that in the case of Phishing, e-mails may also invite the recipient to click on a link in the message, which will take him to a counterfeit site, very similar to that of the institution or entity in question.

Vishing attacks can also consist of activating a VoIP account and initiating an automated calling system that contacts potential victims. When one of them responds, the system plays a recording informing them of the unfortunate existence of a bank account or credit card problem and will ask them to contact an additional number to resolve it. The indicated number is the VoIP number of the visher, calling it you receive a recorded request to enter your confidential personal data.

The phenomenon of fake call centers on VoIP is strongly growing, being that scammers rely on the fact that there is less distrust in communicating personal information verbally to a person who apparently works for a real call center, rather than answering a simple email.[343] Undoubtedly, the mediation of the human voice, especially if reassuring and partially seductive, contributes to slightly reduce the common inhibiting factors of distrust that every individual, for its intrinsic nature, implements, even unconsciously, to every new relationship or interpersonal exchange.

The typical fraud of a Vishing attack characterizes it as a typical fraudulent crime against the patrimony, sanctioned in the Italian Penal Code by the article 640 that expressly foresees the punishability of whoever with artifices or deceptions, inducing someone in error, procures to himself or to

343 L. SAMBUCCI, *Falsi call center sul VoIP: la nuova truffa si chiama Vishing*, in www.anti-phishing.it, 2006.

others an undue profit with damage to others.[344] This type of crime is characterized by the deception through which a person is induced to carry out an act whose consequence is a *deminutio patrimonii* with consequent profit for the agent or for other parties. In jurisprudence, the case in question is defined as "contractual fraud," whenever one of the contracting parties carries out artifices or deception aimed at concealing or hiding facts or circumstances which, if known, would have induced the other party to conclude the contract. In particular, the artifice is a "*mise en scene*" or the transformation of reality to make believe that the non-existent exists; the deception, instead, consists in an aggression of the psyche of others, through a lying and ingenious activity.[345]

Through the internet, individuals can therefore expose themselves to the risk of providing their bank details, for example mistakenly believing to regularize their position with the bank, authorizing on the contrary a money transfer in favor of the visher, with a consequent economic damage. An important question that comes to mind is how does the attacker know that the user, who suffered the vishing attack, has an account with the bank indicated in the message-cause. The answer is provided by the common evidence that normally the visher does not know whether the victim has an account with the service targeted by his action, but simply sends the same e-mail to an indeterminate number of e-mail addresses, in the hope and statistical probability of reaching some user who actually has an account with that service.

Since a Phishing or Vishing attack carried out against a company could cause a loss of funds deposited in current accounts, which are often difficult to recover, it is absolutely necessary to take adequate countermeasures to reduce this danger. If the illegal Phishing or Vishing attack involves a company or bank, it is essential that employees are informed about these forms of fraud and the precautions to be taken to recognize them (for example, some rules could be included in the internal regulations for the use of company computer equipment). It is also possible to equip oneself with technological tools that limit the possibility of being the target of phishing attacks (such as spam filters) or that alert the user to navigation on inauthentic sites.

---

[344] Article 640 Italian Penal Code "*Chiunque, con artifizi o raggiri, inducendo taluno in errore, procura a sé o ad altri un ingiusto profitto con altrui danno, è punito con la reclusione da sei mesi a tre anni e con la multa da euro 51 a euro 1.032.*"

[345] Cass. pen., sez. VI, 13/2/87, in Cass. pen., 1988, p. 1449.

4.1.1. The Relationship between Phishing and the Crime of Money Laundering

We have previously analyzed and identified Phishing as an illegal activity through which, with the use of various expedients (spamming of deceptive e-mail messages, computer programs, malware) a subject manages to fraudulently take possession of electronic codes (username and password) of a user in order to commit computer frauds. These frauds usually consist of accessing bank or postal currency accounts in order to make a profit.[346] In these cases, we have seen that the data provided by the unfortunate user is immediately read and recorded by the phishers, who can then access the victim's bank account and steal the funds. However, in such circumstances, besides the phisher, it is often possible to ascertain the presence of another subject, the so-called financial manager. That is the subject who lends himself to the fact that the sums that the hacker steals from the current account where he has illegally entered, are credited on his own current account to be finally transferred abroad with money transfer operations.[347]

At regulatory level, it should be noted that currently in Italy there is no specific legal framework on the subject, in other words, this system not only does not provide a definition of Phishing, but also does not punish per se such activity as described above. In this regard, unlike French legislation, the Italian Criminal cìCode does not have a specific discipline of computer crimes as they are scattered far and wide in the code and in special laws.[348] The creation of a specific legislative space dedicated to the matter could be based on the above-mentioned statement that computer crime has led to the emergence of a new interest deserving protection, which is that of computer intangibility, understood as a triadic relationship between the data, the reality that the data asserts and the data owner.[349]

However, this does not prevent some single conducts from assuming a specific criminal relevance. In order to evaluate which cases can be integrated in each of the phases of the conduct, it is good to consider that some of them, even if they do not immediately attack the victims' assets, express a strong

[346] Cass. Pen. Sent. 9891/11 dell'11/03/2011.

[347] FLOR, *Permanenza non autorizzata in un sistema informatico o telematico, violazione del segreto d'ufficio e concorso nel reato da parte dell'extraneus*, in cass. Pen., 2009, p. 1502.

[348] On the fragmentation of our penal system and on decoding, see PADOVANI T., STORTONI L., *Diritto penale e fattispecie criminose. Introduzione alla parte speciale del diritto penale*, 2006.

[349] V.MILITELLO, *Nuove esigenze di tutela penale e trattamento elettronico delle informazioni*, in Rivista trimestrale di diritto penale dell'economia, 1992.

offensive dimension that takes the form of identity theft, or in a theft of data fraudulently collected and illicitly used.

In this sense, the jurisprudential orientation can be considered certainly shareable. In fact, according to it, whoever, using Phishing techniques, introduces himself into the home banking service of the victim in order to carry out unauthorized online withdrawal or transfer operations, is considered responsible for the crimes of impersonation,[350] abusive access to a computer or telematics system[351] or fraud.[352] Abusive access to a computer or telematics system.[353] This is the case in the event of retrieval, reproduction, diffusion, communication, delivery to others of access codes or information useful for the above-mentioned purposes and the undue use of credit and payment cards on the Internet, under the conditions indicated in Article 55, paragraph 9, of Legislative Decree 231/2007.[354]

On the other hand, the question of quid juris has arisen with reference to the position of the so-called financial manager. The problem is whether the cases referred to in articles 648 or 648bis of the criminal code are contestable. In this regard, after stealing the money from the fraudster's account, the phisher has the criminal impulse to clean up the traces of the cybercrime-scene and especially of the stolen money. This is technically possible thanks to a complex series of bank transfers that are often facilitated by unsuspected users such as financial managers.

The criminological literature and the most recent jurisprudence have established a proven mechanism that involves a sort of "phase 2" of the phishing attack. Phishers send electronic messages in which they promise, for example, easy earnings or job opportunities. Through brief correspondence, in which logos or names of well-known companies are used, the senders of the messages ask the victims (who are now bewitched by future earnings) to

---

[350] Article 494 of the Criminal Code: When he has illegitimately substituted his own person for that of others or has given himself a false name or a false status, or in any case assumed another virtual one, even non-existent, provided that there is the element of induction into error and the specific fraud consisting in the purpose of procuring an advantage for oneself or others or of causing damage to others and that the fact does not constitute another crime against public trust.

[351] Article 615 - *ter* of the Criminal Code.

[352] Article 640 of the Criminal Code; Court of Milan, 7 October 2011 (sent.), Pres. Pellegrino, Est. Corbetta, maximized by Tommaso Trinchera in Contemporary Criminal Law, 5 December 2011. See also Gip at the Milan Court, in Corriere del Merito, 2009, 3, 285, with a note by Francesco Agnino.

[353] Article 615 quater of the Criminal Code.

[354] Court of Milan, 7 October 2011 (sent.), Pres. Pellegrino, Est. Corbetta, maximized by Tommaso Trinchera in Contemporary Criminal Law, 5 December 2011. See also Gip at the Milan Court, in Corriere del Merito, 2009, 3, 285, with a note by Francesco Agnino.

receive a transfer to their bank account. They are then asked to transfer the promised sums to other bank accounts (managed by the phisher's trustees) withholding a percentage recognized as a reward for their cooperation. The victims send the money to the phisher's bank account, through international channels suitable to interrupt any traceability, however they will never receive the transfer initially promised.

In this way, the doctrine has defined the financial manager as the one who makes himself available to carry out this operation. This has led to its legal position being the subject of pronouncements of merit and legitimacy. The jurisprudential debate focuses on whether or not the offence of money laundering can be attributed to him. In particular, in the examples mentioned above in which the absence of intent or direct intent to launder, the compatibility of the case of art. 648bis penal code with the so-called possible intent is quite evident.

However, jurisprudence has clarified that the financial manager is liable as an accomplice in the same crimes committed by the phisher (articles 494, 615ter and 640 of the Italian Criminal Code) only if he has acted being aware of the overall fraudulent activity carried out to the detriment of the account holders. If, on the other hand, he is unaware, he is liable for receiving stolen goods[355] or money laundering,[356] depending on whether he has merely received the sums of money, being aware of their illegal origin, or has also transferred them abroad in such a way as to hinder the identification of such origin. The offence of receiving or laundering can be said to exist for the financial manager only when it is clear that he was aware of the illicit origin of the money and, nevertheless, was determined to receive it and transfer it abroad in the manner indicated by the phisher.[357] This orientation was authoritatively sanctioned with sentence no. 25960/2011,[358] in which the Supreme Court recalled the teaching of the United Sections on the compatibility of possible fraud with the crime of receiving stolen goods.[359]

This last pronouncement plays a particular role in the jurisprudential review of recent years, not only for the authoritativeness of the judgment that has quelled a long jurisprudential conflict, but especially because it has three important features. First, it affirms that the debate on the distinction between

---

[355] Article 648 of the Penal Code.

[356] Article 648*bis* of the Penal Code.

[357] Tribunale di Milano, 7 ottobre 2011 (sent.), Pres. Pellegrino, Est. Corbetta, massimata da Tommaso Trinchera in Diritto penale contemporaneo, 5 dicembre 2011. See also Gip presso Trib. Milano, in Corriere del Merito, 2009, 3, 285, with note by Francesco Agnino.

[358] Cass. pen., Sez. II, 17.6.2011 (dep. 1.7.2011), n. 25960, Pres. Fiandanese, Est. Gallo.

[359] Cass. SS.UU., Sent. N. 12433 of 26/11/2009.

intentional wrongdoing and fault with foresight concerns only "blood crimes." Secondly, it states that intent and conscious guilt can relate not only to the event but also to one of the conditions of the incriminated conduct. Finally, it distinguishes the subjective situations of certainty, doubt or mere suspicion in relation to the requirement of the illicit origin of the thing or sums of money.

In particular, in the aforementioned judgment, the United Sections of the Supreme Court clearly excluded mere suspicion from the possible intent. In this regard, the Court noted that even receiving stolen goods can be supported by a possible intent. However, it remains to be established how it should be ascertained and what its characteristics should be, since it cannot be inferred from mere suspicion and cannot consist in mere suspicion, if it is true that this is not incompatible with the incautious purchase.[360]

For the receipt of stolen goods more substantial circumstances are required than those that simply give reason to suspect that the thing comes from a crime. Therefore, the reasonable belief that the agent has consciously accepted the risk of the criminal provenance of such goods can only derive from the presence of unequivocal factual data, which make clear the concrete possibility of such illicit provenance. In subjective terms, this means that the possible intent in receiving stolen goods requires a psychological attitude which, although not reaching the level of certainty, is placed on a level immediately higher than that of mere suspicion, being configured, in terms of representation by the agent, the concrete possibility of the criminal origin.

In short, something more than a mere reason for suspicion is required in order to recognize a possible intent. With respect to which the agent could have a psychological attitude of inattention, negligence or simple disinterest. Therefore, a factual situation of unequivocal significance is required, requiring the agent to make a conscious choice between acting, accepting the possibility of committing theft, and not acting.

In conclusion, it is possible to state that the possible intent is compatible with both the case of receiving stolen goods and that of money laundering. However, it must be verified each time, as it is not integrated by doubt or mere suspicion. In the latter case, in the cases of purchase or acquisition of suspicious objects, the crime of receiving stolen goods is not configured, but the lesser crime of "careless purchase."[361] In cases where goods or money are transferred with the mere suspicion of their criminal origin, the subjective element of conduct will be "guilt with foresight."[362] In this case, the

[360] Cass. pen., Sez. II, 17.6.2011 (dep. 1.7.2011), n. 25960, Pres. Fiandanese, Est. Gallo.
[361] Article 712 of the Italian Criminal Code.
[362] Article 61, no. 3 of the criminal code.

perpetrator, therefore, will be considered punishable under the combined provisions of articles 42, paragraphs 1 and 2, and 648bis of the Penal Code since the act does not constitute a crime.

4.2. Pharming

The Pharming - mystification derived from the English verb "to farm" - consists in illegally stealing data from the users in order to cheat them, but in this case the deception can be implemented following two means: move an attack against the user or simply hit a "DNS server." The DNS server is a system that transforms the name of the website written in the address bar (the "domain name," i.e., the one preceded by the classic "www") into a numeric code ("IP address") that indicates where exactly on the web what we are looking for is located. To better understand how it all works, let's make a practical example: when we write the address www.mybank.com on the "search bar," the DNS server translates it in an IP address and brings us to visit exactly what we want, (in this specific case the portal of the bank where we have an account).

Therefore, the term Pharming is used to refer to a site similar to that of a bank, so that the access keys to online accounts are stolen. To do this, the agent has to insert a virus capable of changing the list of the main sites. Therefore, the main solution that should be taken to avoid such a crime is not to include the Internet address used to connect to the personal home banking site among the top sites.

Pharming is very similar to Phishing,[363] in the sense that these are two methods used to implement computer scams, the purpose of which is to steal sensitive data, such as account numbers and passwords, although there are differences between the two crimes. In fact, Phishing is carried out only through the client, e.g., exploiting the naivety of the victim who is encouraged to click on links that direct to sites similar to those of private banks, where it is required to enter personal data that are then stolen. Pharming, on the other hand, is done through servers or clients, so it's much harder to defend yourself. Unfortunately, large companies or even Internet Service Providers can be attacked through Pharming, which directs a company's users to fake sites without having to access each computer. Thus, both Pharming and Phishing

---

[363] M.C. DE VIVO, G. RICCI *Diritto, crimini e tecnologie. Informatica e diritto*, Vol. XXI, 2012, n. 2, pp. 25-112.

are fraudulent acts, but what distinguishes them is the fact that in Pharming, a site's traffic is altered so that users can be redirected to fake sites with software that can damage users' computers or steal personal data.

We can recognize two types of Pharming. The first is characterized by the use of different methods to install viruses or other malware on the victim's computer. Viruses that allow the computer to redirect the user from a real site to a fake one, created specifically to resemble the fake site. The second type of Pharming, which is considered the most dangerous, uses infected computers to redirect any user who wants to visit a real site to a fake one.

Unfortunately, if the crime is committed by experienced criminals, it is very difficult to recognize a fake site from a real one, although there are some aspects that can make users able to detect fake features, starting from how the URL of the site is written. In order to prevent Pharming attacks from causing damage, the best thing to do is to install an effective antivirus that can find and completely eliminate malware present on computers.[364]

As for the other methods you can use to prevent Pharming, the simplest one is to be careful about the sites you visit and, therefore, be sure of their reliability. The best way to protect yourself is always to use advanced internet protection that is able to ensure safety when visiting sites. Unfortunately, the danger of Pharming is that if attacks occur on the system, even if the affected user has a computer that does not have malware, he or she can still be a victim of such an attack. This implies the fact that while using tricks such as manually entering the address of a web page or safer bookmarks, this may not be enough, as the manipulation occurs after the computer sends a connection request. That is why it is always good to pay attention to the websites you visit, especially those that contain personal data and passwords. If you notice possible anomalies in the website, as in the case of the disabled address or strange requests from the site, you should make sure that there is an image of a padlock indicating that the site is secure.

Pharming is said to be a very subtle crime, being that instead of using a trick to hide the true destination of a link, the victim is directed to a fake website by typing in a web address that they believe to be real.

A scammer, who is particularly computer savvy, however, can also break this mechanism. He can make sure that even if the victim types in the exact name of the bank's website, he is automatically directed to another site. Unaware of the scam in progress, the victim types in the data used to access

---

364 See http://www.crime-research.org/news/09.11.2005/1614/. http://www.csoonline.com/article/221737/phishing-thebasics, Conference "La sicurezza dei cittadini nelle aree metropolitane" (Rome, 25 October 2010).

personal accounts on the fake site. The scammer will then get hold of this information and use it for illegal purposes. The scammer succeeds in his illegal purpose by damaging the DNS server - which consequently does not translate the domain name into the exact IP address - or simply the user. Through a spam mail with a dangerous attachment, for example, the scammer can secretly install programs on a person's PC that can change certain things and make sure that the person is always redirected to fake websites when surfing the net.

Also in relation to the possible episodes of Pharming, the hypothesized crimes are many. It goes from the illicit treatment of personal data to the online fraud, passing for the crime of violation of the copyright. The scammer, in fact, by falsifying a site, commits a further offence: he illegally copies a creative work considered original and therefore protected by law,[365] specifically by the laws on intellectual property.

4.3. Final Remarks on the Impact That Evolving IT Techniques Have on Cybercrimes

The reliability of the means of computer defense and the security perceived by the citizen based on a specific and sanctioning legislation of the crimes committed in this field, seem to be the essential defense tools in front of the growing diffusion of these phenomena. Which undermine the already low trust that the individual has towards new technologies and that indirectly aim to break down the confidence in their use.

The only defenses that the citizen can activate of forehead to such situations are dictated mainly from the farsightedness and from the activation of one greater caution in the comparisons of the anomalous demands. In other words, the phenomenon is fought with knowledge, with the elimination of that threshold of ignorance that makes Internet users, at times, mediocre users of an instrument whose actual modus operandi is little known. The development of new technologies that facilitate computer communications is therefore accompanied by their use to commit crimes. As a consequence, this poses serious problems with regard to computer security, especially in the corporate environment where computer violations can cause very significant economic damage.

---

[365] See http://teca.elis.org/2716/prevenzione-repressione-crimini-informatici-2009-12-02.pdf.

It is interesting to note that in the case of activities carried out through the use of computers and the web, people's behaviors seem to take place in a virtual place that is different from everyday reality. A sort of "no man's land" where everything seems lawful, everyone is free and anonymous and no one can be held responsible for the consequences of their actions. However, nothing is more false than this feeling.[366]

A scam carried out through the web has the same negative legal and ethical value as a live scam, but information technology has an impact on the cognitive schemes of individuals that can cause perceptual alterations. Criminal action develops in parallel with the subject's thinking, a process that can be summarized in a "five-step model."[367] This pattern begins with a precise motivation and ends with the execution of the criminal behavior. However, fear of criminal and social consequences, fear of guilt, awareness of causing harm and estimation of the risk of being sued could interrupt the circuit that leads individuals to commit these crimes. However, "technomediation" may alter some of these relevant factors in criminal decision making, such as by reducing perceptions of the severity of behavior and the risk of detection, thereby increasing the number of crimes committed. Indeed, social perceptions of some cybercrimes may be skewed to the point that some individuals do not consider what is normally considered a crime under criminal law to be a crime. On the other hand, many individuals are aware that some behaviors are illegal but justify engaging in them because they perceive such actions as impersonal.[368] The use of information technology has not changed the values around which our society identifies. Therefore, it is a mistake to think that behaviors that violate fundamental human rights cannot be sanctioned, just because they are perpetrated through the use of new technologies.

The new information and communication technologies have a revolutionary and fundamental impact on Europe's growth and competitiveness, but also profound legal and social implications.

---

366 M. STRANO, F. BATTELLI, M. BOCCARDI, R. BRUZZONE, B. FIAMMELLA, M. MATTIUCCI, A. RIGONI, *Inside attack, tecniche di intervento e strategie di prevenzione*, Roma, 2005, introduzione di Corrado Giustozzi.

367 M.STRANO, *Modello a 5 fasi*, 2002, www.criminologia.org.

368 M. STRANO, F. BATTELLI, M. BOCCARDI, R. BRUZZONE, B. FIAMMELLA, M. MATTIUCCI, A. RIGONI, *Inside attack, tecniche di intervento e strategie di prevenzione*, Roma, 2005, introduzione di Corrado Giustozzi.

Chapter 3

Digital Identity Theft: Not Only a Financial Crime

1. The Need to Renew Criteria and Rules for the Attribution of Legal Responsibility in Cyberspace

The complex reality of cyberspace, which is constantly evolving and expanding, requires the continuous adaptation of criminal law, which nonetheless must maintain its typical regulatory and protective functions. This need for our legislation to evolve, also in terms of an analogical interpretation of existing laws, must necessarily respect the exclusion of the malam partem analogy, enshrined within the Italian constitution by the "principle of legality."[369] According to this principle, the stated rules do not apply outside the expressly established cases, and no one can be punished for a fact that is not expressly provided for as a crime by a law that entered into force before its commission. Therefore, the current challenges for criminal law are both to adapt the legal instruments by modifying existing laws while respecting the constitutional indications and to elaborate new norms, which nonetheless also respect the existing conceptual and dogmatic categories.

The activities that take place within cyberspace seem to redefine the relationship between technology and law since the operating conditions and functions of this new area in which lawful and illegal actions take place are at risk of being in competition with the primary regulatory rules of the law. The risk, also feared by authoritative scholars such as Lessig,[370] relies on the fact that the "technical code," which is endowed with its intrinsic universality, is progressively credited and presented as a "new legal" code for the globalized world.[371] The technological self-protection rules and self-developed regulation, autonomously adopted by the private business enterprises and

---

[369] Article 25 paragraph 2 of the Italian Constitution; Art.1 Italian Criminal Code.
[370] Lessig, *Code and other laws of cyberspace, 1999.*
[371] *Ibidem.*

particularly by the large commercial monopolists of the web such as Facebook, Google, Amazon, in many cases tend to become de facto "law" and go as far as replacing existing laws or fill in possible legislative gaps. This is mainly due to the capability of these private commercial organizations to act fast, with no legal contradictory and, basically, with no legal guarantees for the recipient of the sanction. In fact, they are quickly able to intervene and provide a variety of sanctions, such as the drastic exclusion of private or public subjects from services or access to the network, thus conditioning users', competitors' or third parties' behavior to the point of limiting the exercise of even fundamental rights. Furthermore, on many occasions, these private commercial monopoly organizations, which de facto control and manage the network, have provided a very particular definition of cyberspace, defining it as a "space of freedom," as a space free from the law and legal impositions, therefore, a "space," the "cyberspace," where the individual's legal rights are not constitutionally protected.[372] Instead, skillfully, yet maliciously, the commercial monopolists of the web promote cyberspace as a free space for users who will not be oppressed or in any case limited by the nations, who naturally are anchored to the materiality of their territories and their geographical borders, within which they exercise their authority. However, the general analysis of the numerous and often serious illegal activities committed within cyberspace and the danger that they represent not only for private citizens but also to commercial activities, working within the net, demonstrate the emerging need for a truly effective legal protection not only at the local national level but also and most importantly at the international level.[373]

The fundamental criteria must be that what is illegal offline cannot be lawful online, even if it occurs in new ways and forms that were previously unimaginable. For this reason, there is a need to develop a general systematic legal framework in which to place renewed criteria and rules for the attribution of responsibility, which takes into account the peculiar characteristics of the behaviors and criminally relevant "facts" that are committed or manifested in cyberspace.

The complexity of the network makes it necessary to establish and regulate by law multiple situations related to various subjects of different

---

[372] See G.ZICCARDI, *Hacker – Il richiamo della libertà*, Milano, 2011.

[373] In particular, the project of an internet bill of rights was promoted, elaborated and shared in order to recognize and guarantee globally the fundamental rights of anyone in cyberspace, starting from those contained in international documents and conventions; See also T.B.LEE, *internet Magna Carta*; also Italian Parliament committee, *The declaration of rights on the internet*, in www.camera.it.

natures, such as private and public organizations (i.e., business companies and public administrations) that carry out their activities in cyberspace. In fact, data breaches and the consequential possible illegal use or misuse of the information included in their websites or cyber-archives could be potentially dangerous for the rights and legal interests of the data owners and third parties. Therefore, it is of primary importance for private and public organizations to recognize, evaluate and adopt all possible measures finalized at limiting the risks of their activities carried out within cyberspace. In this regard, they should be able to first control, ex ante, the sources from which they derive the data in their possession and at the same time enhance expert systems' and artificial intelligence's potential, which can operate within the new technological context with a special awareness aimed at risk reduction and crime prevention.

2. The Dematerialization of Individuals and Juridification of Their Virtual Identity

Over the past few decades, the concept of personal identity has evolved in parallel with technological advancements. In fact, technological progress has created new "territories" such as cyberspace, where actors and victims are dematerialized although equipped with a new, different form of identity—their digital identity. In cyberspace, victims and offenders often confront each other, highlighting the need to identify rights, duties and respective responsibilities and therefore to "juridify" an individual's personal identity.

In the years preceding the technological revolution, jurisprudence was of fundamental importance in describing the subjective right to personal identity made by the Court of Cassation [374] The position expressed by the Court represents the point of reference for any redefinition of the concept of identity and for addressing and resolving the issues related to a possible conceptual and legislative overlap between the notions of "digital identity" and "personal identity." In fact, the Court fully included the concept of personal identity among the aspects of personality that are protected by the legal system alongside those envisaged by the long doctrinal tradition, such as name, image, reputation or, in a broader sense, privacy.

The right to personal identity has thus progressively been enriched with sociological elements that have been acknowledged by the legislator and that

---

[374] Cass., 22.6.1985, n. 3769, in Foro it., 1985, I , 2211.

have as their object that specific good-value constituted by the social projection of the individual's overall personality. That said, we could describe personal identity as the social projection of the personality of the individual, who has an interest in being represented in his/her relational life with his/her true identity. Particularly, the rights for any individual that his/her intellectual, ideological, political, ethical, religious and professional assets, as they have been already manifested and known in the social environment, will not be modified, obfuscated or in any way altered.[375]

In this perspective, the misrepresentation of identity can consist both in the attribution of non-existent or different characteristics and qualities from the real ones as well as in the omission of existing elements, whether they are ameliorative or pejorative, as long as they are substantial and not accessory. Therefore, it is important to consider and keep in mind that even an alteration for the better can be considered illegitimate if it affects the personality, regardless of the possible damage to one's honor, reputation, image, privacy or other personal rights.

In this regard, the opinion that one might have of him/herself is not relevant in defining one's personal identity, digital or non-digital, given that this would describe identity based on mere subjective elements and not on objective ones. Instead, an individual's identity is in direct reference to their personality as it is perceived in the social reality based on objective findings and explicit behaviors typical of the "relational dimension."[376]

Therefore, from this short analysis, it is clear how the jurisprudence currently protects personal identity with reference to specific differentiating elements particular to the subject in his/her public activity, such as the publication of false news in a newspaper about the assets declared by a professional. In this regard, the legal foundations for the protection of personal identity have been identified in the specific provisions relating to the name (Articles 6–9 of the Italian Civil Code), to the image (Article 10 of the Italian Civil Code), to the right of rectification (Article 8, Law n. 47/1948 and article 32, Legislative Decree n. 177/2005) and in general to the protected rights recognizable in Article 2 of the Constitution.

The specificity of the interest in reference to personal identity can be more easily understood and delineated with reference to the personality aspects connected to it, especially with respect to an individual's distinctive signs (name, pseudonym, image) that identify the subject on the level of material

---

375 See Cass., 7.2.1996, n. 978, in Corr. Jur., 1996, 3, 264.

376 G.ALPA, *I diritti della persona e la cronaca giornalistica*, in Giur. merito, 1987, 1311.

existence and of the civil condition or evoke his/her physical features. Personal identity, in contrast, is a global expression of personality, including in a moral sense. For example, with respect to the protection of ones "reputation," which involves a judgment on the person with the attribution of facts likely to cause a negative judgment, this type of protection implies the need to avoid the dissemination and representation of private events outside the personal private life. Alternatively, the protection of personal identity is finalized to a positive defense and guarantees that the representation of the individual is made by reflecting reality.

However, despite the evolution of the notion of personal identity having occurred during recent years, there is still a part of the doctrine that excludes the possibility to develop an autonomous law for its protection. In this regard, according to some authors, personal identity is qualified simply as a good aimed at satisfying an interest that the legal system protects only through single specific norms, which refers to other rights of the personality due to the fear that a generalized protection may excessively compress the "freedom of thought" pursuant to Article 21 of the Constitution.[377]

However, the debate on the issues of personal identity that characterized the final years of the last century has been impacted and somehow transformed by the technological advances of the last 20 years and by the development of the new notion of digital identity. Personal identity and digital identity are therefore two notions that have somewhat overlapped and have required the legislator to make an innovative effort to adapt and reformulate existing legislation and recently even to consider the possibility and need to develop legislation specifically dedicated and adequate to contrast a number of new types of crime.

In the era of big data, our very personal real and virtual identities are both made up of information. As a matter of fact, information such as nicknames, sentimental statuses and professional qualifications are now part of an individual's real and virtual identity and represent their tangible and intangible property or assets. All data identifying a person today constitutes a real database, which typically is regularly monitored and constantly updated by the respective owners. Any type of illegal intrusion not only may damage the individual in his/her personal sphere but might also undermine the information system itself, on whose security the users have relied.

---

[377] A.PACE, *Branca Constitution Commission*, p.196 ss; F. MACIOCE, *Civil protection of the person and personal identity*, Padua, 1984, p. 7 et seq.

The multiplication of personal identity in multiple digital projections, as well as the pervasiveness of social media as privileged means of human interaction and as a tool for the development of personality, has led some scholars to speak of a "right to digital identity."[378] As emphasized above, in our legal system, the notion of "digital identity" is now distinguished from the traditional "personal identity" that includes the basic registry information related to individuals (e.g., name, date of birth) and a set of features, such as their personal characteristics and marks. However, it does not include a normative definition, lending itself to multiple meanings and interpretations. One may try to find a correct and adequate definition of this concept in Article 1 of Legislative Decree no. 82 of 2005 (the so-called Digital Administration Code). However, this definition does not seem at all satisfactory, being focused on "computer identification," which entails the validation of user data in a system for the use of digital services. The "Declaration on Freedom of Communication on the Internet,"[379] in Article 9, establishes that every person has the right to the full and updated representation of their identities on the network, the definition of which concerns the free construction of their personality and cannot be subtracted from the intervention and knowledge of the interested party. Each person also has the right to provide only data that is strictly necessary for the fulfillment of those obligations that are established by law for the supply of goods and services as well as for access to platforms operating on the internet. Finally, it is specified that the attribution and management of digital identity by public institutions must be accompanied by adequate guarantees, in particular in terms of security.

---

[378] S. RODOTÀ, *Quattro paradigmi per l'identità*, in Il diritto di avere diritti, Bari, 2012, 298-310; G. RESTA, *identità personale e identità digitale*, in Dir.Informatica, fasc.3, 2007, 511 ss.

[379] Council of Europe, Declaration on freedom of communication on the Internet (Adopted by the Committee of Ministers on 28 May 2003 at the 840th meeting of the Ministers' Deputies); Article 9 states: 1. Every person has a right to the complete and up-to-date representation of his or her identities on the Internet. 2. The definition of identity regards the free construction of personality and cannot take place without the intervention and the knowledge of the data subject. 3. The use of algorithms and probabilistic techniques shall be disclosed to the data subject who, in any case, has the right to oppose the construction and dissemination of profiles regarding him or her. 4. Every person has the right to provide only the information which is strictly necessary for complying with legal obligations, for the supply of goods and services or for accessing Internet platforms. 5. The attribution and management of digital identities by public institutions shall be governed by appropriate guarantees, especially with regard to security.

In fact, the dematerialization of the individual and the juridification of his/her identity[380] sculpt new boundaries of the person's identity with increasing force, to the point of bringing personal identity and digital identity to a level of substantial equivalence.

The novel by the Nobel Prize Luigi Pirandello, "One, No One and One Hundred Thousand,"[381] published at the beginning of the last century, anticipates the sociological profiles of personal identity in the cyberspace dimension. Even the Canadian sociologist Erving Goffman, in his work "The Presentation of Self in Everyday Life," stated that each individual's personality is not an internal quid but the sum of the numerous "masks" through which we represent ourselves in different ways, giving rise to a real "social dramaturgy." In the sociological sciences, this new dimension has been long regarded as "post-human,"[382] however, for at least a decade, the legal doctrine also portrays and registers the evidence of a progressive evolution of the human body in a sort of electronic entity.

The metaphor of the "artistic mask" used to describe the phenomenon of digital identity is perhaps the one that best summarizes such concept,[383] especially from the perspective of identity theft.[384] The image of identity as a mask comes well before the development of information technologies. However, this metaphor is strengthened through the screen. In fact, the individual contributes in the first person to writing his/her profile (or his/her many different profiles, especially on social networks[385]) and the mask is thus reinforced by a style of writing, a specific vocabulary and selected subjects.[386] This artistic mask, however, is at the same time both a representation of the person and the creation of the person's ingenuity,[387] precisely because it is both a factor of identity as well as an element external to it. It is a sort of self-

---

380 G. MARINI, *La giuridificazione della persona. Ideologie e tecniche nei diritti della personalità*, in Riv. dir. civ., 2006, 359 ss.

381 L.PIRANDELLO, *Uno nessuno e centomila*, 1926.

382 A. KROKER-M. WINSTEIN, *Data Trash*, trad.it. G. e A. Cara, Milano, 1996, XI.

383 G. RESTA, *Identità personale e identità digitale*; J. ARESTY, *Digital identity and the lawyer's role in furthering trusted online communities*, in Toledo Law Review.

384 P. CIPOLLA, *Social Network, furto d'identità e reati contro il patrimonio*, in Giur. merito., 2672B ss.; Also see S.TURKLE, *La vita sullo schermo. Nuove identità e relazioni sociali nell'epoca di Internet*, Milano, 2005, 210 ss.

385 *Ibidem.*

386 D. WISZNIEWSKI-R. COYNE, *Mask and Identity: The Hermeneutics of Self-Construction in the Information Age., Building Virtual Communities*, 2002, 191-214; S. TURKLE, *La vita sullo schermo. Nuove identità e relazioni sociali nell'epoca di Internet*, Milano, 2005, 210 ss.

387 P. SAMUELSON, *Samuelson, privacy as intellectual property?,* in Stanford Law Review, 52, 1125 ss.

portrait that deserves a double form of protection: in reference to the identity itself and to the expression of the identity provided by the person.[388] In addition, not only does the latter deserve protection against their illegal use by a third party visitor of the cyberspace but also against the provider of the online platform, who could claim the rights of intellectual property on digital products or on the elements originated by the creativity of the user[389]—that is, a claim to be avoided, just as the fact of being, even if partially, in someone else's property is to be avoided.

However, this situation is at the same time an element from which to draw an important concept: that our digital identity is—also—the creation of our intellect.

Because of these comments and reasoning, it is perhaps necessary to refer to personal data not as "identification data"—which helps to identify—but as "identity data" because they express personal identity, translating the concept of identity information coined by common law tradition.[390]

The continuous development of the internet is offering new possibilities to create multiple identities, often based on self-perception, and orienting the interactions of the subject on the basis of how he himself imagines that others (i.e., public/audience) perceive and judge him, especially in the era and field of social media platforms, where it is very likely that people, hidden behind a monitor, tend to create "false cybernetics" distant from their way of being and representing themselves in a different way from their daily life.

Parallel to the creation of multiple "masks" through which we are seen by the outside world, we are witnessing a capitalization or "ownership" of the consumer's personal data, an increasing commercial interest in the acquisition of those data, to the point of pushing the doctrine to speak of "digital gold."[391] This is the "cost" of free services on the internet[392] —and not just on the

---

[388] F. MONTALDO, *Il ritratto fotografico digitale tra diritto d'autore, diritti della persona e tutela della privacy*, Resp. civ. e prev., 2010.

[389] See also J. ARESTY, *Digital identity and the lawyer's role*, in Toledo Law Review; and S.P. CRAWFORD, *Who's in charge of who I am?*, 9 N.Y.L. Sch. L. Rev., 2004/2005, 22.

[390] J. CLOUGH, *Principles of Cybercrime*, Cambridge, 2010.

[391] P. CIPOLLA, *Social network, furto d'identità e reati contro il patrimonio*, in Giur. merito, par. 7.

[392] W.J. ROBINSON, *Free at What Cost?: Cloud Computing Privacy Under the Stored Communications Act,* in Georgetown L.J., Vol. 98, 2010, 1195.; A. MANTELERO, *Il costo della privacy tra valore della persona e ragione d'impresa,* Milano, 2007; Cfr. L.C. UBERTAZZI, *Riservatezza informatica ed industria culturale*, in AIDA, Milano,1997, 530 ss; R.S. MURPHY, *Property Rights in Personal Information: An Economic Defense of Privacy*, in 84 Geo. L.J., 1996, 2381; P. MELL, *Seeking Shade in a Land of Perpetual Sunlight: Privacy as Property in the Elecrtonic Wilderness*, in Berkeley Tech. L.J., vol. 11, 1996.

internet if we think of the recent business model experiment in Denmark in which half of the goods in a shop are free as long as you register with your own data and indicate your tastes and interests.[393]

This new concept of "digital human heritage" is divided into access keys to material assets (ATMs, credit cards, etc.), tools for commercial gain (the economic value of personal data itself), virtual domicile, the manifestation of intellectual property and tools for social relations (online): a complex projection, economically more attractive and more easily reproducible of personal identity.

Therefore, as will be seen, neither the crime against the person (in his/her identity and confidentiality), nor the crime against property, nor that of supra-individual goods (public faith, administration of justice[394]) are able to faithfully photograph the phenomenon in question. Therefore, it is necessary to rethink the current schemes of criminal protection of the digital asset, thanks also to a reorganization of the current cases' criminal acts, starting with digital identity theft.

The dematerialization of the human person, transformed into bits and projected into the virtual world, constitutes the ontological risk that digital identity might become a victim of cybernetic "predators." The various computer alter egos can be cloned when the identity of others is illegally assumed (identity theft), it can be created ad hoc with invented generalities or it can be partially "disguised" when using genuine personal data connected to other fictional data (synthetic identity theft).

It is no coincidence, therefore, that the concept of "digital identity theft" has recently been introduced in our criminal law system as an aggravating circumstance of Article 640ter.[395] This novelty ("novella") was introduced by Article 9 of Legislative Decree n. 93 of 2013, the so-called "femicide" legislative decree, converted with amendments by law no. 119 of 2013.[396] As already analyzed in previous chapters, the legislative decree in question sets as a new aggravating circumstance of computer frauds, pursuant to Article

393 C. ACCOGLI, In Danimarca c'è un negozio dove si compra senza pagare, in www.repubblica.it, (http://www.repubblica.it/tecnologia/2014/09/03/news/freemarket_in_danimarca_compri_gratis_in_cambio_di_pubblicit-94917875/).

394 P. CIPOLLA, *Social network, furto d'identità e reati contro il patrimonio*, in Gir. Merito, 2012, par. 4.

395 Article 640ter disciplines the so-called "frode informatica."

396 Law 15 October 2013, n. 119, Conversion into law, with modifications, of the decree-law 14 August 2013, n. 93, containing urgent provisions on safety and for the fight against gender-based violence, as well as on civil protection and the commissioner of the provinces (13G00163) (GU n.242 of 15-10-2013).

640ter of the Criminal Code, that the fact is committed with the theft or improper use of a person's digital identity. The manifest purpose of this new rule was to fill a legislative void denounced by several parties,[397] also considering the increasing spread of the use of social networks (unknown to the legislator in 1993 as well as in part also to that of 2008) and new forms of cybercrimes[398] that go beyond the classic phishing phenomenon.

That this is an aggravating circumstance is demonstrated by paragraph four, which states that the crime is punishable upon complaint by the injured person unless one of the circumstances referred to in the second and third paragraphs or another aggravating circumstance occurs, thus implying that the circumstances referred to in the second and third paragraphs are aggravating with special effects.[399]

Therefore, based on the genus-species principle, which links the general hypothesis to the aggravating ones, it must be concluded that the theft or improper use of digital identity is a specification of an element of the case, namely the conduct.[400] It is therefore necessary to analyze the terms in which the common hypothesis takes place and then evaluate the consequences in terms of the protection of digital identity to intervene in any way on data, information or programs.[401] As will be seen, the case in point places strong

---

397 Communication from the European Commission "Towards a general policy of combating cybercrime "(COM (2007) 267); Digital Agenda for Europe, (COM (2010) 245). The IX Commission of the Chamber of Deputies (DOC XVII, n. 26, of 22 January 2013), argued that "in order to effectively combat digital identity theft, in addition to preventive measures , it appears necessary to equip institutions with adequate regulatory tools, introducing the crime of digital identity theft into the law, providing for adequate criminal sanctions." Furthermore, in the session of 19 September 2012, the director of the Postal and Communications Police service had stated that "Digital identity theft today does not have a specific regulatory provision in Italy: it would be appropriate to give autonomous legislative configurations from this point of view> >.
See Dossier of the Senate Studies Service on the A.S. n. 1079, October 2013, n. 64, 102. See also A. DEL NINNO, *Il furto d'identità, in Trattato sui nuovi danni*, Vol. V, a cura di P. Cendon, Padova, 2011, 940; R. BARTOLI, *La frode informatica tra modellistica, diritto vigente, diritto vivente e prospettive di riforma*, in Dir.Inf., fasc.3, 2011, 383 ss; C. PECORELLA, *Diritto penale dell'informatica, , II ed., Padova, 2006.*
II ed., Padova, 2006, 277 ss. Als; Cass, section V, 29 April 2013, n. 18826, C., in Cass. pen., 2014, 146 et seq. with note by G. STAMPANONI BASSI.

398 See J. CLOUGH, *Principles of Cybercrime*, Cambridge, 2010.

399 A. DI TULLIO D'ELISIIS, *Frode informatica commessa con sostituzione d'identità digitale: i profili applicativi*, in Altalex,; L. PISTORELLI, Relazione n. III/03/2013 del 16/10/13, consultabile su www.dirittopenalecontemporaneo.it, 6-7.

400 T. PADOVANI, *Diritto Penale*, X ed., Milano, 2012, 252-253.

401 A. DELLO IACOVO, *Articolo 640 ter: truffa o furto?, La frode informatica e il modello 640,* 1996, 597. For a specific analysis of the individual elements proposed by the various sanctioned hypotheses, see. C. PECORELLA, *Diritto Penale dell'informatica*, cit., 61 ss.

limits on the full protection of digital identity.[402] A first limitation can be seen in the description of the sanctioned conduct in the case of computer fraud. The improper use of data cannot alone integrate the crime of computer fraud, requiring a modifying "intervention" on the data structure and therefore, at least, an illicit transfer of money from one asset to the other.

Following this approach, we should conclude that the theft or undue use of digital identity (as illicit use of data) can only constitute instrumental factors to the realization of the "typical fact" ("fatto tipico"), therefore those human conducts, events and causal links that binds the conduct to the event.

In reality, the formulated rule protects digital identity at least in cases in which it is "stolen" or improperly used through a hacking action, the latter falling within the alteration of the functioning of a telematics system or in any case in an intervention without rights on data, information or programs.[403]

Given the syntactic formulation of the law, there seems to be no doubt that the profit is to be considered as the main object of the conduct governed by the law—that is to say, the conduct of procuring, and not as a mere accidental or closing element. This is also confirmed by the fact that the legal asset protected by the crime of computer fraud is undoubtedly that of economic assets.[404] This is also evident from its placement Title XIII of Book II, among crimes against property. Therefore, in other words, the crime of computer fraud in its aggravated manifestation does protect digital identity, but it only protects it from a patrimonial point of view. This specification therefore demonstrates how it cannot be separated from an economic impoverishment of the victim for the benefit of the offender. Therefore, it is necessary to find alternative options in criminal law in order to protect digital identity in its multiform heterogenesis of values.[405] In this regard, it is possible to compare the rule in question with the other criminal provisions that sanction conducts similar to that of digital identity replacement in order to find effective solutions in search of adequate protection for new forms of digital identity theft that are not strictly patrimonial.

---

[402] A. DI TULLIO D'ELISIIS, *Frode informatica commessa con sostituzione d'identità digitale: i profili applicativi,* in Altalex.

[403] C. PECORELLA, Diritto penale dell'informatica, II ed., Padova, 2006, p. 82-83; P. CIPOLLA, *Social network, furto d'identità e reati contro il patrimonio,* cit., par. 4.

[404] A. DELLO IACOVO, *Articolo 640-ter: truffa o furto?,* cit., 597; G. PICA, *Diritto penale delle tecnologie informatiche*, Torino, 1999, 154-156.

[405] G. MALGIERI, *Il furto di "identità digitale": una tutela patrimoniale della personalità*, in R.FLOR-D.FALCINELLI-S.MARCOLINI, *La giustizia penale nella "rete," Le nuove sfide della società dell'informazione nell'epoca di Internet*, Perugia, 2014 p. 37 ss.

Firstly, an adequate solution could be to extend the discipline of impersonation pursuant to Article 494 of the Criminal Code. This rule does not provide for the realization of a damage and a profit but only the specific willful misconduct of damage or "advantage." The reason for the lack of "damage" among the requirements of the case in point can be inferred from the placement of this crime among those against "public faith," an asset that is already damaged when one or more subjects are misled, without the need to further demonstrate the offensiveness of the fact, if not in the criminal will of the agent (for which the specific intent).[406] In sentence no. 12479 of 12/15/11, the "Ermellini" have precisely established that the crime of impersonation, pursuant to Article 494 of the Criminal Code, is integrated by the conduct of the person who creates and uses an email account falsely attributing the personal details of a different subject, misleading the users of the internet, against whom the false personal details are declined and with the aim of causing damage to the person whose personal details have been illegally spent. In addition, in sentence no. 46674 of 8/11/07, the Supreme Council likewise noted that the crime of impersonation is perfected by the conduct of the person who creates and uses an email account falsely attributing to him/herself the personal details of a different subject, misleading the users of the internet, against whom the false personal details are declined, with the aim of causing damage to the subject whose personal details have been illegally spent, subtly included in a correspondence suitable to harm image and dignity. Alternatively, even part of the doctrine has recognized this phenomenon in terms of the replacement of a digital person consisting precisely in the creation of another "digital identity."[407]

However, a difficulty arose immediately in extending the scope of application of the case of impersonation for the protection of digital identity. These difficulties can be clearly seen in the judgment of the Court of Cassation, Section V, no. 18826 of November 28 2012, which states the opportunity to adopt "organic legislative measures" in order to adapt the scope of the traditional case to the new forms of online aggression of the assets subject to protection. Despite this, the legitimacy of the extensive interpretation of the case referred to in Article 494 of the Criminal Code is

---

406 See C. FLICK, *Falsa identità su internet e tutela penale della fede pubblica degli utenti e della persona,* Dir. informatica, fasc.4-5, 2008, par. 2; R. CAPPITELLI, *La sostituzione di persona nel diritto penale italiano*, nota a Cass. sez. V, 26 febbraio 2004, n. 8670, in Cass. Pen., 2005, 1269, 2993 ss.; A.PAGLIARO, *Falsità personale*, voce Enciclopedia del diritto, XVI, 646 ss.

407 P. Cipolla, "*Social network, furto di identità e reati contro il patrimonio,*" in Giur. merito 2012, 12, 2672.

reaffirmed. In this regard, we can understand the reason for this interpretation without violating the principles of analogy in malam partem as the impossibility for the legislator of the time to foresee the memorable revolution induced by information technology, therefore, tracing the attacks to digital identity under the protective hat of Article 2 of the Constitution.

Hence, from this we can see how the reaction and contrast mechanism developed by the jurisprudence, which extended the scope of the crime of impersonation in order to protect digital identity, does not seem entirely satisfactory to protect the new forms of aggression against identity in its virtual dimension. The sanctioning treatment provided for by Article 494 of the Criminal Code (up to one year of imprisonment) does not understand the seriousness of the consequences suffered by the victims and therefore by default is disproportionate compared to the aggression of the "new" legal asset to be protected. The crime in question, being placed in the title relating to "Crimes against public faith," is mainly focused on the protection of third parties who fall into error and not on the protection of those who are stripped of their identity projected into cyberspace. The littera legis expressly provides for the conduct of anyone misleading someone, supported by specific intent to procure an advantage for oneself or others or to harm others; consequently, the dispossessed of digital identity remains in limbo awaiting recognition.

Another rule that we can consider as a launch pad in seeking alternative solutions to the protection of the conduct of digital identity theft is Article 167 of the privacy code, which sanctions the unlawful processing of data. It is noted that it, too, requires the same specific intent of damage or advantage, but in addition, it also requires the occurrence of a "harm," the latter being interpreted as an objective condition of intrinsic punishment and not as a constitutive element of the case.[408]

Furthermore, it should not be overlooked that this is the only criminal law that explicitly protects the legal good of "personal identity"; therefore, the requirements for verifying the typical fact are particularly related to this object

---

[408] Cass., Section III, 9 July 2004, n. 30134, G.Dir, 2004, n. 35, 67; Cass., Section III, February 17, 2011, rv. 249991, most recently Court of Cassation, section II, 24 May 2012, n. 23798, in Law & Justice, fasc. 0, 2012, 487, with a note by A. FERRETTI. Doctrine See L. MANNA, Comment on Legislative Decree 196/03, DPP, 2004, 17; V. DESTITO, *Tutela dei dati personali,* Digesto Online, 2008 which have interpreted the harm as an objective condition of punishment since the presence of the specific intent of profit "or" of damage would not be explained if the damage itself were a constitutive part of the case, moreover, if this were not the case, the harm would have to fall within the subjective representation, even if only the specific fraud of "profit" is necessary (and not also of damage, given the presence of a disjunctive). Of contrary opinion D. IELO, V. SAPONARA, in AA.VV., *Codice della Privacy*, II, Milano, 2004, 710 ss.

of protection and should be taken as a model for a possible future standard that deals with protecting digital identity.[409]

From this analysis, we can therefore examine even more deeply how computer fraud is the only rule among all those analyzed so far that protects (thanks to the new aggravating circumstance of identity substitution) the digital personal identity from a patrimonial perspective, and therefore it cannot disregard the concrete demonstration of the economic shift from victim to offender. However, it is a question of assessing the terms in which the "damage" and "unfair profit" are actually obstacles to a "pure" protection of digital identity (that is, not a substitute for economic issues) and whether there is therefore room for an interpretation—not merely patrimonial—of these two elements.

The case of computer fraud, as formulated, seems to leave room for broad interpretations of the concepts of damage and profit; however, this must not leave the field to arbitrary manipulative interpretations, but rather a greater effort is needed in bringing the constituent elements in question to determination and consistency.

It must be emphasized that Article 640ter of the Criminal Code is the only one on the international scene to use these broad terms in a rule that has the purpose of protecting the victim's assets.[410] In fact, the German penal code at §263a expresses itself in these terms: "anyone with the intention of procuring an unfair financial advantage damages the assets of others." In addition to the peculiarity of introducing the advantage as a mere element of specific intent, one cannot help but note the explicit reference to the patrimony in the legal rule.[411] The provisions stated in Article 386A of the Greek Penal Code[412] are quite similar. Also very similar is §148a of the Austrian penal code, which speaks of "unjust enrichment" and "damage to the patrimony of others,"[413] as well as the Portuguese one, which differs only in the expression "illicit enrichment."[414] The Spanish penal code in Article 248 (estafa via

---

[409] G. MALGIERI, *Il furto di "identità digitale": una tutela patrimoniale della personalità*, in R.FLOR-D.FALCINELLI-S.MARCOLINI, *La giustizia penale nella "rete," Le nuove sfide della società dell'informazione nell'epoca di Internet*, Perugia, 2014 p. 37 ss.

[410] C. PECORELLA, *Diritto Penale dell'Informatica*, 64 ss.

[411] K.TIEDMANN, *Strafgesetzbuch. Leipziger Kommentar*, XI ed., Berlin, 1998, sub § 263a.

[412] E. VASSILAKI, *Computer Crimes and Other Crimes against Information Technology in Greece*, in Rev.Int.dr.pén. (vol.64), 1993, 367 ss.

[413] G.F. SEILER, *Kritische Anmerkungen zum StrÄG 1987 den Besonderen Teil des StGB*, in KBkm 1989m 751 ss.

[414] J. FIGUEREDO DIAS, *Introduzione al codice penale portoghese* (transaltion by G. Torre), Padova, 1997.

procedimentos informaticos) refers to a "profit purpose,"[415] and the Swiss penal code explicitly speaks of a "transfer of assets."[416] In contrast, it should be noted that the French criminal code does not place computer frauds among the crimes against heritage/patrimony,[417] but against "assets" (and specifically among "damage to automated data processing systems"[418]). This rule, in fact, is similar to our "unauthorized access to a computer system" (Article 615ter of the Italian Criminal Code).[419]

It should be specified that the expressions mentioned in the foreign penal codes mentioned above are not frequent in Title XIII of the Italian criminal code, whereas the expressions "profit" and "damage" with asset value are always used. Specifically, the word "profit" occurs in almost all crimes against property, and the word damage is not infrequent when the pecuniary damage is not already an implicit requirement in the case. The jurisprudence is unanimous in considering the "damage" in financial terms only, while it is more flexible on the meaning of profit.[420] Regarding the undue profit with the damage of others,[421] the damage must therefore explicitly involve a deminutio patrimonii for the victim.[422] Excluding isolated cases,[423] the doctrine also stresses that the damage must always be economically appreciable since it cannot include strictly personal or moral benefits—to the point that it has been stated that even the transfer of an asset with only personal or emotional value

---

415 T.S. VIVES ANTON, J.L. GONZALES CUSSAC, in AA.VV., Comenta*rios al Còdigo Penal de 1995*, vol II, Valencia, 1996, sub. art. 248.

416 N. SCHMID, *Computer-sowie Check und Kreditkarten-Kriminalität*, Zurigo, 1994, 215 ss.

417 Loi n° 88-19 du 5 janvier 1988 relative à la fraude informatique, oggi Article 323-1 code pénal, "Le fait d'accéder ou de se maintenir, frauduleusement, dans tout ou partie d'un système de traitement automatisé de données est puni de deux ans d'emprisonnement et de 30000 euros d'amende. Lorsqu'il en est résulté soit la suppression ou la modification de données contenues dans le système, soit une altération du fonctionnement de ce système, la peine est de trois ans d'emprisonnement et de 45000 euros d'amende."

418 Livre III, Titre II, Chapitre III, "Des atteintes aux systèmes de traitement automatisé de données.

419 L.SAENKO, *Le nouveau délit d'usurpation d'identité numérique*: RLDI juin 2011, n° 72, 63 ss.

420 G. PICA, Diritto penale delle tecnologie informatiche, cit., 148 ss.

421 Cass., sez. III, 2 maggio 2012, n. 23798, in Guida dir., 2012, 38, 81; Cass. pen. sez. II, 11.11.09,
Gabbriellini, rv. 245696.; Cass., sez. VI, 4.10.99, De Vecchis, Rv. 214942; conf. Cass., sez. V, 24.11.03, Rv. 227459.

422 Cass., Section II, April 3, 1986, in Cass. Pen., 1987, 2137; Cass., Section V, September 20, 1989, in Giust.pen., 1990, II, 438 for which "the damage must have a patrimonial content, that is, it must materialize in a detriment of the patrimony." Similarly Cass., Section II, 05-03-2008, n. 10085, rv. 239508.

423 A. DI TULLIO D'ELISIIS, *Frode informatica commessa con sostituzione d'identità digitale: i profili applicativi,* in Altalex, whom states that the "damage" can also be non-pecuniary.

for the victim cannot integrate the damage required for the existence of the crime.[424] As for "unfair profit," however, the situation is very different. In fact, despite the fact that the 1930s legislator aimed (for the scam) at an idea of profit that was totally patrimonial, jurisprudence has always interpreted the concept of "profit" in a broader sense, including in it any utility, even of a non-patrimonial nature, pushing up to only psychological or moral advantages.

In fact, the crime against assets is expressed in a detriment to the victim's assets but not necessarily in a tradition, that is, in an operation of perfect transfer from one asset to another.[425]

From this analysis, it can be deduced that digital identity theft today no longer needs to be analyzed from an exclusively patrimonial point of view as in this way we would risk finding ourselves faced with a protection gap, especially when one considers cases in which the offender acts with a direct aim only to steal the victim's trust and to alter or even destroy the perception that others have of him/her.

3. Digital Identity Theft Affecting Intangible Personal Assets

As already seen in the analysis concerning cyber security and particularly identity theft, the new forms of technological violence mostly involve intangible properties, meaning those valuable non-material personal assets, such as a good reputation, and those individual properties commonly known as "soft assets," which include the skills, ideas or knowledge that a career or a business depends on to be successful. Intangible properties, therefore, differ from tangible properties, which describe a physical asset whose value can be easily measured, such as cash, property, goods or machinery.

The methods and outcomes of illegal actions committed by technological means may involve violent circumstances that often characterize digitally perpetrated crimes, making them much more dangerous than expected or envisaged.

To the extreme, if it is possible to defend against or escape from an attacker, it is difficult to escape the illicit dissemination of a photograph or video that violates the intimacy of the represented subject. As well, it is much more difficult to prevent an act of terrorism organized by the use of the internet's "dark zones."

---

[424] G. PICA, *Diritto penale delle tecnologie informatiche*, p. 154 ss.
[425] Criminal Cassation court at SS.UU., 29.9.11, Rossi, rv. 251499.

As discussed in previous chapters, besides traditional cybercrimes directed against tangible assets, there are also a variety of criminal offenses that may involve an individual's intangible assets. Therefore, in this regard, cybercrimes may also involve actions directed at harming a person, not in their partisan sphere but in their moral and relational sphere, as in cases of cyberbullying, cyberstalking or revenge porn as well as actions directed at harming the civil society or a nation, as in the case of terrorist acts that can be organized by the auxiliary use of the identity theft.

3.1. Cyberbullying

With the entry into force of Law No. 71/2017 containing two provisions for the protection of minors for the prevention and contrast of the phenomenon of cyberbullying, a new case, defined as "non-case," commonly known as "cyberbullying," was introduced into our legal system. This normative intervention has responded to the urgent and unfailing need to provide effective instruments of protection against widespread conduct accompanied by an increasing social alarm.

In the analysis of this new case history, it seems useful to start from an examination of its etymology. The term "bullying" generally indicates the implementation of intimidating or oppressive behaviors carried out in order to frighten another person and abuse him. The term "cyberbullying" comes from the fusion of the verb "to bully" and "cyberspace" which, as we have seen, is nothing but the virtual space where this phenomenon can occur. Cyberbullying is therefore a variant of the classic form of bullying capable of spreading through the network with extreme ease and in a seriously invasive way.

Cyberbullying[426] is nothing but a phenomenon that is spreading exponentially especially in the Western world involving many minors. According to the definition proposed in 2006 by Peter Smith together with other English-speaking jurists, cyberbullying indicates a form of voluntary and repeated abuse, implemented through an electronic text, made against an individual or a group with the aim of hurting and making uncomfortable the victim of such behavior who is unable to defend himself.

Prior to the introduction of the 2017 novella, there was no legislative definition of bullying or its possible digital variant in our system. Nor was

[426] Equivalent expressions such as "online bullying," "electronic bullying" or "internet bullying" can be found.

there any specific legislation against such conduct. However, the rapid access to instant messaging tools and social networks, the lack of awareness of the scope and consequences of the offense when it occurs online, as well as the amplification of the injury due to the peculiarity of the medium by which the action is carried out have imposed a regulatory intervention that provided for integrated actions. In fact, the use of the computer tool generally blurs the perception of reality and the anonymity that the author believes to enjoy, thus making cyberbullies more fearless and overbearing, as they are sure of their impunity. The perception of the gesture is loose as it is filtered by the screen, which prevents any empathic realization with the victim.[427]

A technical-juridical definition of the term cyberbullying has been provided by the legislator in the law n. 71/2007 containing provisions for the protection of minors for the prevention and contrast of the phenomenon of cyberbullying. Article 1 paragraph 2 of this law states that "cyberbullying" means any form of pressure, aggression, harassment, blackmail, insult, denigration, defamation, identity theft, alteration, illegal acquisition, manipulation, illegal processing of personal data against minors, carried out electronically, as well as the dissemination of online content relating to one or more members of the child's family whose intentional and predominant purpose is to isolate a child or a group of children by enacting a serious abuse, harmful attack, or ridicule them.[428]

Regardless of the possible initiation of criminal proceedings, the legislature intended to give specific protection to the victims of cyberbullying through the provision of an instrument aimed at quickly erase the tangible consequences of the phenomenon, removing the offensive material posted online. This is a novelty that demonstrates the will of the legal system to intervene urgently to protect the dignity and reputation of the child.[429] The victim of cyberbullying - who is at least 14 years old - and the parents or those who exercise responsibility for the child, may submit to the data controller or manager of the website or social media a request to obscure, remove or block any other personal data of the child, spread on the Internet. If this does not happen within 48 hours, the interested party may apply to the Privacy Guarantor who will intervene directly within the following 48 hours. The

---

427 FRIGENI, *Bullismo e aspetti processuali*, in PENNETTA, *la responsabilità giuridica di atti di bullismo*, Torino, 2014, p. 109 ss.

428 Article 1 paragraph 2, Law no. 71 on "Provisions for the protection of minors for the prevention and contrast of the phenomenon of cyberbullying."

429 M.C.PARMIGGIANI, *Il cyberbullismo*, in A.CADOPPI-S.CANESTRARI-A.MANNA-M.PAPA, *Cybercrime,* 2019, p. 642 ss.

person responsible for the site or the owner of the treatment can present a request for removal even after having kept the original data, even if the conduct does not constitute a crime.[430] The request for removal may be made after retaining the original data, in order to ensure those requirements of an evidentiary nature. In addition, a contact person for initiatives against cyberbullying will be identified in each school. The school manager will immediately inform the families of minors involved in acts of bullying and, if necessary, will convene all stakeholders to take measures to assist the victim and sanctioning and rehabilitation paths for the offender. The Ministry of Education has the task of preparing guidelines for the prevention and contrast, focusing, among other things, on the training of school staff and the promotion of an active role of students, while individual institutions are entrusted with the education to legality and conscious use of the Internet.

With the introduction of the new law, the legislator has therefore created a system that is not so much punitive as preventive. It implements an inclusive and educational intervention plan, in the awareness that an effective action against cyberbullying can only pass through a large-scale consideration of the phenomenon.

Cyberbullying is a specific case of non-intentionality. It requires a particular purpose or intent on the part of the agent, i.e., an intentional and predominant purpose to isolate the subject, typically a minor or group of minors, by enacting serious abuse,[431] a harmful attack[432] or their ridicule.[433] t is therefore necessary that the author's volitional spectrum includes the representation of one of the three typical events contemplated in the normative definition as a consequence of the conduct. The provision of specific intent

---

430 ZORZINI, *Cyberbullismo e reclamo al Garante per la Privacy*, in www.personaedanno.it.

431 In this case, the “serious abuse” ask by the case in point, must be understood as a non-physical, but psychological and functional abuse of harming a subject electronically. The qualification of the type of abuse perpetrated is doubtful, which according to the dictates of the law must be "serious," because it would seem paradoxical to think of the existence of abuses not qualified as "serious."

432 With reference to the event of the “harmful attack,” the Legislator intended to evoke an assessment of the suitability of the conduct to "attack" the minor not only on the basis of subjective parameters, but also taking into account objective considerations, in terms of effectiveness.

433 This requirement extends the sphere of application of the law to those conducts of prevarication which, if they do not constitute a serious abuse or a harmful attack, in any case heavily affect the quality of the social life and mental well-being of the victim. See SELLAROLI, *Il nuovo reato di cyberbullismo, l. 29 maggio 2017, n. 71*; in Il penalista, Milano, 2017, p. 30 ss.

therefore implies that conduct that does not assume this specific purpose of isolation must be excluded from the application of the law.[434]

The new legislation, as previously noted, does not introduce ex novo a new crime. The choice of the legislator with the introduction of this new criminal conduct was in fact that of not providing for a specific penalty, thus giving rise to a so-called "non-existent circumstance" (non-factispecies). Analysing this case, its objective element is integrated by the implementation of one or more behaviours listed by the legislator, in a clear attempt to include any means of implementation. In most cases, the behaviors described constitute already existing crimes or, otherwise, facts that are not criminally relevant, if considered individually. Ultimately, therefore, the description of the ways of implementation of the phenomenon of cyberbullying includes multiple behaviors, explained through the use of various terminology and characterized by the psychological element that has the form of specific malicious intent.[435]

As we can see, Cyberbullying can be easily implemented through behaviors attributable to identity theft. Behaviors better known as "masquerading." In these cases, the aggressor replaces the real person by creating an internet profile with a fictitious identity using personal information, photos and access data, such as passwords and usernames, related

---

[434] M.C.PARMIGGIANI, *Il cyberbullismo*, in A.CADOPPI-S.CANESTRARI-A.MANNA-M.PAPA, *Cybercrime,* 2019, p. 642 ss.

[435] Some of the behaviors that may integrate the objective element of cyberbullying are harassment; injury; defamation; blackmail and so on. Article 660 of the Italian Criminal Code, sanctions the conduct of who publicly harasses or disturbs an individual. In its IT form, this scope is achieved for example by sending two text messages with offensive content. These offensive messages must pose the victim in a condition of severe discomfort and must alter the normal conditions of his personal and family tranquility. The Cassation has also clarified that for the purpose of better sanctioning this crime in its It form, Facebook is to be considered a public area. Therefore, posting offensive messages on the public pages of individuals will integrate the above-mentioned sanction.
Another conduct by which cyberbullying can be carried out is that of obloquy or defamation. In its telematics aspect, the conduct of obloquy may consist in sending violent, vulgar and offensive messages within a chat where the victim is present. This conduct can be particularly afflictive if it is carried out frequently or by several subjects at the same time. Defamation instead is generally integrated when the offense occurs through a communication addressed to several people. According to case law, the dissemination of a defamatory message through the use of a Facebook page integrates an hypothesis of an aggravated defamation as it is a conduct potentially capable of reaching an undetermined number of people.
Finally, even blackmail can be considered a conduct through which cyberbullying can be committed. In such specific case, the content of the intimidation, typical of blackmail, will not be money, but rather a sexual type of service or conduct. Such intimidation is primarily aimed at determining a state of discomfort or affliction in the offended person.

to someone's account, in order to send messages or publish questionable content to damage the image and reputation of the victim. In fact, this conduct is primarily aimed at damaging the reputation of the person whose identity is stolen.

It is extremely complex to find a real form of protection and prevention of the phenomenon. This is because in the eyes of the aggressor has many positive aspects.

Typical of bullies is their ability to cover up who they really are, which makes it difficult to catch them. They develop stories and are able to deceive their victims through the use of different identities, which are often stolen. Therefore, more often than not, victims do not know or recognize the identity of the bullies. In this regard, it is important to note that there are at least two victims in this masquerade: the person committing the act but also the person they choose to represent.

Examples of digital identity theft used to realize the phenomenon of cyberbullying can be, for example, the case in which a person takes possession of the passwords of others thus entering the profile of the victim or even the case in which false accounts are created by third parties to make fun of the victim.

A typical example of cyberbullying through digital identity theft, mainly studied by the US discipline, is the phenomenon of "Catfishing." The term catfishing is still a foreign work for many online users. Catfish is commonly defined as "a person who creates a false personal profile on a social networking site for fraudulent or deceptive purposes."[436]

Online impersonation can be committed through the methods of phishing and catfishing, both of which involve a perpetrator pretending to be someone else. Typically, in phishing, the perpetrator lures victims through fake websites, emails and phone calls, with the goal of stealing their sensitive personal data and information, including online banking passwords or social security numbers, which are used to exploit the victims financially. "Catfish" describes the act of creating fake online profiles by portraying someone else's identity.[437]

It is a growing social illicit phenomenon of constructing a false virtual identity using fake or stolen data and images in order to deceive people or perform online scams.[438] It is a practice used to lure victims, in many cases

---

436 Catfish: In Merriam-Webster.com Dictionary.

437 M.SIMMONS-J.S.LEE, Catfishing: A Look into Online Dating and Impersonation, 2020.

438 See L.REICHART SMITH-K.D.SMITH-M.BLAZKA, *Follow Me, What's the Harm? Considerations of Catfishing and Utilizing Fake Online Personas on Social Media*, in

minors, online, arrange meetings with adults, establish dishonest relationships, but also defame other people, up to real blackmail and scams, with the sale of products of any kind that are never delivered. The list of illegal actions committed by catfishing is very long.

The reasons that lead individuals to choose false identities in order to relate with users on the web can be sought in problems of insecurity, low self-esteem or psychological distress. In this case, pretending to be someone else or showing photos of a more attractive person helps them to overcome fears and anxieties and to approach others in a different way, even if incorrectly. Those who resort to catfishing leverage on the vulnerability and fragility of victims, to engage in relationships, take revenge on partners or acquaintances, spoil their cries and humiliate them. In addition, posing as other individuals is the most common method used by sexual predators and pedophiles to connect with adolescents.

Catfishing is often used to hide one's true identity in order to extort money or commit other crimes, such as defamation, stalking up to revenge porn.

3.2. The Crime of Persecutory Acts Ex Article 612*bis* of the Italian Criminal Code

The crime of "persecutory acts," contemplated by Article 612 bis of the Italian Penal Code, was introduced in Chapter III of Title XII, Part II of the said Penal Code, in the section relating to "crimes against moral freedom," by Law 38/2009. This crime was introduced mainly to sanction those harassing or threatening behaviors, which put the victim in a serious state of physical and mental discomfort, of real subjection. Such behaviours are therefore put in place in order to determine a justified fear for the safety of the victim or for the safety of a person particularly close to the latter and that can also be prodromal to serious acts of aggression. If the protection of moral freedom - understood as the faculty of self-determination of the subject - is the primary objective of the right, it must be considered that with it is protected the further legal good of individual security. At least when the threats or the persistent and serious state of anxiety or fear, which, if understood as a pathology medically ascertainable, involves the injury of the good health.[439] Not only

Journal of Legal Aspects of Sport, 2017; p. 33-34; Y.F PAAT-C.MARKHAM, *Digital crime, trauma, and abuse: Internet safety and cyber risks for adolescents and emerging adults in the 21st century.* Social Work in Mental Health 2021 pages 18-40.

[439] See A.BARBAZZA-E.GAZZETTA, *Il nuovo reato di atti persecutori* in www.altalex.it.

that, it has also been argued that this new crime also aims to protect the "psychological serenity" as well as the privacy of the individual.[440]

The case referred to in Article 612bis of the Criminal Code provides for three events caused by the harasser. These events are: the creation of a persistent and serious state of anxiety or fear; the generation of a well-founded fear for one's own safety or that of a close relative or a person linked to him by an emotional relationship or the obligation to change one's habits of life.

To understand the conduct exercised we must first understand the general meaning of what constitutes a threat. In general, a threat is a limitation of the psychic freedom of an individual by any means. It is an external manifestation that, for the purpose of intimidation, represents in any form to the passive subject the danger of an unjust evil, which is "contra ius," which in the more or less near future may be caused by the perpetrator or others for him in the person or property.[441] We are faced with a habitual crime for the existence of which a plurality of conducts of a similar nature is required, consisting in repeated harassment or threats productive of the three typified events that affect the psychic sphere or the habits of life of the offended person. With reference to the concept of threat, it should be considered the doctrinal and jurisprudential elaboration concerning the crime of threat referred to in Article 612. Moreover, the threat as a means of coercion in the crimes of private violence and sexual violence. In these circumstances, "threat" means the prospect of hostile action by the agent. As far as "harassing conduct" is concerned, it is, on the other hand, necessary to refer to the jurisprudence of the Court of Cassation on the crime referred to in art. 660 c.p. in which the concept of harassment has been identified with the disturbance or interference in the private life or relations of others.

The legislator has deliberately described the conduct in very broad terms, using general concepts that constitute the common heritage of the penal system. This is a "typification" more apparent than real of such conduct, since both harassment and threats can occur in the most disparate forms. Forms that in practice could not be provided for and described by the legislator, who has thus focused his attention on the consequences of such conduct. A crime, therefore, substantially free-form, characterized in particular by the necessary repetition of such conduct and above all by being structured as a so-called event crime. It is precisely the description of these possible alternative events that poses the most problematic profiles for the interpretation of the regulation.

---

440 A.CADOPPI, *Efficace la misura dell'ammonimento del questore*, in Guida al Diritto, 10/2009, 52.

441 Cass. Sez. V, 23 aprile 1986 (dep. 12 agosto 1986) n.8275, CED 173578.

The crime referred to in art. 612bis does not derive sic et simpliciter from the sum of the crimes referred to in art. 612 c.p. and in art. 660 of the same code. A peculiar characteristic of the crime of persecutory acts is in fact the provision of the necessary repetition of the individual conducts. The regulation does not specify the frequency with which the repetition must occur, nor the time frame within which the conduct must be repeated. Therefore, it can be excluded that the crime set forth in art. 612-bis c.p. falls within the category of the so-called complex crimes.

The crime in question can be defined as a case of generic intentional crime (malicious intent), in which a particular purpose or intention of the agent is not required, but only the consciousness and will of the "typical material fact."

We have introduced the analysis of this crime just because also in this case all the instruments of telematic communication, in the most varied forms, can vehiculate both typologies of conduct with particular effectiveness, easily allowing forms of repetition.

3.3. Cyberstalking

With the coming into force of the law 38/2009 containing urgent measures in matter of public security and contrast to sexual violence, as well as in matter of persecutory acts, the phenomenon of stalking has been finally and specifically taken into consideration. Stalking is not an obsessive manifestation typical of our times, a bitter consequence of a distortion of emotional relationships, of the affirmation of a psychotic virulence of interpersonal relationships. This phenomenon has always been present in our history as we can see in Manzoni's "Promessi Sposi" (The Betrothed) where the act of stalking is contemplated with the figure of Don Rodrigo who in this case is a stalker. Also in the Odyssey we have the configuration of this phenomenon with Penelope and her suitors - the so-called "proci." This may be enough to convey the idea of the "antiquity" of the phenomenon.[442]

On a strictly lexical level, the Anglo-Saxon term to "stalk" can be translated as "hunting," "stealthy hunting," or "approaching stealthily."

The stalker would then be the hunter in ambush, studying and waiting for his prey under cover. In many cases, he lurks and pursues his victim openly, letting his cumbersome presence "weigh" on the victim's life. A presence that

---

[442] C.PARODI, *La tutela della persona nella realtà telematica: revenge porn e cyberstalking*, p. 7, in www.magistraturaindipendente.it.

is certainly destined to become, in the intentions of the stalker a real interference in the private life of the victim and as such become a source of distress, even before a direct form of contact between "hunter" and "hunted."

An attempt to understand this phenomenon can only begin with a quick examination of the phenomenology of the perpetrator of the conduct. A basic tripartition is conceivable, being understood that the highlighted categories can well coincide or overlap at least in part. Undoubtedly the stalker can be identified with a subject affected by mental disorders, for whom the persecutory attitude originates from the belief to have a relationship with the other person. In such situations, stalking represents the manifestation of a predefined pathology and finds its origin in it. A second perspective concerns subjects who live in terms of personal discomfort within a "physiological" state. These are subjects with problems of social interaction, for whom the obsessive persecutory activity becomes the primary way to establish an interpersonal relationship with third parties, imposing their presence and insisting even in the face of unequivocally negative responses. In these first two situations, given the circumstances, the stalker is generally a stranger to the harassed subject, or at least the "owner" of a relationship that is not particularly qualified. In the third case, most likely, the harasser may be the victim's ex-spouse, ex-partner or otherwise an acquaintance or colleague.[443]

The diffusion of electronic communications, the possibility of being "present" in the lives of others in a manner as constant as anonymous, has favored the exponential growth and therefore the exponential "damage" resulting from this phenomenon. Following the entry into force of Legislative Decree 93 of 2013, the second paragraph of the article in question provides for the tightening of the penalty in case of harassment or threats persecutory committed through computer or telematic tools, criminalizing also the so-called Cyberstalking.

Today is widespread and alarming the phenomenon of cyber stalking, which manifests itself when the obsessive attentions of the stalker find space via computer in the most disparate forms. From the obtuse and repeated sending of e-mails to the publications on sites or areas shared by other subjects of data and information about the victim, to forms of abusive computer access in the computer of the "attacked," up to the fraudulent appropriation of the account of the victim and of the identification data of this last one, the telematic stalker has, inevitably, sociological and characterial characteristics

---

[443] *Ibidem.*

different from the common stalker. He tends to reveal himself by hand, but he is probably more constant and maniacal in his behavior.

The rationale of this aggravating circumstance resides in the greater social disvalue of the harassing or threatening action, committed with instruments that make much easier the contact with the victim wherever he is. Not only the passive subject feels the presence of the stalker in a ubiquitous way, but it is also impossible to get rid of him given the multiplicity of means through which it is possible to perpetrate the crime.

Identity theft may constitute a non-secondary element in the determinism of the events described in Article 612bis of the Criminal Code. In reality, the crime of identity theft is not contemplated, at least with this meaning, by our legal system, even though the phenomenon is particularly widespread and equally particularly perceived at a general level.[444] The phenomenon in question occurs in particular in the context of social networks, however, as a result of several factors, this undoubtedly due to inadequate methods of custody of authentication credentials of users, both in the face of an autonomous will to create false accounts by third parties. This second hypothesis could often be evaluated in relation to cyberstalking. Not, therefore, identity theft as an instrument to seek economic profit, but to attribute to the victim of the illicit conduct, communications and messages that can put him/her in a "bad light" on the web or to falsely attribute personal "attacks" to third parties to subjects who are actually extraneous to the facts.

3.4. Revenge Porn

Among the many innovations contained in Law 69 of July 2019, which establishes the amendments to the Criminal Code, the Code of Criminal Procedure and other provisions on the protection of victims of domestic and gender-based violence,[445] the new cases provided for in Article 10, which

---

[444] The concept of "digital identity" has already been introduced in the criminal system with Legislative Decree n. 93/2014 (converted by Law 119/2014), whose art. 9 entitled "Computer fraud committed with the replacement of digital identity" has amended art. 640-ter of the Criminal Code, with the insertion of a third paragraph, where the legislator has provided for the penalty of imprisonment for two and six years and the fine from € 600.00 to € 3,000.00 in the event that the offense is committed by means of theft or improper use of digital identity to the detriment of one or more subjects; this is a crime for which the complaint of the injured person is envisaged unless the hypothesis referred to in the 2nd or 3rd paragraph of art. 640-ter or other aggravating circumstance.

[445] Published in the Official Gazette No. 173 of 25 July 2019, in force since 9 August 2019.

introduced Article 612ter of the Criminal Code on the unlawful dissemination of sexually explicit images or videos, assume significant importance. This crime is generally known, especially in the media, as "revenge porn."[446]

With this expression is meant, in a broad sense, the consensual creation of intimate or sexual images generally within a context of a couple and the subsequent non-consensual publication of the same by one of the components, usually the man, aimed at taking revenge for the often "stormy" breakup of the intimate relationship (revenge porn in the strict sense). The publication of images or recordings usually occurs with the sole purpose of humiliating the person involved, for retaliation or revenge. Dissemination results in significant damage to the reputation and personal dignity of the person involved.

The expression "revenge porn" is used in common language, especially in the media, in a broad sense, to indicate any form of non-consensual dissemination of pornographic images or images/videos with any kind of sexual content, regardless of the previous existence of a romantic relationship or the retaliatory purpose of the person who publishes the images. Part of the broad notion of revenge porn, for example, is the posting of sexually explicit images and videos of celebrities online after their iCloud accounts have been hacked.[447]

It is undoubtedly a multi-offensive crime - aimed at protecting not only the freedom of self-determination of the individual, but also the dignity, reputation and right to privacy, in relation to sexual life - introduced in the system as part of an organic intervention aimed at facing, in its various forms, gender violence.

Revenge porn is part of a wider phenomenon, known as "non-consensual pornography" (NCP). A phenomenon that is not necessarily related to "relational revenge" and that concerns the digital sharing/dissemination without the consent of the person portrayed in said shared images. These images are generally those taken consensually or voluntarily during sexual intercourse or a sexual act and intended to remain private or to be shared privately; images captured by hidden cameras; images stolen from electronic devices; images taken during a sexual assault, and so on.

This phenomenon, which has spread especially in the last decade, due to significant technological developments, had raised serious questions about the

---

[446] On this topic see also S. RECCHIONE, *Codice Rosso. Come cambia la tutela delle vittime di violenza domestica e di genere con la legge 69/2019*; R. A. MANCUSO, *Revenge porn: la nuova fattispecie di reato*, in altalex.it.

[447] As stated in 2019 by the Senate Research Department in its relations on the measures for the contrast of the so-called revenge porn.

criminal protection concretely applicable, often considered insufficient to counter these behaviors. These problems were mainly due to the fact that the author of the crime is not motivated by any motive of profit, intended in a strictly patrimonial sense, and does not use any violence or threat on the victim. For this reason, the criminal framework of the conduct was particularly complex. In fact, it was not possible in the Italian legislation to configure a hypothesis of extortion pursuant to art. 629 c.p.,[448] lacking both the threatening or violent conduct and the event of profit. Nor was the crime of dissemination of fraudulent filming and recording integrated, which presupposes that the recordings are made in a fraudulent manner.[449]

Therefore, the debate had begun on the advisability of introducing in the criminal code an autonomous ad hoc case that would sanction the conduct of dissemination of sexually explicit images and videos, following the example of many legal systems that already provide for a similar crime hypothesis. However, it is only in 2019 with the reform of the "Red Code" that we have the introduction of the new article 216-ter of the Criminal Code. This new article aims to protect the illicit dissemination of sexually explicit images or videos by punishing anyone who, after having made or stolen them, sends, delivers, transfers, publishes or disseminates images or videos with sexually explicit content, intended to remain private, without the consent of the subjects represented. The same punishment also applies to those who, having received or otherwise acquired the images or videos referred to in the first paragraph, send, deliver, transfer, publish or disseminate them without the consent of the persons represented in order to damage them.

Analyzing the new article 612ter, we see that it is a "common crime" in which the agent does not necessarily have to correspond to the person who makes the video or image, as it can also be the person who has appropriated it

---

[448] Article 629 Italian Criminal Code; according to which anyone who, by means of violence or threat, by forcing someone to do or omit something, obtains an undue profit for himself or others with damage to others, by means of violence or threat. "*Chiunque, mediante violenza o minaccia, costringendo taluno a fare o ad omettere qualche cosa, procura a sé o ad altri un ingiusto profitto con altrui danno, è punito con la reclusione da cinque a dieci anni e con la multa da euro 1.000 a euro 4.000.*"

[449] Article 617*septies* Italian Criminal Code: "*Chiunque, al fine di recare danno all'altrui reputazione o immagine, diffonde con qualsiasi mezzo riprese audio o video, compiute fraudolentemente, di incontri privati o registrazioni, pur esse fraudolente, di conversazioni, anche telefoniche o telematiche, svolte in sua presenza o con la sua partecipazione, è punito con la reclusione fino a quattro anni.*" In other words with this case point Anyone who, in order to damage the reputation or image of others, disseminates, by any means, audio or video footage, made fraudulently, of private meetings or recordings, even if they are fraudulent, of conversations, including telephone or telematics conversations, carried out in his presence or with its participation, is punished.

with violence or other fraudulent means. The particular status of the author of the crime (that is, his subjective qualification given by a relationship of proximity with the victim) will be relevant, in fact, only for the purposes of the effectiveness of the aggravating circumstance. The subjective element consists in the generic intent, being required the simple representation and volition by the agent in relation to the conduct considered as a whole.

The case in question envisages three "ordinary" aggravating circumstances and two with special effect. In the first case, the third paragraph establishes that "the punishment is increased if the facts are committed by the spouse, also separated or divorced, or by a person who is or has been linked by an affective relationship to the offended person or if the facts are committed by means of computer or telematic instruments."

The fourth paragraph of art. 612ter of the Italian Penal Code provides for aggravating circumstances of a special nature - with an increase from one third to one half of the penalty when the crime is committed to the detriment of a person in a condition of physical or psychic inferiority or to the detriment of a pregnant woman. These are aggravating factors of an objective nature, pursuant to art. 70 of the Italian Penal Code, concerning the personal conditions and qualities of the offended person; they do not pose a particular problem of verifying the assumption of the fact or how much the offender knows about it.

The provision of art. 612ter of the Penal Code opens with a safeguard clause unless the fact constitutes a more serious crime. It is an absolutely necessary indication, considering that the behaviours described in the two "basic" hypotheses contained in the article - as well as the subsequent aggravated ones - overlap in various ways to other cases, for which the conduct referable to revenge porn was or could be sanctioned. In the first place, in fact, the problem of understanding the exact boundaries of the new crime could be one of the most delicate. This under a threefold profile: to understand when the aforementioned reserve clause must be applied, but also when it is necessary to assume a concurrence with other crimes or when the dispute of the case of which at the article 612ter of the penal code can exclude the existence of hypothesis of minor gravity, exhausting the negative value.

As an example, it could be referred to a hypothesis of formal competition between revenge porn and the crime of substitution of person of which at the art. 494 c.p..[450] If the agent replaces the victim, using his credentials and publishing sexually explicit contents on his Facebook profile.[451]

However, the legal assets protected in the two cases are different: the crime referred to in art. 494 c.p. has a multioffensive nature, protecting not only the public faith but also the person on whose concrete legal position the fact directly affects.[452] Furthermore, the sanctioning treatment foreseen by the legislator for the case of impersonation turns out to be far inferior to that of art. 612-ter of the Italian Penal Code, so that there appears to be an undoubted concurrence between the two crimes. It is a multioffensive crime, since, besides the public faith, the user also undermines the trust of the single victims. When false virtual identities or false Facebook profiles are created, not only is the trust that the individual user places in the Net undermined, but a wider balance is disturbed, that of the entire community of users who must be able to count on the fidelity of the identities with which they have virtual relations.

3.5. Cyberterrorism

More recently, data breaches have raised troubling questions about the possibility that terrorists may be using identity theft and related techniques to further their efforts to harm nations. In this regard, stolen identities provide criminals, including terrorists, with access to critical infrastructure such as airports and military facilities. Terrorists also use stolen identities to obtain money or credit needed to fund their operations to further their violent aims, exchange information, and use stolen identities to directly organize terrorist acts.

After the fall of the Twin Towers in 2001, in Italy, unlike many transnational countries, it was only in 2015 that it was definitively acknowledged that cyber tools constitute a part of the modern war heritage in use by terrorists. The intrinsic characteristics of cyberspace offer enormous

---

450 *"Chiunque, al fine di procurare a sé o ad altri un vantaggio o di recare ad altri un danno, induce taluno in errore, sostituendo illegittimamente la propria all'altrui persona, o attribuendo a sé o ad altri un falso nome, o un falso stato, ovvero una qualità a cui la legge attribuisce effetti giuridici, è punito, se il fatto non costituisce un altro delitto contro la fede pubblica, con la reclusione fino ad un anno."*

451 On the point Cass. pen., Section V, 8.06.2018, n 33862: "It integrates the crime of substituting a person (art.494 of the Criminal Code) the creation and use of a profile on social networks, abusively using the image of a completely unaware person, since it is a conduct suitable for the representation of a digital identity that does not correspond to the person who uses it."

452 L. PICOTTI, *Sistematica dei reati informatici tecniche di formulazione legislativa e beni giuridici tutelati*, 2004, p. 21 ss.

potential for financing and proselytizing terrorist associations, delocalizing and globalizing even territorially circumscribed phenomena. The network is the ideal arena to reach a global audience, spread radical ideology and recruit new followers.

It is clear that cyberterrorism represents a threat and the use of internet for terrorist purposes is particularly alarming. The need to find solutions that bridge the gap between the speed of media evolution and the regulatory response is critical in the field of high-tech investigations. As we read in the report computers at risk by the US National Research Council in '91:

> "we are at risk. [...] The modern thief can steal more with a computer than with a gun. Tomorrow's terrorists may be able to do more damage with a keyboard than with a bomb."[453]

The term cyberterrorism was coined in the 1980s by security and intelligence researcher Barry Collin, defining it as a simple convergence of cybercrime and the classic act of terrorism. However, while cyberspace can be defined as that place where "computer programs work and data moves,"[454] it is much more difficult to comprehensively define what is meant by terrorism. This definition can be easily found in the one provided by the Italian legislator in article 270-sexies. In this article, terrorist activities are defined as all those conducts that, by their nature, can cause serious damage to a country or an international organization. Such conduct must be carried out with the aim of intimidating the population or forcing public authorities or international organizations to perform or refrain from performing any act. Furthermore, they can be aimed at destabilizing or destroying the political, constitutional, economic and social structures that are fundamental to a country or an international organization. Community sources, on the other hand, follow a different path in the compulsory typification of conduct potentially capable of being classified as terrorist. To be considered as such, these actions must be aimed at seriously intimidating the population; unduly compelling public authorities or an international organization to perform or refrain from performing any act; seriously destabilizing or destroying the fundamental

[453] National Research Council (U.S.). Computer Science and Telecommunications Board. System Security Study Committee, Computers at risk: safe computing in the information age, 1991, in https://www.nap.edu/read/1581/chapter/1#iv.

[454] COLLIN, *The future of Cyberterrorism, in Crime and Justice International*, 1997.

political, constitutional, economic or social structures of a country or an international organization.[455]

In any case, it still seems difficult to identify a true definition of cyberterrorism. An early country where this term was defined comprehensively was the United States. According to American literature, "cyberterrorism is the convergence of cyberspace and terrorism. It refers to unlawful attacks and threats of attack against computers, networks, and the information stored in them, when done to intimidate or coerce a government or its people to pursue political or social goals.

In addition, to qualify as cyberterrorism, an attack should result in violence against people or property, or at least cause enough damage to generate fear. Attacks that result in death or personal injury, explosions, or severe economic loss would be examples. Serious attacks against critical infrastructure could be acts of cyberterrorism, depending on their impact. Attacks that disrupt non-essential services or are primarily a costly nuisance would not be."[456]

Italian doctrine considers it necessary to distinguish a few key elements or components that characterize cyberterrorism. They include: a) Attacks carried out through the telematic network and technologies able to cause the damage or the alteration of the functioning of sensitive computer systems or communication systems. b) The diffusion of illegal contents through the network aimed not only to provide information on the preparation of a terrorist attack but also to incite, publicize, spread ideas, opinions or recruit militants. (c) The use of the network and technologies as tools for communication between terrorists or terrorist groups must make possible the use of systems of anonymity or delocalization of the data flow as well as the operation of the timing of communication, which can also be managed through automated procedures and programmable *ex ante*.[457]

Directive 541 of 2017 introduces ex novo a hypothesis of cyberterrorism in the proper sense with the textual reference to the cases of unlawful interference to systems and/or data referred to in Articles 4 and 5 of European Directive 40 of 2013, in case they are committed with the intent to damage an information system of a critical infrastructure.

---

455 F.CAJANI, *Le indagini informatiche per I reati di cyberterrorismo*, in A.CADOPPI-S.CANESTRARI-A.MANNA-M.PAPA, *Cybercrime*, 2019, 1521 ss.

456 See DENNING, *Cyberterrorism: The Logic Bomb versus the Truck Bomb*, in Global Dialogue, vol. 2, 2000.

457 FLOR, *Cyber-terrorismo e diritto penale in Italia*, in Dritto Penale Contemporaneo, 2019, p. 333 ss.

In a broad sense, the notion of cyberterrorism can therefore encompass two distinct types of conduct: target-oriented ones, in which the Internet is the tool to carry out the terrorist act, and tool-oriented ones, in which the Internet is a means of supporting the life of the association and the dissemination of the terrorist creed.[458]

Currently, terrorist organizations or individual terrorists use the Internet for various purposes, either to damage or compromise the computer systems or critical infrastructure of a given country; or to carry out all the activities related to the management and survival of the terrorist organization, such as propaganda, fundraising, communication, proselytizing and recruitment. (cyberterrorism in a broad sense).

[458] P.SEVERINO, Cybersecurity course, Luiss, 2019.

Conclusion

The Evolving New Concept of Personal Assets

In all the digital identity theft cases reviewed above, we can appreciate how the conduct used by criminals to perpetrate digital crimes does not have a financial gain as its main goal. Most often, their purpose is to make the victim look bad, cause trouble, cause danger, or damage the victim's reputation or friendships both in cyberspace and in real life. Perpetrators may also involve their unwitting victims in cyber attacks directed at other people.

The phenomenon of identity theft occurs particularly in the context of social media networks as a result of several factors. It is often due to inadequate methods of keeping users' authentication credentials or the willingness of third parties to create fake accounts.

Therefore, identity theft must be considered not only as a tool for the pursuit of a financial gain, but also as a means to discredit people or to blame others for false communications, devious messages or fraudulent conduct.

As numerous observations of the judicial reality show, it is wrong to believe that the web can be used only and exclusively to commit computer crimes of an economic nature. More and more evidences show that the web is not only used to perpetrate the crimes introduced and described in the Italian Penal Code by Law no. 547/93 as "violence on things." Therefore, it is essential to rethink all the numerous cases provided by the Penal Code or by ordinary special laws, whose constitutive elements and means of perpetration are generally forms of communication. In this regard, it is important to consider that the constant technological evolution and in particular the evolution of the means of communication made available to the community, as well as the number, quality and quantity of communications carried out electronically, play a role in the increase of crimes perpetrated through the web.

A full understanding of the criminal phenomena related to the web implies a careful re-evaluation, in legal and technical terms, of the traditional modes of interpersonal communication currently provided for by the Criminal Code. In fact, advances in computer knowledge allow potential perpetrators to use new and increasingly sophisticated means to carry out various types of crimes, not necessarily of an economic nature.

Therefore, all criminal offenses in which the main offending behavior is related to any form of communication must be examined in relation to the new and more advanced technological tools now available to consumers. Furthermore, they must be evaluated in light of the current telematics scenarios in which digital communications take place, including chats, blogs, electronic bulletin boards or web pages. All of the various forms of web communication possibly related to crime need to be considered and evaluated carefully, as they may reflect a technological update of traditional methods or represent a new phenomenon peculiar to the use of new cyber tools. However, all new criminal phenomena and related criminal activities perpetrated through the web with advanced or new computer tools also require a careful assessment of the subjective and objective elements of the crime, as well as a cautious evaluation of the time and place in which the crime occurred.

In this regard, the publication of news or any kind of information on web pages represents the most modern, effective and potentially insidious form of dissemination, especially if the data entered is of a personal nature or published against the owner's will. The information published on web pages is usually viewed by users who are familiar with the web pages where the news is reported. However, it can also be reached and viewed by unaware and casual users who can be directed to those pages by entering one or more keywords in one of the available search engines. Search engines are in fact powerful multipliers of the diffusion of any kind of data or information reported on the web.

As of today, article 494 of the Italian Penal Code is considered the most used norm in the protection of an individual's personal digital identity.[459] This article specifically punishes those who, in order to procure for themselves or others an advantage or to cause damage to others, mislead someone by illegally substituting their own identity with that of another person, or by attributing to themselves or others a false name or false status, or a quality to which the law attributes legal effects. According to the Supreme Court, the legal asset to be protected is that of "public faith," as the rule aims to punish any possible deception relating to the true essence of individuals. In the event that the illicit conduct is perpetrated online, the protection granted to potential victims could be extended well beyond the narrow circle of the single

[459] Cass., sez. V, November 28 2012, n. 18826; See E. MENGONI, *Chattare con un nickname riconducibile ad altri (e comunicare il loro numero telefonico) integra il reato di sostituzione di persona* , in Cassazione Penale, fasc.1, 2014, 148; Trib. Bari, sez. Molfetta.

individual identified as the recipient or object of an illicit communication, up to and including all other users who share the illicit content online.[460]

However, in other proceedings the Supreme Court has stated how there are many doubts about the adequacy of this rule[461] in sanctioning all possible cases of violation of the right to digital identity that are not accompanied by an economic profit.[462]

The crime of impersonation, presenting itself as a residual case and with a derisory penalty (up to one year of imprisonment), does not seem to capture the seriousness of a possible injury to our digital identity. Especially in the world in which social networks and, in general, the web have assumed an increasingly pervasive role.[463] It also doesn't seem to grasp the ease with which someone's identity can be stolen or duplicated through computer technology. The so-called "nebulization" of infrastructure in the world of the internet, allows one to replace another person simply by entering a username and password, without any additional simulation effort. In this regard, the exponential increase of a danger has not been matched so far by an adequate reaction of the legal system.

In addition, there is a problem of interpretation in the application of article 494 of the Criminal Code in cases of identity theft. The article in question expressly protects primarily those who fall into error and not those who are dispossessed of their identity. The central conduct is to deceive an individual,

---

[460] The SC has on the one hand recognized the applicability of art. 494 c.p. in a case in which a person has been replaced by online chat lines (Cass., Cass., Sez. V, 28/11/2012, n. 18826, CED 255086). Furthermore, the crime in question was recognized in the conduct of the person who carries out and uses a specific profile on a social network that reproduces the photo of the victim by ascribing to the same a degrading description and, through this identity, uses the site by communicating with other subscribers and sharing their contents (Cass., Sez. V, 23./4/2014, n. 25774).

[461] Conceived in the Rocco code to protect "public faith," See also R. CAPPITELLI, *La sostituzione di persona nel diritto penale italiano*, in Cass.pen. 2005, 1269, 2993 ss.

[462] Cass., Section V, April 29 2013, n. 18826, cit., For which "*the profound and, in some ways, revolutionary changes that technological evolution has produced through the affirmation of new information technologies, which, thanks to the well-known Internet telematics network, allow for the dissemination of information and almost unlimited direct communication between users, have unfolded their effects (...)also in criminal matters, posing many problems, among which the ones underlying an extensive interpretation activity appear which, in the absence of organic legislative interventions, allowing to adapt the scope of operation of the traditional types of crime, such as that referred to in art. 494 of the Criminal Code, to the new forms of online aggression of the legal assets subject to protection, without violating the principles of the mandatory nature of the legal case and the prohibition of analogical interpretation of criminal law.*"

[463] See P. CIPOLLA, *Social Network, furto d'identità e reati contro il patrimonio, in Giur. Merito, 2012.*

not to usurp his or her identity. Thus, the deceived is not considered a victim of usurpation, although the Supreme Court has strongly revised this idea.

These ideas offer an interesting perspective on untying computer fraud committed through digital identity theft from its purpose of obtaining a pure economic benefit: profit. Even if profits were to impart legal, moral, and social benefits, the interpretation of "harm" will remain closely tied to the negative economic effects induced. Therefore, reconsidering the notion of "good" as a whole offers a viable approach to extending the criminal implications of cyber fraud committed through digital identity theft beyond its narrow economic link. This approach may enable the development of a new concept of global personal property. In this regard, the creation of a global personal asset will create a much-needed balance in terms of privacy and freedom of negotiation between the rights of the provider to make a profit and the extreme importance of intangible assets granted to its custody, such as an individual's personal data.[464] In many cases, doctrine has also insisted on reconceptualizing what is an asset. Considering it no longer only in "economic-material" terms, but also in its possible "legal" terms.[465]

With reference to the above hypothesis, US economic and legal doctrine had already provided a sketch of the possible monetization of the average value of the typical consumer's personal data.[466] Each person has passive control (as the only person who originally owns and can dispose of that data) and active control (as the only person who can create and modify that data over time) over these valuable intangible assets. Control over these is a concept borrowed from notions of intellectual property law. In addition, "data collectors" sell consumers' personal data through "databases"[467] over which providers can claim an intellectual property right.[468] It had also been specified how the identification of fraud aims not only to protect economic assets *tout*

---

[464] A. RICCI, *Il valore economico della reputazione nel mondo digitale. Prime considerazioni,* p. 1297; P. CIPOLLA, *Social network, furto d'identità e reati contro il patrimonio, i profili dei social network, "oro digitale"*

[465] A first important reconsideration of the concept of assets was made by the Pagliaro. Project which stressed the need for its reinterpretation in "personalistic" terms . In addition to representing the dogmatic platform in which the prevailing doctrine is recognized the Pagliaro project, constitutes the most important attempt at a possible reform of the Rocco Code. On this point see also G. FORTI, *L'ordinamento lessicale dei beni giuridici personali nella parte speciale del codice penale. Un'analisi quantitativo-strutturale sui codici di 20 paesi secondo la prospettiva delle "capacità,"* in L. PICOTTI, *Tutela penale della persona e nuove tecnologie*, Padova, 2013, p. 459.

[466] See R.S. MURPHY, *Property Rights in Personal Information.*

[467] See P. MELL, *Seeking Shade in a Land of Perpetual Sunlight.*

[468] G.PICA, *Diritto penale delle tecnologie informatiche*, which specifically analyzes in such context, the meaning of the "undue" of profit.

court, but also to ensure the freedom of negotiation of individuals and guarantee the right of each person to freely dispose of his or her assets.[469]

Another conceivable solution could be to reconsider not the concept of property but rather that of "damage," which should not be interpreted in the sense derived from the discipline of fraud, but rather in a non-strictly patrimonial sense. However, such terminological interpretations *sic stantibus rebus* do not fit the principle of strict legality of criminal law.

The recent introduction, in the legal system, of the circumstance of "digital identity theft" can therefore be considered as a profitable opportunity for a radical rethinking of the role of criminal law in information technology. By introducing the crime of digital identity theft into the Criminal Code, legislators have certainly aimed to protect the assets of information technology users. However, lawmakers have also consistently aimed to protect the digital projection of human identity. Once it has been ascertained that the traditional incriminatory cases fail to capture the peculiarity of the phenomenon in question, neither considered individually nor together with the new aggravated computer fraud, one can only hope for a solution to this protection gap.[470]

These are fields still largely to be explored, which require a continuous reflection and elaboration of concepts, even dogmatic ones, by scholars of criminal law, who must be able to adapt the cognitive and systematic tools of their conceptual categories to this new reality. Adaptation to evolving social and technological realities will allow criminal law scholars to better reaffirm and enforce effective criminal protection and at the same time preserve the fundamental principles and guarantees that characterize a legally constituted state.

European and national legislation currently appears to be insufficient in combating cybercrime. Therefore, the role of the legislature remains essential due to the need to update and/or develop legal rules to regulate activities that take place within cyberspace. The regulation of cyberspace is of paramount importance, as it is a social space in which digital identity theft can pose a very serious risk to citizens in the presence of a legislative vacuum and therefore in the absence of effective regulation and enforcement. While waiting for an acceptable reformulation of the rule found in article 640*ter*,[471] all that remains

---

[469] E. PALOMBI, G. PICA, *Diritto penale dell'economia e dell'impresa*, Vol.1, Torino, 1996, 687 ss.

[470] A.FURLANI-F. LUTMAN, *Social innovation. Reti sociali: le nuove protagoniste dell'innovazione. Una guida pratica per le aziende italiane*, Milano, 2012, 111; Also see P. CIPOLLA, *Social Network, furto d'identità e reati contro il patrimonio.*

[471] A. DI TULLIO D'ELISIIS, *Frode informatica commessa con sostituzione d'identità digitale: i profili applicativi,* in Altalex.

is to enhance the innovative meaning of the article in question without manipulating it, while searching for current alternative tools to protect digital identity.

References

Accogli C., *In Danimarca c'è un negozio dove si compra senza pagare*, in www.repubblica.it. [*In Denmark there is a shop where you can buy without paying*]

Adiconsum, *Guida al Furto d'Identità, Informativa per il consumatore sui rischi e le tutele da adottare a difesa dei propri dati personali*, in www.adiconsum.it. [*Guide to Identity Theft, Information for consumers on the risks and safeguards to be adopted in defense of their personal data*]

Agnino F, *Fino a che punto è possibile disporre contrattualmente dei propri diritti?*, in Giur. mer., 2012. [*To what extent is it possible to contractually dispose of one's rights?*]

Alessandri, *Criminalità informatica*, in Riv. Trim. dir. pen. Economia, 1990. [*Cybercrime*]

Alighieri D., *Divine Comedy*, Inferno, Canto XXX.

Alpa G., *I diritti della persona e la cronaca giornalistica*, in Giur. merito, 1987. [*The rights of the person and the news*]

Alpa G., *L'identità digitale e la tutela della persona. Spunti di riflessione*, in Contr. e impr., 2017. [*Digital identity and personal protection. Food for thought*]

Alpa G., *Privacy e statuto dell'informazione*, Riv. dir, civ., 1980. [*Privacy and information statute*]

Antolisei F., *Manuale di diritto penale, Parte Generale, VIII ed. revisionata da L. Conti, Milano, 2000.* [*Criminal Law Manual, General Part, VIII ed. revised by L. Conti, Milan*]

Apruzzese A., *La prevenzione e la repressione dei crimini informatici, Le nuove forme di criminalità informatica Dal Computer crime al Computer related-crime*, in www.teca.elis.org. [*The prevention and repression of cybercrime, The new forms of cybercrime From Computer crime to Computer related-crime*]

Aresty J., *Digital identity and the lawyer's role in furthering trusted online communities*, in Toledo Law Review.

Astorina Marino P., *Sub. art. 494 c.p., in Commentario breve al codice penale, directed by G. Forti, S. Seminara, G. Zuccalà, VI ed., Padova, 2017.* [*Sub. art. 494 c.p., in Commentario breve al codice penale, directed by G. Forti, S. Seminara, G. Zuccalà, VI ed., Padova, 2017*]

Barbazza A., Gazzetta E., *Il nuovo reato di atti persecutori* in www.altalex.it. [*The new crime of stalking*]

Bartoli R., *Brevi considerazioni sulla responsabilità penale dell'Internet Service Provider*, in Dir. Pen. e Processo, 2013. [*Brief Considerations on the Criminal Liability of the Internet Service Provider*]

Bartoli R., *La frode informatica tra modellistica, diritto vigente, diritto vivente e prospettive di riforma*, in Dir.Inf., fasc.3, 2011. [*Computer fraud between modeling, current law, living law and prospects for reform*]

Bettiol G., Pettoello Mantovani L., *Manuale di Diritto Penale*, Padova, 1986. [*Criminal Law Manual*]

Bianca C. M., *Note introduttive*, cit., XXXIII, in Trolli F., *La successione mortis causa nei dati personali del defunto e i limiti al loro trattamento*, in www.juscivile.it. [*Introductory notes*, cit., XXXIII, in Trolli F., *La succione mortis causa in the personal data of the deceased and the limits to their treatment*]

Bignardi F., *IT: Hacker attack on pharmaceutical company Zambon. April, 29.2021*, in www.databreaches.net.

Bonavita S., Poli V.; *La tutela civilistica della reputazione online*, in Cyberspazio e diritto, 2017. [*The civil protection of online reputation*]

Bosco F., C. Cocciadiferro, *L'evoluzione del crimine informatico: dall'hacking all'underground economy* - Unicri, Emerging Crimes Unit, 2011. [*The evolution of cybercrime: from hacking to the underground economy*]

Briat M., U. Sieber, *Computer Related Criminality; Analysis of Legal Policy in the OECD Area,* Parigi, 1989.

Brugi M., *Dall'identità personale all'identità digitale. Una necessità per il cittadino del terzo millennio, in Informatica e diritto*, 2008, 167 ss. [*From personal identity to digital identity. A necessity for the citizen of the third millennium, in IT and law*]

Cadoppi A., Canestrari S., Manna A., Papa M., *Cybercrime,* Milano, 2019.

Cadoppi A., *Efficace la misura dell'ammonimento del questore*, in Guida al Diritto, 10/2009. [*The measure of the warning given by the commissioner is effective*]

Cajani F., Costabile G., Mazzaraco G., *Phishing e furto d'identità digitale. Indagini informatiche e sicurezza bancaria,* Milano, 2008. [*Phishing and digital identity theft. Computer investigations and banking security*]

Cajani F., Le indagini informatiche per I reati di cyberterrorimo, in A. Cadoppi-S. Canestrari-A. Manna-M. Papa, *Cybercrime*, 2019. [Computer investigations for cyberterrorism offenses]

Cajani F., *Profili penali del phishing,* in Cass.pen, 2007, 2294 ss. [*Criminal profiles of phishing*]

Camardi C., *L'eredità digitale*, 2018. [*The digital legacy*]

Cappitelli R., *La sostituzione di persona nel diritto penale italiano*, nota a Cass., sez. V, 26 febbraio 2004, n. 8670, in Cass. Pen., 2005. [*The replacement of a person in Italian criminal law*]

Carli E., *la politica di sicurezza e difesa comune dell'UE*, Torino, 2019. [*the EU's common security and defense policy*]

Cataldo A., Peluso F.: *Cybersecurity, La nuova disciplina italiana ed europea alla luce della direttiva NIS, 2018.* [*Cybersecurity: The new Italian and European discipline in the light of the NIS directive*]

Cencetti C., *Cybersecurity: Unione Europea e Italia, prospettive a confronto*, 2014, Roma. [*Cybersecurity: European Union and Italy, comparing perspectives*]

Chawki M., *A Critical Look at the Regulation of Cybercrime: A Comparative Analysis with suggestions for Legal Policy*, 2004.

Chitarro A., R. Setola, Nuova direttiva per la protezione cibernetica e la sicurezza informatica, in *Sicurezza e giustizia*, 2017. [New directive for cyber protection and information security, in *Security and Justice*]

Choucri N., *What is cybersecurity? Explorations in automated knowledge generation*, in political science department working paper, 2012.

Ciacci G., *La firma digitale*, Il Sole 24 ore, 1999. [*The digital signature*]

Ciclosi F., *La normative europea e italiana in materia di protezione di dati personali*, Milano, 2019. [*European and Italian legislation on the protection of personal data*]

Cipolla P., *Social network, furto di identità e reati contro il patrimonio,* in Giur. merito 2012. [*Social networks, identity theft and property crime*]

Clough J., *Principles of Cybercrime*, Cambridge, 2010.

Cocuccio M. F., Il diritto all'identità personale e l'identità "digitale," in *Diritto di Famiglia e delle Persone*, 2016. [The right to personal identity and "digital" identity in *Family and Personal Law*]

Colapietro C., *I principi ispiratori del Regolamento UE 2016/679 sulla protezione dei dati personali e la loro incidenza sul contesto normativo nazionale,* 2018. [*The inspiring principles of EU Regulation 2016/679 on the protection of personal data and their impact on the national regulatory context*]

Collin, *The future of Cyberterrorism, in Crime and Justice International*, 1997.

ContaldO A., *ENISA e le competenze comunitarie per la cybersicurezza,* Pisa, 2020. [*ENISA and community skills for cybersecurity*]

Cooley T., A *Treaties on the Law of Torts. Or the wrongs which Arise Independent of Contract*, Chicago, 1888.

Cosio R., Natura del contratto tra utente e social, in *Ricerche giuridiche*, 2017. [Nature of the contract between user and social network, in *Legal research*]

Costantini P., *Il regolamento UE 679/2016 sulla protezione dei dati personali,* in www.commercialistacostantini.com. [*The EU regulation 679/2016 on the protection of personal data*]

Crawford S. P., *Who's in charge of who I am?*, 9 N.Y.L. Sch. L. Rev., 2004/2005.

Crescioli C., *Una sentenza della Cassazione sulla sostituzione della persona online*, in www.penalecontemporaneo.it. [*A sentence of the Supreme Court on the replacement of the person online*]

Cristiani A., *Falsità,* 1955. [*Falsehood*]

Cushing T., *Spanish Government Moves Ahead with First 'Fake News' Prosecution*, in www.techdirt.com.

De Angelis S., L. Aniello, R. Baldoni, F. Lombardi, A. Margheri, V. Sassone. *PBFT vs proof-of-authority: applying the CAP theorem to permissioned blockchain*, 2017.

De Benoist A., *Identità e comunità,* 2015. [*Identity and community*]

De Vivo M. C., Ricci G., Diritto, crimini e tecnologie. *Informatica e diritto*, Vol. XXI, 2012. [Law, crimes and technologies. *IT and law*]

Del Ninno A., *Il furto d'identità, in Trattato sui nuovi danni*, Vol. V, curated by P. CENDON, Padova, 2011. [*Identity theft, in the Treaty on new damages*]

Dello Iacovo A. A., *Articolo 640 ter: truffa o furto?, La frode informatica e il modello 640,* 1996. [*Article 640b: Scam or theft ?, Cyber fraud and the 640 model*]

Delsignore S., La tutela dei minori e la pedopornografia telematica: i reati dell'articolo 600ter c.p., in Cadoppi-S.Canestrari-A.Manna-M.Papa, *Cybercrime*, Milano, 2019. [The protection of minors and telematic child pornography: the offenses of article 600ter of the criminal code]

Denning, *Cyberterrorism: The Logic Bomb versus the Truck Bomb*, in Global Dialogue, vol. 2, 2000.

Destito V., Dati personali (tutela penale dei), *Digesto Online*, 2008. [Personal data (criminal protection of), *Digesto Online*]

Di Tullio D'elisiis A., *Frode informatica commessa con sostituzione d'identità digitale: i profili applicativi*, in Altalex. [*Computer fraud committed with digital identity replacement: application profiles*]

Ducato R., *I social network, in Il diritto dell'era digitale*, a cura di G. Pascuzzi, Bologna, 2015. [*Social networks, in The law of the digital age*]

Emilio C. Viano, *Cybercrime: Definition, Typology, and Criminalization*, 2016.

ENISA, Bolstering ENISA in the EU Cybersecurity certification framework, in www.enisa.europa.eu, 2019.

Faralli C., Il diritto alla privacy, in Diritti e nuove tecnologie, 2019. [The right to privacy, in *Rights and new technologies*]

Fiandaca G., Musco E. *Diritto Penale, Parte Generale, Roma, 2018.* [*Criminal Law, General Part, Rome, 2018.*]

Fiandaca G., Musco E., *Diritto Penale parte speciale, vol.1, Roma, 2017.* [*Criminal Law special part, vol. 1, Rome, 2017*]

Fiandaca G., Musco E., *Diritto penale. Parte special, vol. II/2, Roma, 2015.* [*Criminal law. Special part, vol. II / 2, Rome, 2015.*]

Figueredo Dias J., *Introduzione al codice penale portoghese* (transaltion by G. Torre), 2007. [*Introduction to the Portuguese Criminal Code*]

Finocchiaro G., Documento informatico e firma digitale, in *Contratto e impresa*, 1998. [IT document and digital signature, in *Contract and company*]

Finocchiaro G., *Identità personale su internet: il diritto alla contestualizzazione dell'informazione*, in Dir. inform., 2012. [*Personal identity on the internet: the right to contextualize information*]

Flick C., *Falsa identità su internet e tutela penale della fede pubblica degli utenti e della persona*, in Dir. inf. inf., 2008. [*False identity on the internet and criminal protection of the public faith of users and the person*]

Flor R., Cyber-terrorismo e diritto penale in Italia, in *Dritto Penale Contemporaneo*, 2019. [Cyber-terrorism and criminal law in Italy, in *Contemporary Criminal Law*]

Flor R., *Permanenza non autorizzata in un sistema informatico o telematico, violazione del segreto d'ufficio e concorso nel reato da parte dell'extraneus*, in cass. Pen., 2009. [*Unauthorized stay in an IT or telematic system, violation of official secrecy and participation in the crime by the extraneus*]

Flor R., *Phishing e profili penali,* 2012. [*Phishing and criminal profiles*]

Flor R., Phishing, identity theft e identity abuse. Le prospettive applicative del diritto penale vigente, in *Rivista it. dir. proc. pen.*, 2007. [Phishing, identity theft and identity abuse. The applicative perspectives of the criminal law in force]

Floridi L., *The fourth revolution. How the infosphere is transforming the world*, Milan, 2017.

Fonsi A., *Cybersecurity Act: l'Unione europea costruisce un sistema di sicurezza informatica by design*, in www.iusinitinere,it, 2019. [*Cybersecurity Act: the European Union builds an IT security system by design*]

Forti G., L'ordinamento lessicale dei beni giuridici personali nella parte speciale del codice penale. Un'analisi quantitativo-strutturale sui codici di 20 paesi secondo la prospettiva delle "capacità," in L. Picotti, *Tutela penale della persona e nuove tecnologie*, 2013. [The lexical ordering of personal legal assets in the special part of the criminal code. A quantitative-structural analysis on the codes of 20 countries from the perspective of "capabilities," in L. Picotti, *Criminal protection of the person and new technologies*]

Frigeni L., Bullismo e aspetti processuali, in Pennetta, *la responsabilità giuridica di atti di bullismo*, Torino, 2014. [Bullying and procedural aspects, in Pennetta, *the legal responsibility for bullying*]

Frosini T., *Telematica e informatica giuridica*, in Enc. dir., XLIV, Milano, 1992. [*Telematics and legal informatics*]

Fumo M., *La condotta nei reati informatici,* in Arch. Pen., 2013. [*Conduct in computer crimes*]

Furlani A., Lutman F., *Social innovation. Reti sociali: le nuove protagoniste dell'innovazione. Una guida pratica per le aziende italiane*, Milano, 2012. [*Social innovation. Social networks: the new protagonists of innovation. A practical guide for Italian companies*]

Gaeta M. C., La protezione dei dati personali nell'internet of things: l'esempio dei veicoli autonomi, in *Dir. informaz, e informatica*, 2018. [The protection of personal data in the internet of things: the example of autonomous vehicles]

Genghini R., La ricerca di un diritto naturale per una società digitale, in *codice e altre leggi del cyberspazio*, 2021. [The search for a natural right for a digital society, in *code and other laws of cyberspace*]

Gercker M., *The Convention on Cybercrime,* in MMR, 2004.

Gibson W., *Burning Chrome, in Omni magazine, 1982.*

Gibson W., *Neuromancer*, 1984, in www.defense.gov.

Giovannangeli S. F., la violazione dei dati o data breach, in *Circolazione e protezione dei dati tra libertà e regole del mercato, Commentario al regolamento UE n.679/2016 e al d.lgs. 101/2018, Milano, 2019*. [data breach or data breach, in *Circulation and data protection between freedoms and market rules, Commentary on EU regulation n.679 / 2016 and on legislative decree 101/2018, Milan, 2019*.]

Giustozzi, Nuove norme cybersecurity, tutto ciò che bisogna sapere, in *Agenda Digitale*, 2017, in www.agendadigitale.eu. [New cybersecurity regulations, everything you need to know, in the *Digital Agenda*]

Goffman E., *The Presentation of Self in Everyday Life*, 1959.

Gottijng I., *Risk Based Security. 2020 Q3 Report - Data Breach QuickView*, 2020, in www.pages.riskbasedsecurity.com.

Grabrosky P. N.; *Global Dimension of Cybercrime, Global Crime*, 2004.

Graham-Harrison E., *50 million Facebook profiles harvested for Cambridge Analytica in major data breach, in* The Guardian, 2018.

Grotto, Reati informatici e convenzione Cybercrime. Oltre la truffa e la frode informatica: la frode del certificatore, in *dir. informaz. e informatica*, 2009. [Cybercrime and Cybercrime Convention. Beyond scam and cyber fraud: certifier fraud]

Guzzo A., *Data breach nel GDPR: cos'è e come fare segnalazione e prevenzione*, P4 Hub Innovation Editor, 2021. [*Data breach in the GDPR: what it is and how to report and prevent*]

Hailes N. K., *How we became Posthuman, virtual bodies in Cybernetics, Literature and Informatics*, London, 1999.

Holmesa., *Facebook users' phone numbers and personal data have been leaked online*, Insider, 2021, in www.businessinsider.com.

Id., La privacy tra individuo e collettività, in *Tecnologie e diritti,* Bologna, 1995. [Privacy between the individual and the community, in *Technologies and rights*]

Ielo D., Saponara V., in AA.VV., *Codice della privacy,* II, Milano, 2004. [*Privacy Code*]

Ielo D., Saponara V., in AA.VV., *Codice in materia di dati personali*, Milano, 2004, in www.javapoint.com. [*Code regarding personal data*]

Jacovone V., *Il delitto di sostituzione di persona*, Napoli, 1974. [*The crime of substitution of person*]

Karif O., *Cybersecurity: 2016 was a record year for data breaches*, IN www.bloomberg.com.

Kaspersky E., *What is cybersecurity?, in* www.kaspersky.com.

Kroker A., Winstein M., *Data Trash*, trad.it. G. e A. Cara, Milano, 1996, XI.

Lamanuzzi M., *Diritto penale e trattamento dei dati personali*, 2017. [*Criminal law and personal data processing*]

Landini S., Identità digitale tra tutela della persona e proprietà intellettuale, in Riv. *Dir. industriale*, 2017. [Digital identity between personal protection and intellectual property]

Lanza M. L., *Non-Physical Violence*, in AAOHN Journal, 2006 Sep;54(9).

Lanzara, Osservazioni sul delitto di sostituzione di persona, in *Riv. pol., 1970.* [Observations on the crime of substitution of person]

Lasalvia F. P., La diffamazione via web nell'epoca dei social network, in Cadoppi S. Canestrari, A. Manna, M. Papa, *Cybercrime*, Milano, 2019. [Defamation via the web in the age of social networks]

Lessig L., *Code and other laws of cyberspace, 1999.*

Lessig L., *The Law of the Horse. What Cyberlaw Might Teach*, in Harvard Law Review, 1999.

Limone D. A., *Elementi di diritto dell'informatica, Lecce,* 1999. [*Elements of IT law, Lecce*]

Limone D. A., DataBreach: Zambon farmaceutica. 23 April, 2021. *ICT, cybersecurity,* in www.edoardolimone.com.

Lopriore P., Dalla firma digitale alla firma elettronica qualificata, in *Firma informatica: dalla firma digitale alla firma elettronica qualificata,* 2012.

[From digital signature to qualified electronic signature, in IT *signature: from digital signature to qualified electronic signature*]

Losana C., Reato complesso e "ne bis in idem" sostanziale, in *Riv. It. dir. proc. pen.* 1963. [Complex crime and substantial "ne bis in idem"]

Maalouf A., *Les identités meurtriéres*, Parigi, 1998. [*The killer identities*]

Macioce F., *Civil protection of the person and personal identity*, Padua, 1984.

Malgier G. I., *Il furto di identità digitale: una tutela patrimoniale della personalità, in La giustizia penale nella rete. Le nuove sfide della società dell'informazione nell'epoca di Internet, curated by R. Flor, D. Falcinelli, S. Marcolini, Milano, 2015.* [*Digital identity theft: a patrimonial protection of the personality, in Criminal justice on the net. The new challenges of the information society in the age of the Internet, curated by R. Flor, D. Falcinelli, S. Marcolini, Milan, 2015.*]

Malgieri G., La nuova fattispecie di "indebito utilizzo d'identità digitale, in *Diritto Penale Contemporaneo*, 2015. [The new case of "improper use of digital identity, in *Contemporary Criminal Law*]

Manacorda S., Flor R., Oh Jang J., *Cybercriminality,* Milano, 2012.

Mancuso R. A., *Revenge porn: la nuova fattispecie di reato*, in altalex.it.

Manna L., *Comment on legislative decree 196/03*, in www.diritto.it, 2004.

Mantelero A., *Il costo della privacy tra valore della persona e ragione d'impresa,* Milano, 2007. [*The cost of privacy between the value of the person and the business purpose*]

Mantovani F., *Concorso e conflitto di norme nel diritto penale*, Padova, 1966. [*Competition and conflict of rules in criminal law*]

Mantovani F., *Diritto penale*, PS, vol. II, *I delitti contro il patrimonio*, IV ed., Padova, 2016. [*Crimes against property*]

Mantovani F., *Diritto penale*. Parte speciale II, Padova, 2019. [*Criminal law*]

Manzini V., *Sostituzione di persona*, in Annali 1935. [*Person replacement*]

Manzini V., *Trattato di diritto penale italiano,* vol. VI, 5ª ed., curated by G. Pisapia, 1983. [*Italian criminal law treaty*]

Margiocco M., *Frode informatica*, in G. Finocchiaro – F. Delfini, Diritto dell'informatica, Assago, 2014. [*Computer fraud*, in G. Finocchiaro - F. Delfini, IT law]

Marini G., *La giuridificazione della persona. Ideologie e tecniche nei diritti della personalità*, in Riv. dir. civ., 2006. [*The juridification of the person. Ideologies and techniques in the rights of the personality*]

Marini G., Truffa, in *Digesto pen*. 1999. [Fraud]

Marraffino M., La sostituzione di persona mediante furto di identità digitale, in A. Cadoppi-S.Canestrari-A. Manna-M. Papa, *Cybercrime*, 2019. [Person replacement through digital identity theft]

Matteucci N., *Privacy e banche di dati, Bologna*, 1981. [*Privacy and databases, Bologna*]

Mei-Ling Huang, *Deepfakes and the Law – What Can You Do If Your Face Appears in a Deepfake Video?,* 2019, www.roydswithyking.com.

Mell P., *Seeking Shade in a Land of Perpetual Sunlight: Privacy as Property in the Elecrtonic Wilderness*, in Berkeley.

Metthey L., B. Steiner, *Les associations de migrants et la formation de l'identité: une approche internaliste,* in Nous, mois – les autres, 2009. [*Migrant Associations and Identity Formation: An Internalist Approach*]

Michael-Ross F., *France Passes Controversial 'Fake News' Law EURONEWS*, 2018, in www.euronews.com.

Militello V., Nuove esigenze di tutela penale e trattamento elettronico delle informazioni, in *Rivista trimestrale di diritto penale dell'economia*, 1992. [New needs for criminal protection and electronic processing of information, in the *Quarterly Review of Economic Criminal Law*]

Mincucci G., Le frodi informatiche, in A. Cadoppi-S. Canestrari-A. Manna-M. Papa, *Cybercrime,* 2019. [Computer fraud]

Miquelon M. F., *The Convention on Cybercrime: an Harmonized Implementation of International Penal Law*, in J. M. *Comp. & Info* L., 2005.

Montaldo F., *Il ritratto fotografico digitale tra diritto d'autore, diritti della persona e tutela della privacy*, Resp. civ. e prev., 2010. [*The digital photographic portrait between copyright, personal rights and privacy protection*]

Mosca G., Strategia Europea di cybersecurity, quale impatto sulle PA, in *Agenda Digitale*, www.agendadigitale.eu. [European cybersecurity strategy, what impact on PA]

Mucciarelli, Computer (disciplna giuridica del) nel diritto penale, in *Digesto penale*, 1988. [Computer (legal discipline of) in criminal law, in *criminal digest*]

Murphy R. S., *Property Rights in Personal Information: An Economic Defense of Privacy*, in 84 Geo. L.J., 1996.

National Research Council (U.S.). Computer Science and Telecommunications Board. System Security Study Committee, *Computers at risk: safe computing in the information age*, 1991, in www.nap.edu.

Nava G., Blockchain: tassonomia di un "hype" o "it's here to stay"?, in *Associazione Italiana di Diritto e dell'Energia (AIDEN)*, 2019. [Blockchain: taxonomy of a "hype" or "it's here to stay" ?, in the *Italian Association of Law and Energy (AIDEN)*]

Nicholas J. P., *Developing a Framework to Improve Critical Infrastructure. Cybersecurity. Response of Microsoft Corporation to Request for Information,* Before the United States Department of Commerce National

Institute of Standards and Technology. Docket No. 130208119-3119-01-April 8, 2013.

Nucci G., *Protezione dei dati personali e GDPR: dai precetti giuridici ai processi organizzativi,* 2018. [*Personal data protection and GDPR: from legal precepts to organizational processes*]

OECD*, Scoping Paper on Online Identity Theft*, June 18 2008, Section I.

Olivo F., *Dati personali e situazioni giuridiche soggettive*, in Giust. civ., 2002, II. [*Personal data and subjective legal situations*]

Ottoli A., *Privacy e social networks: profili evolutivi della tutela dei dati personali*, in Aida, 2011. [*Privacy and social networks: evolutionary profiles of the protection of personal data*]

Paat Y. F. Markham C., *Digital crime, trauma, and abuse: Internet safety and cyber risks for adolescents and emerging adults in the 21st century*. Social Work in Mental Health 2021.

Pace A., *Branca Constitution Commission.*

Padovan D., *Data breach e GDPR: gestire la crisi con procedure corrette*, in Network Cybersecurity360, www.cybersecurity360.it. [*Data breach and GDPR: managing the crisis with correct procedures*]

Padovani T., *Diritto Penale*, X ed., Milano, 2012. [*Criminal law*]

Padovani T., Stortoni L., *Diritto penale e fattispecie criminose. Introduzione alla parte speciale del diritto penale*, 2006. [*Criminal law and criminal offenses. Introduction to the special part of criminal law*]

Pagliaro A., Falsità personale, *voce Enciclopedia del diritto*, XVI. [Personal Falsehood, *Encyclopedia of Law entry*]

Palombi E., Pica G., *Diritto penale dell'economia e dell'impresa*, Vol.1, Torino, 1996. [*Criminal law of economics and business*]

Pardolesi R., *I diritti della personalità*, 2005. [*The rights of the personality*]

Parmiggiani M. C., Il cyberbullismo, in Cadoppi A.- Canestrari S.- Manna A.- Papa M., *Cybercrime*, 2019.

Parodi C., *La tutela della persona nella realtà telematica: revenge porn e cyberstalking*, in www.magistraturaindipendente.it. [*The protection of the person in the telematic reality: revenge porn and cyberstalking*]

Pascuzzi G., *Internet*, in Dig. disc. priv., Torino, 2000.

Pecorella C., *Diritto penale dell'informatica,* II ed., Padova, 2006. [*Criminal law of information technology*]

Pica G., *Diritto penale delle tecnologie informatiche*, Torino, 1999. [*Criminal law of information technology*]

Pica G., *Reati informatici e telematici,* Digesto pen., 2000. [*IT and telematic crimes*]

Picotti L. La proposta di una nuova direttiva sulle misure per un elevato livello comune di cybersecurity nell'UE (c.d. NIS 2), in sostituzione della vigente direttiva (UE) 2016/1148, c.d. Direttiva NIS (Network and Information Security). In *Diritto di Internet. Newsletter Osservatorio Cybercrime n.12 2020/31 gennaio 2021.* [The proposal for a new directive on measures for a high common level of cybersecurity in the EU (so-called NIS 2), replacing the current directive (EU) 2016/1148, so-called NIS (Network and Information Security) Directive. In *Internet Law. Cybercrime Observatory Newsletter n.12 2020/31 January 2021.*]

Picotti L., Commento alla sentenza del tribunale di Firenze, January 27 1986, in *Dir. Dell'informatica*, 1986. [Comment on the sentence of the court of Florence, January 27 1986]

Picotti L., Cybercrime e tutela penale dei diritti della persona e della privacy nel web, *AIAF*, issue 1, 2020. [Cybercrime and criminal protection of personal rights and privacy on the web]

Picotti L., *I delitti di sfruttamento sessuale dei bambini, la pornografia virtuale e l'offesa dei beni giuridici*, Napoli, 2007. [*The crimes of sexual exploitation of children, virtual pornography and the offense of legal assets*]

Picotti L., I diritti fondamentali nell'uso e abuso sui Social Network. Aspetti Penali, in *Giur. di Merito*, 2012. [Fundamental rights in the use and abuse on Social Networks. Criminal Aspects]

Picotti L., Internet e responsabilità penali, in G. Pascuzzi (a cura di), *Diritto ed informatica*, Milano, 2002. [Internet and criminal liability, in G. Pascuzzi (edited by), *Law and IT*]

Picotti L., *Online child pornography offences. A brief overview*, in Festschrift fur Frieder Dunkel zum 70. Kriminologie und Kriminalpolitik im Dienste der Menschenwürde, Forum Verlag Godesberg, Monchengladback, 2020.

Picotti L., Presentazione, in ID., *Il diritto penale dell'informatica nell'epoca di Internet*, Padova, 2004. [Presentation, in ID., *The criminal law of information technology in the age of the Internet*]

Picotti L., Profili di diritto sostanziale, in *Dir. pen. E processo*, 2008. [Profiles of substantive law]

Picotti L., Profili penali del cyberlaundering: le nuove tecniche di riciclaggio, in *Riv.trim.dir.pen.ec.*, 2018. [Criminal profiles of cyberlaundering: the new money laundering techniques]

Picotti L., *Profili penali delle comunicazioni illecite via internet, in Il diritto dell'informazione e dell'informatica,* 1999. [*Criminal profiles of illicit communications via the internet, in Information and IT law*]

Picotti L., Ratifica della Convenzione Cybercrime e nuovi strumenti di contrasto contro la cirminalità informatica e non solo, in *Dir. Internet*, 2008. [Ratification of the Cybercrime Convention and new instruments to combat cyber crime and more]

Picotti L., *Sistematica dei reati informatici, tecniche di formulazione legislativa e beni giuridici tutelati,* 2004. [*Systematics of computer crimes, legislative formulation techniques and protected legal assets*]

Picotti L., *Studi di diritto penale dell'informatica,* Verona, 1992. [*Criminal law studies in information technology*]

Picotti L., Terrorismo e Sistema penale: realtà, prospettive, limiti, in *Riv. trim. Dir. Pen. Contemporaneo*, 2017. [Terrorism and the criminal system: reality, perspectives, limits]

Pino G., *Il diritto all'identità personale, ieri e oggi. Informazione, mercato, dati personali, in Libera circolazione e protezione dei dati personali*, edited by R. Panetta, Milano, 2006. [*The right to personal identity, yesterday and today. Information, market, personal data, free circulation and protection of personal data*]

Pino G., *L'identità Personale*, extract from the volume: *Trattato di Biodiritto, ambito e fonti del biodiritto*, edited by S. Rodotà; P. Zatti, 2010. [*Personal identity*, extract from the volume: *Treaty of bio-law, scope and sources of bio-law*]

Pioletti U., Possesso o utilizzo abusivo di carte di credito, in *Giur. Merito*, 2012. [Abusive possession or use of credit cards

Pirandello L., *Uno nessuno e centomila*, 1926. [*One none and one hundred thousand*]

Pistorelli L., *Prime note sulla legge di conversione, con modificazioni*, del d.l. n. 93 del 2013, in Dir. pen. cont., 18 ottobre 2013. [*First notes on the conversion law, with amendments*]

Pistorelli L., *Relazione n. III/03/2013 del 16/10/13*, in www.dirittopenal econtemporaneo.it.

Pizzacalla M., Firma digitale: le novità legislative e regolamenti, in *Impresa*, 2001. [Digital signature: the new laws and regulations, in *the Company*]

Pizzetti F., *Privacy e il diritto europeo alla protezione dei dati personali*, 2016. [*Privacy and the European right to the protection of personal data*]

Pollicino O., *Internet nella Giurisprudenza delle Corti Europe,* 2013. [*Internet in European Court Jurisprudence*]

Rasi G., *Il nuovo codice sulla protezione dei dati personali tutela la dignità della persona*, in www.garanteprivacy.it. [*The new code on the protection of personal data protects the dignity of the person*]

Recchione S., *Codice Rosso. Come cambia la tutela delle vittime di violenza domestica e di genere con la legge 69/2019.* [*Red Code. How does the protection of victims of domestic and gender-based violence change with law 69/2019*]

Reichart Smith L., Smith K. D., Blazka M., F*ollow Me, What's the Harm? Considerations of Catfishing and Utilizing Fake Online Personas on Social Media*, in Journal of Legal Aspects of Sport, 2017.

Resta G., Identità personale e identità digitale, in *Dir. Informaica*, 2007. [Personal identity and digital identity]

Resta G., Le perosne fisiche e i diritti della personalità, in *Tratt. Sacco, Torino*, 2006. [Individuals and personality rights]

Ricci A., Il valore economico della reputazione nel mondo digitale. *Prime considerazioni,* 2011. [The economic value of reputation in the digital world. *First considerations*]

Robinson W. J., *Free at What Cost?: Cloud Computing Privacy Under the Stored Communications Act,* in Georgetown L. J., Vol. 98, 2010.

Rodotà S., *Il mondo della rete. Quali diritti, quali vincoli*, Roma-Bari, 2014. [*The world of the network. What rights, what constraints*]

Rodotà S., Quattro paradigmi per l'identità, in *Il diritto di avere diritti*, Bari, 2012. [Four paradigms for identity, in *The right to have rights*]

Rodotà S., *Tecnopolitica: la democrazia e le nuove tecnologie della comunicazione*, Roma- Bari, 1997. [*Technopolitics: democracy and new communication technologies*]

Rodotà S., Tra diritti fondamentali ed elasticità della normativa: il nuovo codice sulla privacy, in *Eur. dir. priv.*, 2004. [Between fundamental rights and the elasticity of the legislation: the new privacy code]

Rodotà S., Trasformazioni del corpo, in *Politica del diritto*, 2006. [Transformations of the body, in *Politics of law*]

Rodota' S., Persona, riservatezza, identità`. *Prime note sistematiche sulla protezione dei dati personali*, 2004. [Person, confidentiality, identity. *Systematic first notes on the protection of personal data*]

Rodota' S., *Tecnologie e diritti*, Bologna, 1995. [*Technologies and rights*]

Rovegno A. O., Identità digitale: tra esigenze di condivisione e necessità di tutela, in *Cyberspazio e diritto, rivista internazionale Giuridica*, 2013. [Digital identity: between sharing needs and protection needs, in *Cyberspace and law, an international law magazine*]

Saenko L., *Le nouveau délit d'usurpation d'identité numérique*: *RLDI juin 2011*, n° 72 . [*The New Crime of Digital Identity Theft: RLDI June 2011*]

Salvadori I., I reati contro la riservatezza informatica, in A. Cadoppi-S. Canestrari-A. Manna-M. Papa, *Cybercrime*, 2019. [Crimes against IT confidentiality]

Sambucci L., *Falsi call center sul VoIP: la nuova truffa si chiama Vishing*, in www.anti-phishing.it, 2006. [*Fake call centers on VoIP: the new scam is called Vishing*]

Samuelson P., Samuelson, privacy as intellectual property?, in *Stanford Law Review*, 52.

Santoro F., *Cooperazione internazionale in materia di criminalità informatica*, Roma, 2011. [*International cooperation on cybercrime*]

Santoro F., Sostituzione di persona, in *Enciclopedia forense*, v. VII. [Person Replacement, in *Encyclopedia Forensics*]

Sarzana Di Sant'ippolito, Note sul diritto penale dell'informatica, in *Giustizia penale*, 1984. [Notes on IT criminal law, in *Criminal Justice*]

Scalzini S., I servizi di online social network tra privacy, regole di utilizzo e violazione dei diritti dei terzi, in *Giur. mer.*, 2012. [The online social network services between privacy, rules of use and violation of the rights of third parties]

Schmid N., *Computer-sowie Check und Kreditkarten-Kriminalität*, Zurigo, 1994. [*Computer as well as check and credit card crime*]

Scognamiglio P., *Criminalità informatica. Commento organico alla Legge 18 marzo 2008, n. 48*. [*Cybercrime. Organic commentary on Law no. 48.*]

Seiler G. F., Kritische Anmerkungen zum StrÄG 1987 den Besonderen Teil des StGB, in *KBkm 1989m.* [Critical comments on the StrÄG 1987 the special part of the StGB]

Sellaroli V., Il nuovo reato di cyberbullismo (l. 29 maggio 2017, n. 71); in *Il penalista*, Milano, 2017. [The new crime of cyberbullying (Law 29 May 2017, n.71); in *The criminal lawyer*]

Senigaglia R., Reg. UE 2016/679 e diritto all'oblio nella comunicazione telematica.Identità, informazione e trasparenza nell'ordine della dignità personale, in *Nuove leg. civ. comm.*, 2017. [EU Reg. 2016/679 and right to be forgotten in telematic communication. Identity, information and transparency in the order of personal dignity]

Severino P., "Cybersecurity: Regulation and Policy," *Luiss Law School seminar*, 2019-2020.

Severino P., *Le leve e le sfide per il rilancio del paese. Le frontiere della sicurezza. Sicurezza informatica e prevenzione del Cybercrime*, Cernobbio, 2017. [*The levers and challenges for the relaunch of the country. The frontiers of security. Cyber security and Cybercrime prevention*]

Sica S., Giannone Codiglione G., *Social network sites and the "labyrinth" of responsibilities*, in Giur. Merit, 2012.

Simmons M., Lee J. S., *Catfishing: A Look into Online Dating and Impersonation,* 2020.

Soafer A. D., Goodman S. E., *The Transnational Dimension of Cyber Crime and Terrorism,* Hoover Press, 2005.

Stanzione M. G., *Il nuovo regolamento Europeo sulla protezione dei dati personali: Genesi ed ambito di applicazione,* in www.comparazione dirittocivile.it, 2016. [*The new European regulation on the protection of personal data: Genesis and scope of application*]

Stea G., La responsabilità penale dell'internet provider, in *Giur. Penale*, 2016. [Criminal liability of the internet provider]

Strano M., Battelli F., Boccardi M., Bruzzone R., Fiammella B.-Mattiucci M., Rigoni A., *Inside attack, tecniche di intervento e strategie di prevenzione*, Roma, 2005, introduzione di Corrado Giustozzi.

Strano M., *Modello a 5 fasi*, 2002, www.criminologia.org. [*5-step model*]

Tanwar S., Q. Bhatia, P. Patel, A. Kumari A, P. K.Singh, Wc. Hong; *Machine learning adoption in blockchain-based smart applications: the challenges, and a way forward*. IEEE Access 2020.

Taylor C., *Le malaise de la modernité*, 2015. [*The malaise of modernity*]

Terenzi P., Identità, in S. Belardinelli, L. Allodi, *Sociologia della cultura*, Milano, 2011. [*Sociology of culture*]

Tiedmann K., *Strafgesetzbuch. Leipziger Kommentar*, XI ed., Berlin, 1998, sub § 263. [*Criminal code. Leipzig Commentary*]

Tirino N., *Cambridge Analytica. Il potere segreto, la gestione del consenso e la fine della propaganda*, Lecce, 2019. [*Cambridge Analytica. Secret power, consensus management and the end of propaganda*]

Torrente A., Schlesinger P., *Manuale di Diritto Privato*, 2015. [*Private Law Handbook*]

Tosoni L., *Cybersecurity Act, ecco le nuove norme in arrivo su certificazione dei prodotti e servizi ICT*, in www.agendadigitale.eu, 2019. [*Cybersecurity Act, here are the new regulations on the certification of ICT products and services*]

Turkle S., *La vita sullo schermo. Nuove identità e relazioni sociali nell'epoca di Internet*, Milano, 2005. [*Life on the screen. New identities and social relationships in the age of the Internet*]

Ubertazzi L. C., Riservatezza informatica ed industria culturale, in *AIDA*, Milano, 1997. [IT and cultural industry confidentiality]

Vadala' R. M., La direttiva UE 2019/713 del 17 aprile 2019 e la tutela penale dell'uso legittimo delle valute virtuali, in *Osservatorio Cybercrime*. [The EU directive 2019/713 of April 17, 2019 and the criminal protection of the legitimate use of virtual currencies, in *Cybercrime Observatory*.]

Vadala' R. M., La disciplina penale degli usi e abusi delle valute virtuali, in *Diritto di Internet*, 2020. [The criminal discipline of the uses and abuses of virtual currencies, in *Internet Law*]

Vassalli, Nuove e vecchie incertezze nel reato complesso, in *Riv, It*. 1978. [New and old uncertainties in the complex crime]

Vassilaki E., *Computer Crimes and Other Crimes against Information Technology in Greece*, in Rev.Int.dr.pén. (vol.64), 1993.

Vincent J., *Deepfakes for Dancing: You Can Now Use Ai to Fake Those Dance Moves You Always Wanted*, 2018, www.theverge.com.

Vives Anton T. S., Gonzales Cussac J. L., in AA.VV., *Comentarios al Còdigo Penal de 1995*, vol II, Valencia, 1996, sub. art. 248. [*Comments to the Penal Code of 1995*]

Voigt P., Von Dem Bussche A., *The EU General Data Protection Regulation (GDPR)*, London, 2017.

Warren S., L. Brandeis, *The Right to Privacy, in Harvard Law Review*, in www.groups.csail.mit.edu.

Wasik M., *Crime and the computer*, Oxford, 1991.

Weinreich P., W. Saunderson, *Analyzing Identity: Cross-Cultural, Societal and Clinical Contexts*, London, 2003.

Wiener, *Humans and the use of Human Beings*, 1950.

Wiszniewski D., Coyne R., *Mask and Identity: The Hermeneutics of Self-Construction in the Information Age., Building Virtual Communities*, 2002.

Wylie C., *Il mercato del consenso: come ho creato e poi distrutto Cambridge Analytica*, Milano, 2020.

Xingan L., *International actions against cybercrime: Networking legal systems in the networked crime scene,* 2007, in www.webology.org.

Zagami, *La firma digitale e sicurezza giuridica,* 2000.

Zeno-Sencovich V., Identità personale, *Dig.disci.priv.*, sez.civ., IX,1993. [Personal identity]

Zeno-Zencovich V., Informatica ed evoluzione del diritto, in *Dir. Inform.*, 2003. [Information technology and evolution of law]

Zeno-Zencovich V., voce Personalità, in (diritti della), in *Dig. Disc. Priv. Sez. civ.*, vol.XIII, Torino, 1995. [Personality voice]

Ziccardi G., Hacker, *Il richiamo della libertà*, Milano, 2011. [*The call of freedom*]

Zorzini, *Cyberbullismo e reclamo al Garante per la Privacy*, in www.personaedanno.it. [*Cyberbullying and complaint to the Privacy Guarantor*]

About the Author

Clara Pettoello-Mantovani*, JD, LLM

Trainee Lawyer at the Law Firm "Bongiorno", Rome, Italy

Clara Pettoello-Mantovani received her law degree, with a specialization in criminal law, from the LUISS Guido Carli School of Law in Rome, Italy. Her formal training includes law course for international scholars at Fordham University School of Law, New York, USA. She has based her academic studies on the study of digital identity, cybersecurity and cybercrime, actively contributing to the European Parliament's project for the development of a digital signature legislation in the EU. She has been a legal assistant in European affairs at the Genghini law and notary firm in Milan and internal consultant at e-Witness Milano, an IT company offering services and technological solutions in digital preservation, accredited by the Agency for Digital Italy (AgID). From 2021, she is a trainee lawyer at the distinguished "Bongiorno" law firm in Rome, Italy

* Corresponding Author's E-mail: c.pettoellomantovani@gmail.com.

Index